CHARLES

THE KING AND WALES

T0016136

Huw Thomas is a journalist whose writing and broadcasting covers the beating heart of Welsh life. Born in Maesteg in the post-industrial south Wales valleys, for the best part of twenty years he has reported on the people and places of Wales. He began in local radio, before joining the BBC after a brief stint producing business news for Bloomberg. His work has taken him around Wales and the UK, covering key events from the Queen's Jubilee to the Olympic Games, and the Hay Festival to the National Eisteddfod. Stories have also lured him abroad, allowing him to interview the descendants of Welsh settlers in Patagonia and Bonnie Tyler at the Eurovision Song Contest in Sweden. Huw is an accomplished TV correspondent, having covered the darkest days of the Covid-19 pandemic, while his presenting skills have seen him front programmes for BBC Wales and network radio.

CHARLES

THE KING AND WALES

Huw Thomas

PARTHIAN

Parthian, Cardigan SA43 1ED
www.parthianbooks.com
© Huw Thomas 2023
ISBN 978-1-914595-44-8
Edited by Richard Davies
Typeset by Elaine Sharples
Printed by 4edge Limited
Published with the financial support of the Welsh Books Council
British Library Cataloguing in Publication Data
A cataloguing record for this book is available from the British Library.
Every attempt has been made to secure the permission of copyright
holders to reproduce archival and printed material.
Printed on paper from sustainable sources

For Isobel, Clara and Alys

Parthian started publishing books with a loan from the Prince's Youth Business Trust in 1993. We would like to thank the Trust and particularly Dr Martin Price, for his expertise and engagement in our development through the Trust's excellent programme of support for young people starting a business.

Contents

Acknowledgements

When I first began researching this book, the nature of the polarised responses I received made me question whether it was possible to adequately assess the impact that Charles made on Wales, and to what extent the Welsh had rubbed off on him. Fortunately, dozens of people were prepared to share their own stories of Charles's sixty-four years as Prince of Wales. The resulting interviews, conducted in office blocks and stately homes, created a picture of Charles's Welsh interests and how Wales influenced the man who would be King.

I am indebted to those who gave their time, often on more than one occasion, to discuss their own encounters with Charles. Many of them are named in the chapters that follow. My heartfelt thanks is also extended to those who cannot be identified but whose valuable insight helped to shape the narrative of this book. Others who supported me by checking facts, reading extracts and discussing concepts have also contributed to my story about the King's relationship with Wales. The support of my family in pursuing this book, from Covid lockdown to the eve of the King's coronation, has been an incredible blessing. Having said all of that, any errors or omissions are entirely my own.

Introduction

'For me it is a way of officially dedicating one's life,
or part of one's life, to Wales.
And the Welsh people, after all, wanted it.'

It is a spring morning in 1969 when a blue sports car glides to a stop outside a Welsh country house. From the driver's side a man emerges quickly and fumbles briefly with his light brown suit. A buttoned-up blue shirt and his tie, taut and restrictive, remain unruffled by the short journey. The man is self-conscious, his hands quickly slide into the unstitched pockets of his suit jacket. While the sixties swung, this man remained rigid. He glances at the newsreel camera which whirs its colour film. The glance never fixes on the barrel of the camera lens, instead the eyes scatter until he has turned around on the spot. He takes a small, awkward pirouette towards the back of the car to exchange inaudible small talk with his companion before he returns to the safe space between car door and front door; that sweet spot where the camera can sustain a few more seconds on the face of the man who will be King, but only for as long as he can bear to be on show.

Charles had almost finished a pre-investiture public relations epic when this scene played out on the drive of the manor house on the Faenol estate near Bangor, north-west Wales. His MG sports car, new in 1968, was the ostentatious shell for a shy public schoolboy whose path in life was indelibly etched at the moment of his birth. His friends, at school and at Cambridge, may have shared the great privileges of the aristocracy. But while their gilded paths opened doors to investment banks and the Inns of Court, Charles would take an almost lifelong walk along a deep-pile red carpet. Its destination was the crown of the United Kingdom. It is perhaps unsurprising that when life sets such a singularly simplistic and elusive goal the bearer is forced to define their existence by other achievements. The freedoms offered by great wealth and class are curtailed for royalty by the duties and service that is expected of them. For the heir to the throne, such expectations are closely defined and restrict the liberties that their siblings, cousins and aunts could indulge. But for an heir in need of an agenda, a self-defining role can be created to fill the time between reaching adulthood and reaching the throne.

The Prince's coming-of-age coincided with an awakening in society that swept aside the stuffiness of post-war Britain and celebrated the free-thinking and free-loving that was fostered by the 1960s. Two decades earlier it had seemed radically modern that the Home Secretary had not been present to witness Charles's birth. James Chunter Ede was the first Home Secretary in over a hundred years to have been absent from the arrival into the world of a senior royal, a practice rooted in the fears of Tudor and Stuart monarchs that their line of succession would be stolen by a changeling or a chancer. Despite the dawning modernity, Charles had been born into an ancient system of monarchy and was expected to keep it going. His supporters, while championing the ambitions of a modern prince, also pressed his pedigree. He was fifth in descent from Queen Victoria and could claim a direct route back to all the kings and queens whose names had graced schoolbooks, postboxes and pub signs for centuries. There were connections made, too, with Charlemagne, Vortigern and Cadwallader, although genealogy means most Europeans alive today could probably claim a similar pedigree. Journalists published complex family trees that linked the future Prince of Wales with the ancient and original title-holders. It was possible to claim that Charles was twenty-fourth in descent from Llywelyn the Great, a king of Gwynedd and one of the last native Princes of Wales before the title's thirteenth-century conquest by Edward I. The public relations effort was designed to embed the idea that this was a boy prince whose lineage did not deviate from the warrior men who had gone before him.

While history charted the bloody battles for Welsh territory and Welsh titles by neighbouring rulers, the happy birth of a modern heir focused attention on celebrating tenuous genealogical links, overlooking the murderous conquests that had shaped the family tree. The grandson of Llywelyn the Great suffered a beheading which not only cut off the Welsh claim to the title Prince of Wales, it also created a totem in the story of Wales that bolstered sentiment for independence from the English, and fomented in some an ongoing rejection of the title when worn by any heir to the throne since Edward II.

If Charles had a hereditary connection to the last native Welsh princes, it was a connection that was lost on Welsh historians. 'With the fall of Llywelyn ap Gruffydd an epoch ended – the Wales of the Princes,' wrote Gwyn Alf Williams in *When Was Wales?* 'The Welsh passed under the nakedly colonial rule of an even more arrogant, and self-consciously alien, imperialism. Many historians... have largely accepted the verdict of nineteenth-century Welsh nationalism and identified the house of Aberffraw as the lost and legitimate dynasty of Wales. Llywelyn ap Gruffydd has become Llywelyn the Last,' wrote Williams. Whatever the bloodlines drawn to impress Charles's pedigree, the blood ran clear for some.

And yet the line of succession had never landed during a time of such huge societal change and liberation from the chains of tradition. The relaxing attitudes of the 1960s presented an opportunity for Charles to write his own job description. In 1968 the journalist Dermot Morrah charted the early years of the Prince, having evolved from being a correspondent for *The Times* to occasionally writing the Queen's speeches. His authorised biography of Charles's young life described the upbringing of the Prince and, assuming a long reign for his mother, offered a thesis on the heir's adulthood:

Prince Charles will require to find some new direction of princely activity for the common good, something that grows out of the needs of the modern world as it is, and as it is becoming. He belongs to that world, and, at the end of the thoughtful years on which he is about to embark, will be better able than his elders to judge how best it can be helped.

The prospect of determining his own 'princely activity' must have seemed both daunting and delightful. He had an enviable opportunity to map out a role that allowed his preferred pursuits of culture and countryside to be the anchor points of a period as heir which, even then, seemed to offer a good thirty years before having to worry about becoming King.

As a modern Prince of Wales he could heal the scars left on the House of Windsor by the previous bearer of the title, Edward VIII, who took the throne and handed it back in pursuit of that most uncommon royal commodity: love.

Charles's shoulders would carry the investiture robes a little more sensibly than another Edward, the seventh to bear the regal name when he eventually grasped the crown. Before taking the throne in 1901 Edward VII had spent the best part of sixty years gallivanting the globe as the playboy Prince of Wales. Aged thirteen he had attended a party thrown by Napoleon III in Paris which exposed the young prince to the vices available beyond Victorian England. While his mother's name became a synonym for stuffy conservatism, the young Prince rebelled against his restrictive childhood. He is said to have lost his virginity aged nineteen on a ten-week tour of Ireland with the Grenadier Guards and continued to travel widely in order to indulge his passion for women and gambling. His mother's longevity ensured he could spend decades exploring the attractions of the expanding Empire.

Examples from recent history may have been enough to chasten any of Charles's more radical ideas for his time as Prince of Wales. In fiction, too, there were near-the-bone notes of caution. 'To be Prince of Wales is not a position – it is a predicament!' said Alan Bennett's heir to the throne in *The Madness of King George*.

In 1969 it was Charles's chance to either make it work or mess it up. He would proceed in plain sight of those who wished him to fail, and knew not only that there were a minority of committed anti-monarchists who were determined to protest his path to the title of Prince of Wales, but also that there existed a largely indifferent majority who may tune in as much for the spectacle of the investiture as they would for his wife's *Panorama* interview twenty-five years later.

Sympathy for a prince can be a struggle as much in the 2020s as it was in the 1960s. When Charles's youngest son told the American television presenter Oprah Winfrey in 2021 that he had felt 'trapped' in the clutch of the royal family, she responded to Prince Harry with a jaw-dropping call for clarity. 'Please explain how you, Prince Harry, raised in a palace, in a life of privilege, literally a prince, how you were trapped.' Similarly, ahead of Charles's investiture, there were crocodile tears from the era's cultural critics. The republican Labour MP Emrys Hughes hid many truths in his sarcastic take on Charles's ceremony at Caernarfon Castle. 'If a Society for the Prevention of Cruelty to the Prince of Wales is formed, I will immediately send a subscription,' he told the House of Commons in a debate about the investiture in December 1968. The record of proceedings continued: 'There is no need to drag the unfortunate Prince of Wales through what his predecessor had to undergo. Having seen the photographs in the *Manchester Guardian* I am more convinced than ever. The then Prince of Wales [later Edward VIII] had to appear in a uniform with swaddling-clothes. In one hand he held a wand, in the other a sword, and he had on something that looked a cross between a duffle coat and a mini skirt. It is sheer cruelty to have the Prince of Wales taken to Caernarfon and televised before four hundred million people. I ask the Minister to support me in preventing it.'

It was not prevented, of course. When his MG car arrived on the tarmac of the Welsh country house that morning in a final publicity push, Charles entered a room with a waiting camera and lights rigged by British Pathé. He would provide a soundbite that would play out on newsreels in picture houses around the world as they showed the highlights of his investiture:

I feel that it is a very impressive ceremony. I know that perhaps some people would think it is rather anachronistic and out of place in this world, which is perhaps somewhat cynical. But I think it can mean quite a lot if one goes about it in the right way. I think it can have some form of symbolism. For me it is a way of officially dedicating one's life, or part of one's life to Wales. The Welsh people, after all, wanted it.

1

Creating a Prince of Wales

For thousands of years the birth of a son, and sometimes a daughter, to the chief of a tribe was greeted with celebration and relief. The existence of an heir confirmed the longevity of the line. A strong leader was nothing without a successor, and for millennia the figureheads of countries and continents have corralled their populations around their own superior status to fight wars and to populate new lands. They had the power to persuade and press their followers to fight and die on their behalf in battles from Bosworth Field to Massachusetts and Mumbai. They could command taxes and treasure from their subjects as much as from their conquered territories, and the many wars and land-grabs would often enrich the leader's coffers as much as it would expand their empires. Each ruler had his trusted advisors, from the tribal elders to the royal court, but there were few accessories more valuable to a king's grip on power than the arrival of an heir. For over seven hundred years the Prince of Wales has been heir to the crown – first of England, and then of Britain. But just as monarchy has survived the redrawing of boundaries and the development of democracy, the title of Prince of Wales has endured in spite of the tension of its creation and the indiscretions of some of the men who held it.

And they have always been men. Kind men, mean men, lecherous men, clever men. Men who were empathetic and flawed, men who were clever and conniving. The short-lived, short-tempered and short-trousered. Those who made the title of Prince of Wales a laughing-stock, and those who made the job last a lifetime. Since 1301 the Prince of Wales has been a title and little else – it comes with no land with which to recoup rents, income or taxes. While the Welsh nation is notionally attached, no Prince of Wales has been Welsh since the thirteenth century and no product or place in the country is indelibly tied up with the title. When William was created Prince of Wales in 2022 it was in the gift of his father, the King, to pass it to his eldest son. The more lucrative decoration for the first in line to the throne is the Duchy of Cornwall, a profitable portfolio of assets that immediately passed into the possession of William at the moment of his grandmother's death. The title of Prince of Wales does not come with a prescribed or specific routine, nor an official regalia. Recent centuries have seen the adoption of the three ostrich feathers as an official crest, but items such as the crown worn by Charles at his investiture were a 1960s creation likened more to a sparkling kitchen colander than a symbol of the ancient English throne. Under the British monarchy the Prince of Wales has been a badge worn by the male heir, and a title with which the bearer can do as they please. The very absence of any onerous duties belies the great political significance of its creation under the English Crown, its symbolism a potent and still sometimes toxic reminder of the conquering armies that rampaged across western Britain in the thirteenth century.

The original Welsh Princes of Wales weren't heirs or spares, but the leaders of their kingdoms. The Welsh word for prince, *tywysog*, came to mean a male leader. But it is a word which defines itself as more than the chief of a tribe. Should somebody express in Welsh that they wish to *tywys* you, then their role is that of a guide. They are an experienced companion who can steer you through unfamiliar territory, from darkness into light. They are not second-in-command or a king-in-waiting. In the history of Welsh princes, they were men whose territory was hard-won and fiercely defended, but who were noted, too, for their compassion and desire to improve the lives of their people. Many layers of mythology have been applied to the Welsh Princes of the Middle Ages. The likes of Hywel Dda, Llywelyn ap Gruffydd and Owain Glyndŵr have legacies which are swathed in historical treacle. The goal of creating political unity in Wales and leading resistance to invading armies, is often the sum total of modern Welsh understanding of the princes that ruled around a thousand years ago. It was a Wales that placed itself firmly among the nations of Europe, and which had embraced Christianity and the role of religion in public life.

The Wales that was ruled by Welsh princes had barely a town on the map. Its territory was farmed by labourers and slaves, with the warring princes ruling a number of different kingdoms within the modern map of Wales. The Welsh saw themselves as the natural leaders of Britain, a position earned by being descendants of the Celtic tribes who had settled broadly across the isles of what would become the United Kingdom centuries later. But while the Welsh may have laid claim to much of the island of Britain, the occupiers of modern-day England saw a population now enclosed on its western edge and which was different to the rest of them. Their Celtic genetics gave them a more fierce appearance, while their tongues spoke a Welsh language that bore little relation to the Anglo-Saxon English that developed next door. The Welsh princes, far from edging towards broader domination of Britain, would face a fight to stop their territory being gobbled by an all-consuming England.

This book is not an historical account of all of the princes, but it is important to note the title-holders who came before Charles. The treachery and gruesome torture of the Middle Ages has left scars that run deep in the psyche of many who oppose monarchy, support Welsh independence, or both. The name of Llywelyn ap Gruffydd is incanted by those who despise Charles's embodiment of the role of Prince of Wales and will be as hostile to William in his attempts to carve out his own distinctive path. But even those with milder antipathy and who oppose the title without any personal vindictiveness against the most recent incumbents will invoke the name of Llywelyn ap Gruffydd as the never-to-be-forgotten and final true Prince of Wales.

Llywelyn ap Gruffydd
Prince of Wales 1258-1282

Llywelyn's claim to be Prince of Wales in the thirteenth century was confirmed not just by the extent of the territory he managed to rule – around three quarters of Wales – but by the acknowledgement of the English monarch at the time, Henry III, that Llywelyn deserved the title. Nobody before had ever been called Prince of Wales by a King of England. The official recognition of Llywelyn's status came when both men agreed to the Treaty of Montgomery, signed on 29 September 1267 near the town which sits on the border between the two nations. The treaty required Llywelyn to give homage to the King, but it also gave land and power to the Welsh prince following years of fighting. Such was the significance of the Treaty of Montgomery that it was brokered, in part, by the Pope's representative in Britain and signed by Llywelyn and Henry near the bank of the River Severn at Rhydwhyman.

Generations of princes of the different parts of Wales had fought over land, but only Llywelyn had succeeded in reaching a political deal that would allow him to use the title. The price of the agreement was high, with Llywelyn required to pay the Crown an annual levy which was equivalent to millions of pounds in today's money. The bill was several times higher than Llywelyn's existing annual income from the land he controlled, and in order to pay for the treaty the Welsh people would be required to contribute more to the coffers. Llywelyn's rule was oppressive according to some of the people, predominately those in the north-west territory of Gwynedd, who had to pay the price. Gwynedd was Llywelyn's home, but it was also the most productive of the Welsh land under his control. He appointed tax collectors to recoup the revenue required to satisfy the King, proving that Llywelyn was prepared to pay an eye-watering amount to the English Crown for the right to keep calling himself the Prince of Wales. It also made him Prince of the Princes, a unifying figure for the Welsh following decades of bloody conflict among local leaders and between English and Welsh armies.

The relative tranquillity of those early years of Llywelyn's rule as Prince of Wales came after a brutal campaign that spanned two decades. He had fought with Henry III's armies for most of that time. Llywelyn's grip on power had also pitched him against his brothers; family ties had become obstacles to political dominance. Llywelyn banished his siblings and created alliances with Welsh noblemen to advance his dream of a unified Welsh principality, while Henry had faced his own local revolt. English landowners, led by Henry's brother-in-law Simon de Montford, fought against the King. It was a war that briefly suspended the monarch's grip on some English territory and posed a direct threat to his reign. Nobilities of the Middle Ages seemed to intertwine as much, if not more, than their modern equivalents. Llywelyn backed de Montford and would later marry his daughter Eleanor. When de Montford was eventually cornered and killed in 1265, the King's troubles in England subsided.

Reaching rapprochement with the de facto leader of the Welsh was part of the broader settling of arguments, and two years later Henry and Llywelyn met to sign the Treaty of Montgomery near the banks of the River Severn. While Llywelyn had achieved his ambition, within a decade his principality would be decimated by further battles and a changing monarch. The Treaty of Montgomery had given Llywelyn the right to be called Prince of Wales, but the use of the title by the Welsh leader relied on the continuing approval of the King of England.

In 1272 Henry III died at the Palace of Westminster, his reign of fifty-six years ending with his burial in the grave of Edward the Confessor at Westminster Abbey and his heart removed and despatched to a holy spot at Fontevrault in Anjou, France. His son, Edward I, would construct an ornate tomb at Westminster Abbey to honour his father's legacy. But Edward would also push back against the alliance made in Wales to an ultimately devastating effect.

The relationship between Edward I and Llywelyn was fragile from the beginning. Llywelyn, who had to pay homage to the new monarch as part of the agreement to keep the title of Prince of Wales, did not attend Edward's coronation in Westminster Abbey. He also declined several opportunities to publicly swear allegiance to the new King. Llywelyn's brothers contributed to the worsening relationship, assisting with local rebellions against Llywelyn's rule and being granted sanctuary in England by Edward when they were forced into exile.

Money flowed intermittently from Wales to the Crown, and the Prince of Wales's attempts to quell opposition and fortify his principality led to the building of new castles and extensions to existing battlements. From a high point of Welsh unity, Llywelyn's rule over Wales was eroded until he was largely confined to the north-west territory of Gwynedd, his original fiefdom. Ten years on from the signing of the Treaty of Montgomery in 1267, Llywelyn's principality was curtailed and under threat of being completely consumed by the English Crown. Edward's armies had taken back Llywelyn's territory, and the King's castles began to encircle the Welsh. His grip on Wales was slowed only by an agreement in 1277 to end the fighting, and which stripped away much of the power that the Prince of Wales had managed to consolidate. He was allowed to keep part of Gwynedd and could retain his title, but the Prince had ceded control of the rest of Wales to Edward's armies.

Nursing his reduced realm, Llywelyn continued with his agreed marriage to Eleanor de Montford and they were wed on the feast day of St Edward the Confessor, the patron saint of English monarchs, at Worcester Cathedral. The bride was presented to the groom by Edward I, who also paid for the feast. Despite the warring between them, this was a symbol of the accord that had seemingly been reached. The Prince of Wales finally paid homage to Edward I, but the celebrations at Worcester were the last hurrah for this souring alliance. One final conflict would finish off the last Welsh prince.

In 1282 the total conquest of Wales by Edward would

be triggered not by the King or the Prince of Wales, but by Llywelyn's brother Dafydd. The brothers had been reconciled after previous acrimony, but Dafydd was politically fickle and by 1281 he was both disillusioned by his brother's pursuits and bitter about his own limited success. On Palm Sunday, Dafydd attacked Hawarden Castle, and then raided Rhuddlan Castle, while other rebellions broke out which sought to shake the remaining foundations of Llywelyn's shrinking principality. It riled Edward, whose response was to stage a summer campaign to end the Welsh problem for good. Fighting broke out in several locations until a fleet of Edward's ships captured the island of Anglesey, part of Llywelyn's Gwynedd. The King's troops ruined the harvest on the island, depriving Llywelyn and his men of food. Now besieged, the Prince of Wales was offered the opportunity to surrender to Edward. If Llywelyn agreed, he would be given an earldom in England on the condition that no Welsh prince would rule over Gwynedd again. Llywelyn refused to leave his people to the King's mercy and declined the chance to live in English exile.

Llywelyn raged. 'We fight because we are forced to fight, for we, and all Wales, are oppressed, subjugated, despoiled, reduced to servitude by the royal officers and bailiffs,' he wrote to the Archbishop of Canterbury, John Peckham. The correspondence was clear, and as the archbishop relayed Llywelyn's determination to the King, the Prince of Wales left the vulnerable Gwynedd to concentrate his court in Mid Wales. Llywelyn had been well-supported in the area, but on 11 December 1282 he arrived at Cilmeri near Builth Wells where an English army lay in wait.

Many stories survive about Llywelyn's death, but it seems certain that Edward had placed the elimination of the Prince of Wales as the main objective of the war. He was killed near the River Irfon, a site now marked by a public house – the Prince Llewelyn Inn – and a stone monument often adorned with a Welsh flag and a floral tribute to Llywelyn the Last. While he was slain on this site, his body was mutilated and taken as a trophy. Llywelyn's head was carried to London, to be viewed by the King as confirmation that the Prince of Wales was dead. With Edward's approval the head was then mounted on a pike, and contemptuously crowned with ivy. It was immediately displayed in London and remained in place for a considerable length of time. The skull was said to still be atop a pike some fifteen years later. What remained of Llywelyn's body was buried at the Abbey of Cwmhir, nestled among deep woods near Llandrindod Wells.

Dafydd ap Gruffydd
Prince of Wales 1282–1283

The end of Llywelyn was not the end of the line, with his brother Dafydd seen as the natural successor to the family fight to regain a principality led by a Welshman. While he maintained the rebellion against the Crown, Dafydd's resistance only lasted six months. He was captured in the summer of 1283 and given the grizzly execution that would become the trademark treatment for those considered guilty of treason against the King: he was hanged at Shrewsbury before his entrails were removed and burnt, and his body split in four parts and sent to four English cities. It was one of the first recorded occasions of a person accused of treason being hanged, drawn and quartered for the pleasure of the monarch. The fate of the children of the Welsh princes was less gruesome but just as effective in ending the royal lineage. Llywelyn's only child, his young daughter Gwenllian, was captured and sent to a convent in Lincolnshire where she would live until her death some fifty-five years later. She was a prisoner housed in a religious cage, a Princess of Wales exiled to the furthest reaches of England. Dafydd's daughter was also dispatched to a nunnery, while his two sons were imprisoned at Bristol Castle where the eldest – heir to the Prince of Wales title – would die in what some deemed mysterious circumstances and others deduced was the result of malnutrition; the youngest son would remain captive in Bristol for decades, before he gradually disappeared from any further records.

That Edward would try so deliberately and so determinedly to end Llywelyn's claim to the title of Prince of Wales is unsurprising; the extent to which he sought to round up, entrap and remove Llywelyn's extended family links with the old principality speaks to the paranoia of the age. The prospect of further rebellion was almost guaranteed. Edward's ruthless destruction of the Welsh royal court allowed him to keep the Prince of Wales title for those who would inherit the English Crown.

No pass

Edward II
Prince of Wales 1301–1307

It was no coincidence that the first Prince of Wales to be created by the King of England was born deep inside Welsh territory. Edward was the fourth son of King Edward I when he arrived in April 1284 at Caernarfon Castle. Two of his older brothers had died before he was born, while the third brother Alfonso would die later in 1284 leaving the baby Edward as sole heir to his father's throne. The fortress in Caernarfon was still being built and would grow into an unavoidable reminder to the people of Gwynedd and beyond that an English monarch now ruled in place of their defeated Welsh leader. The completed Caernarfon Castle did not have the more overt defensive capabilities of Harlech and Beaumaris which formed part of the Iron Ring of Edward's network of Welsh castles. But Caernarfon's sheer size allowed it to become a seat of power and crushing dominance over the subdued and reluctantly submissive Welsh.

The King and his Queen, Eleanor, had spent most of the previous summer at Caernarfon as intensive construction work was underway, so there was a chance the young Prince was conceived there too. The time and place of the Prince's birth, and potentially his conception, were politically serendipitous to the ongoing narrative of the English Crown. The new Prince Edward arrived two years after the death of Llywelyn, and a year after the siblings and offspring of the Welsh Court had been killed or contained. While he would not be created Prince of

Wales until he was seventeen, the young Edward's birth in the crucible of Welsh resistance could not have been more auspicious for the Crown's campaign. The birth of the Prince, and the expansion of Caernarfon Castle, did not crush Welsh resistance. The Middle Ages were peppered with skirmishes and bloody battles across swathes of Britain, Ireland and France which contributed to a rather restless childhood for Edward. Dermot Morrah wrote that 'the royal nursery was a peripatetic affair, the young Lord Edward and his five sisters (no more boys were born) being carted about in the wake of the King in his constant journeying to Wales, to the Scottish Border, and on frequent progresses about his English realm'. By 1300 and still a teenager, Prince Edward fought with his father on a campaign in Scotland. His father created him Prince of Wales in 1301, partly to exert further authority over a corner of the realm that still bubbled with resistance. Six years later he became King Edward II.

The tradition of creating a Prince of Wales for every first-in-line did not begin with Edward II but with his grandson, Edward of Woodstock, the Black Prince. He was thirteen when, on 23 May 1343 his father King Edward III invested him as Prince of Wales. Edward III had never been given the title, and so history records that the Black Prince was the first of what Dermot Morrah calls the 'continuous history of the English Princes of Wales'. Despite the pageantry and officialdom surrounding the monarch's use of the title, there would be one final Welsh claim to be Prince of Wales.

Owain Glyndŵr

Over a century after the death of Llywelyn ap Gruffydd, one man made certain that the memory of the Welsh princes had not been wiped from the national consciousness. The endless attempts to repress and subdue the Welsh had granted English kings a level of dominance over Wales and its people that the native princes had failed to accomplish themselves. It had left the population feeling oppressed, and they longed for a new Welsh leader to present himself and represent them. Owain Glyndŵr's rising in the fifteenth century managed to establish more order and authority over Wales than any native prince had achieved in hundreds of years.

At Glyndyfrdwy in north-east Wales a small crowd gathered on 16 September 1400 to create Owain ap Gruffydd, or Owain Glyndŵr, the new Prince of Wales. He was a man with the military skill to beat back the colonial army, while maintaining enough political diplomacy to unite local Welsh lords and rebel leaders in support of his cause. The Welsh had watched Edward I and his heirs exerting power after the death of Llywelyn, and had witnessed the crushing and controlling effects of the castle construction and land-grabbing. Famine and plague worsened what must have been a fairly miserable existence, with failed harvests and the Black Death instilling rebellious anger in those who had yet to succumb to starvation or disease. As well as famine and plague, social tension was spurred by some of the harsh laws that Edward I had imposed on the Welsh population.

The English came to populate the towns that grew around the new castles in Conwy and Caernarfon, and they were given special rights that formed part of the economic element of this military conquest. Only the English could trade within the walled towns around Edward's new castles, with the Welsh kept as outsiders in their own land.

Owain Glyndŵr was in his forties when the stars almost literally aligned for him at the turn of the fifteenth century. He was a member of the Welsh nobility, and could trace his lineage back to the royal rulers of Wales before Edward. Through marriage he was related to the Gwynedd princes, while his father's family were descended from the twelfth-century princes of Powys Fadog in Mid Wales. Through his mother, Glyndŵr was descended from the Princes of Deheubarth in the South West. His pedigree allowed him to claim regal connections across Wales and gave him authority among those who remembered the various Welsh principalities as he embarked on a campaign to reclaim the territory and become a Prince of Wales himself. He was buoyed by a tradition of Welsh political prophecy, heightened by the appearance of a comet in the skies at that time. Anybody reading the runes in medieval Wales could easily place Glyndŵr at the heart of a great rebellion, with soothsayers foreseeing that he could reclaim land and dignity for the people of Wales after their subjugation at the hands of English kings and non-native Princes of Wales. The mythologising of Owain Glyndŵr began before his campaign and would continue for centuries after his defeat. He was a prodigal son who understood his Welsh heritage, while his land-owning under the Crown gave him useful insight into the English colonial attitude. And, like Llywelyn before him, Glyndŵr also saw an opportunity to strike while the Crown was weakened by events in England. Richard II had been deposed in 1399, the raging King overthrown by Henry Bollingbroke – Henry IV – who had schemed to take control of the royal court.

Glyndŵr's land in North and South Wales gave him wealth, and he held a court at Sycharth near Llangollen in north-east Wales which had a legendary splendour. The poet Iolo Goch, to whom Glyndŵr was a patron, composed works in honour of his master and his household that described the gardens, orchards and vineyards that surrounded a manor house of great architectural standard. After Glyndŵr was elevated to be the Prince of Wales in 1400 by the noblemen at his other court, Glyndyfrdwy, he launched a revolt against English rule that would see his lands forfeited in the pursuit of freedom. The rebellion peaked around 1406 when his men captured key battlements in Aberystwyth and Harlech.

Alongside the military victories, Glyndŵr also sought to establish his vision for an emerging Welsh state. France had backed the rebellion, and in a letter to the French King Charles VI in March 1406, Owain Glyndŵr asked for continued support in ridding Wales of its English monarch. It was composed in Pennal, a settlement near the north bank of the River Dyfi on the southern edge of Gwynedd. The letter is a unique record of the potential structure of an independent Wales in the Middle Ages. Known as the Pennal Letter, Glyndŵr's words were written during a meeting of the Welsh church. Glyndŵr said he would swear allegiance to the Pope of Avignon, rather than the Pope in Rome, in return for the establishment and recognition of a formal Welsh church. The Bishop of St Davids would lead a communion whose catchment would spread as far east as Lichfield and Bath. After brutal battles against the English, it was this vision of a decolonised Wales which Glyndŵr presented as the future fruits of his endeavours. Universities would be established in North and South Wales, and he called for the French monarch's support in repelling the English and fortifying a resurgent Welsh nation. But further French support evaporated more quickly than the dream of an autonomous Welsh nation.

In his meditation on Welsh nationhood, *When Was Wales?*, the writer and film-maker Gwyn Alf Williams outlined Glyndŵr's ability to unite a basket of grievances and ingrained wrongs.

It was a quarrel in the March which ignited a race war; it was a civil war; it was an explosion of anger and hatred from the unfree and oppressed; it was a peasant *jacquerie*; it was a rebellion by rising squireens against the restrictions of an archaic regime; it was a revolt of frustrated intellectuals within the church; it was a feudal war to create some kind of Burgundy within Britain. These all fused, like so many rebellions we have seen since, into a war of national liberation against a colonial regime riddled with contradiction.

And yet the many fronts and numerous causes that had spurred his rebellion were beginning to lose their momentum. In the same year that Glyndŵr composed the Pennal Letter, his grip on Wales was loosening. From 1406 territory was lost and some parts of Wales asked for pardons from the King, though it was not the end of Glyndŵr. His campaigns continued sporadically, but this was a rebel on the run and not a princely hero. He faded into the background, with no record of his rebellion after 1415.

The absence of a public spectacle around his death allowed those Welsh who had prophesied his rebellion to romanticise his disappearance. He had been a leader with a vision for Wales and had briefly succeeded in continuing the ambition of Llywelyn that had been so forcefully crushed by Edward I some hundred and thirty years earlier. He was a modern, European leader with a plan for Wales that would not be realised again until the election of members of the National Assembly in 1999. Glyndŵr's strength was ultimately in his ability to remain in the national consciousness, to keep alive the memory of a fighting nation which rebelled for almost fifteen years. The man has been transformed from an historical figure into an almost mythological leader, the ultimate Welsh patriot and an inspiration for modern Welsh nationalism. Most of the other Welsh princes had been focused on gripping power and taking land, but Owain Glyndŵr was a leader with a much broader vision to enrich the principality he ruled. While he succeeded in reviving the ideas of a Welsh nation after the death of

Llywelyn, the death of Owain Glyndŵr was the end of the true last native Welsh Prince. With his disappearance, the very idea of a Welsh monarchy died forever.

Every Prince of Wales since Owain Glyndŵr has been created by the Crown, an institution that has clung to the tradition of bestowing that title on the first-in-line despite happily discarding all sorts of anachronistic decorations over the centuries. The monarchy has frequently modernised to meet changing tastes or challenging circumstances. Yet despite the executions, the merging of the English and Scottish Crowns and the creation of a House of Tudor from Welsh roots, the Prince of Wales has remained the creation of an English and latterly a British monarchy whose foundations cling to a thousand years of history. Its colonial footprints stretch around the world, but the conquering of the Welsh created a trophy that would become symbolic of the continuity of the monarchy. The existence of a Prince of Wales reaffirmed the hereditary principle, decorated the next-in-line and hallmarked the pedigree. Its use has sometimes waned over the centuries, as monarchs changed more quickly than in recent history or in the absence of a male heir. But throughout its creation by the monarch, the title-holders had given very little concern for Wales or any calling to care for the Welsh. Only with the arrival of Charles, and his elevation to be Prince of Wales, did the title-holder show a compassion for the Welsh people that would rival the loyalty shown by Owain Glyndŵr, whether they wanted it or not.

Charles was born at 9.14 pm on 14 November 1948 at Buckingham Palace. Crowds had been building outside throughout the day, finding vantage points on the Victoria Memorial and growing deeper in number against the railings. The Duke of Edinburgh, having become restless at the length of time it was taking for his first child to emerge into the world, 'changed into flannels and a roll-collar sweater' and went to the palace squash court with his private secretary, according to Dermot Morrah. By the evening there were a few thousand people outside, with police officers clearing a space in the crowds for doctors and midwives whose arrival signalled the imminent appearance of a prince. The Duke was still playing squash when he was told that he had become a father. At almost midnight a notice was placed on the palace railings announcing that the Princess Elizabeth had safely delivered a son. On the BBC light programme the announcer Franklin Engleman broke the news. 'It has just been announced from Buckingham Palace that Her Royal Highness, Princess Elizabeth, Duchess of Edinburgh, has safely delivered a prince at 9.14 pm and that her Royal Highness and her son are both doing well. Listeners will wish us to offer their loyal congratulations to Princess Elizabeth and to the royal family on this happy occasion,' he declared in a crisp BBC voice.

After midnight a police car with a loudspeaker sought to hush the crowd as the first baby to be born in Buckingham Palace for sixty-two years risked being kept awake by the revellers outside. Morrah's impeccable account of the night recalls the loudhailer repeating countless times: 'Ladies and gentlemen, it is requested from the palace that we have a little quietness, if you please.' The singing crowds drowned out the announcements.

While the numbers thinned, the news spread around the world. Pre-prepared telegrams were sent to governors and ambassadors overseas, while the newspapers set to work reporting the evening and predicting the little boy's future. They speculated intently about his education, which armed forces he might join and what type of king he may become. Few, if any, journalists appeared to spend time discussing what the boy may do in the years before his accession to the throne. None would have predicted that Charles could spend almost a lifetime as heir, and why would they? The reigns of monarchs had been remarkably short. When Charles was born his grandfather would last another four years as King before dying of cancer in 1952. He had reluctantly taken the throne in 1936 when Edward VIII lasted three hundred and twenty-five days in the role. Before that there was George V: sixteen years, and Edward VII: nine years. Had the newspaper columnists looked to Victoria (almost sixty-four years) then the prospect of a female monarch in Elizabeth II may have led them to realise that this newborn future King faced a significant wait before his regnal qualities could be assessed.

A month after his birth the baby boy was christened in the music room at Buckingham Palace. Charles Philip Arthur George was baptised by the Archbishop of Canterbury with water from the River Jordan. It was the moment at which Charles was tethered to a Christian faith

21

which he would vow to defend at the moment of his coronation. While some royal traditions were essential, some practices were modernised. By the time he was eight years old, and his mother had become Queen, Charles was sent to school. Private tutors had been preferred by royalty, their offspring seemingly above attending even the best schools until the middle of the twentieth century. At Hill House, then a small prep school in London, Charles's teachers and pupils were encouraged to address him by his first name and to treat him as any other boy in class. He was the only boy to be raised in a palace, and despite efforts by his parents and nannies to keep him grounded, there were some experiences the young Prince could not relate to. This included the idea of going to a shop, as Dermot Morrah's well-informed book on Charles's schooling described how 'he knew nothing about money and never handled it. One of the first tasks of the school was to teach him the values of these various bronze and cupro-nickel discs with his mother's head on them. And it was not until six months after he went to Hill House that he made his first journey on a bus'.

A few months later he was wearing the uniform of a new school. An embroidered 'C' marked the centre of his royal-blue school cap, not for 'Charles' but for Cheam School in Berkshire. His first term was notable for an early accusation of press intrusion – dozens of newspaper stories remarked on his school days, his companions and his teachers. An intervention by the Queen's press secretary put Fleet Street on notice, and the attention then focused only on newsworthy matters. Happily, one presented itself for the papers and the Prince in the summer of 1958.

The Queen had been due to attend that year's British Empire and Commonwealth Games in Cardiff, but a recurring bout of sinusitis kept her under medical supervision in London. Instead, the Duke of Edinburgh deputised for the monarch at the official opening on 18 July. A new Wales Empire Pool had been constructed in Cardiff's city centre for the event. Boxing and wrestling events were held at Sophia Gardens across the River Taff, while cyclists raced around Maindy Stadium. By the end of the competitions, England topped the medal table while Wales managed a respectable eleventh place out of the thirty-six nations and territories to take part. The boxer Howard Winstone secured the host country's only gold medal.

Over forty thousand people crammed into Cardiff Arms Park for the closing ceremony on Saturday 26 July 1958. The Band of the Welsh Guards played 'We'll keep a welcome in the hillsides' and 'Auld Lang Syne' as the teams paraded around the stadium, drowned out briefly by the roar of an RAF fly-past. The band would also play God Save the Queen for the guest of honour, and while she was not there in person, the Queen did record a message to be played to the crowd. Prince Charles and some of the other boys at Cheam School were invited to the headmaster's study to watch the ceremony on television. In the stadium, and on the tiny black-and-white set, the Queen's voice closed the event with a sensational twist:

The British Empire and Commonwealth Games in the capital, together with all the activities of the Festival of Wales, have made this a memorable year for the Principality. I have therefore decided to mark it further by an act which will, I hope, give as much pleasure to all Welshmen as it does to me. I intend to create my son, Charles, Prince of Wales today. When he is grown up, I will present him to you at Caernarfon.

It was a moment of acute embarrassment for Charles, his face flushing as his friends turned to congratulate him. 'I remember thinking, "What on earth have I been let in for?" That is my overriding memory,' Charles would later recall. He told his biographer Jonathan Dimbleby that the moment of the announcement confirmed the 'awful truth', and that his fate was sealed. He was nine years and eight months old, but already realised the enormity and, perhaps, the loneliness of his position.

It was a surprise to the introverted Charles and to almost everybody else. The prime minister Harold Macmillan had been informed two days earlier. Beside the PM and the heads of some Commonwealth nations, only around half a dozen other officials were aware of the intention to create a new Prince of Wales at the Games. The announcement in Cardiff completed the creation of the heir apparent with all of the decorations and titles he could be awarded for being the first-born child of the reigning monarch. He was His Royal Highness Prince Charles Philip Arthur George, Prince of Wales and Earl of Chester, Duke of Cornwall, Duke of Rothesay, Earl of

Carrick, Lord of the Isles and Baron of Renfrew, Prince and Great Steward of Scotland, Knight Companion of the Most Noble Order of the Garter. But at school he remained, simply, Charles. His transition from boy to Prince of Wales would only truly resonate with the world and the Welsh when the last of the Queen's words at the Empire Games were enacted at Caernarfon in 1969.

The immediate concern of the self-styled national newspaper of Wales, the *Western Mail*, was the question of Charles's first visit to Wales since being made Prince of Wales. On the Monday after the closing ceremony of the Empire Games, its front-page headline asked: 'Prince of Wales here soon?' and 'We'll keep a welcome next week, says the Land of his Fathers'. A pre-publicised upcoming trip by the Queen and Duke of Edinburgh around the British coastline on the Royal Yacht Britannia now carried the added thrill, for the papers at least, that the newly created Prince of Wales would step ashore when the yacht was due to call at Holyhead on Anglesey the following month. 'All Wales was wondering last night whether the Prince of Wales will pay his first official visit to the Principality on August 9,' the newspaper proclaimed. Charles had been to Wales as a boy, including a surreptitious trip to Milford Haven by motor launch from the royal yacht, where he spent a pleasant few hours playing on the beach with his sister and Prince Michael of Kent. While the speculation filled a page, so too did the messages of congratulations for the new Prince of Wales. They came from heads of state and the individual Lord-Lieutenants of the counties of Wales. These days, what might be considered the most awkward greeting came from the village of Nettleham in Lincolnshire. In 1301 King Edward I was staying in the Bishop's Palace in Nettleham when he created his son – later Edward II – Prince of Wales. Over six hundred and fifty years after the creation of the first Prince of Wales by an English monarch, the vicar of Nettleham sent a telegram to the Queen. 'God bless the Prince of Wales,' wrote the Reverend George Herrington, who conveyed the town's 'loyal greetings' and welcomed the creation of this latest Prince of Wales. Hindsight allows us to view the message as being almost troubling, as it underlined the link between the new Prince of Wales and the bloody struggle which preceded the first use of the title by the English Crown. But Wales in 1958 did not have the national confidence to interrogate the tradition of the title, or to question its continuation. The telegram from Nettleham, just like the one from the premier of South Africa, was printed alongside the good wishes from the four corners of the planet. The praise from Wales was gushing. 'I would like you to know,' wrote the chairman of Glamorgan County Council, 'that your announcement creating Prince Charles Prince of Wales has been received with great enthusiasm and delight by the people of Glamorgan. God Bless the Prince of Wales.' The Lord Mayor of Cardiff pushed the envelope a little further. 'Wales hails with joy Your Majesty's profound announcement,' wrote the Alderman A.J. Williams. There were similar effusive proclamations from lord mayors and council chairmen. A comparison with the conquering of the native Welsh princes by the English Crown came from the unlikely direction of the Archbishop of Wales, though he did so with diplomacy and grace:

> The news that Prince Charles is to be Prince of Wales comes from a Queen who has conquered Wales in very different fashion, namely, a dedication to high service, selflessly and steadfastly maintained, which has evoked the reverent and affectionate loyalty of us all.

Welsh cultural institutions threw some weight behind the announcement. The committee of the 1958 Royal National Eisteddfod of Wales conveyed 'their delight at the news that Your Majesty has this day been pleased to create His Royal Highness Prince Charles, Duke of Cornwall, Prince of Wales'. The *Western Mail* reported that the first to toast the Prince of Wales was the Delhi Welsh Society, who were holding their thirteenth annual reunion in the Park Hotel in Cardiff after the Empire Games closing ceremony. In England, too, the event was marked. Bellringers rang a peal of 'Kent treble bob royal, lasting over three hours, at Chesterfield parish church,' reported *The Times*.

The celebrations prompted Cardiff's lord mayor to suggest the city's imposing Victorian gothic castle should be handed over to Charles for state occasions. Sir Thomas Williams told the press that Cardiff should offer use of the castle to the new Prince of Wales 'so that he could meet his Welsh subjects', suggesting Charles may want to take up residence in the city for a month each year.

If the wave of messages and yards of newspaper

columns proved anything, it was the value of royal news to a nation still hooked on the fairy tale trimmings of a modern monarchy. If there were those who shared Charles's private pang of anxiety at the prospect of a new Prince of Wales, they were not included in the publicised reaction.

Two weeks later Charles arrived at Holyhead on Anglesey on the Royal Yacht Britannia as part of the annual west coast cruise to Scotland. The *Western Mail* reported: 'The Prince of Wales stepped ashore on his own domain on Saturday for the first time since the Queen gave him his new title, and although cosmopolitan Holyhead had the honour of giving him a welcome of warm affection, all Anglesey was delighted at the Prince's unexpected visit to the "Mother of Wales".' The front-page article was accompanied by a photograph of Charles as he 'takes a peep at the *Western Mail* cameraman' over the shoulder of his sister, Princess Anne. The children were taken on a tour of the island by Lord and Lady Mountbatten, and after lunch at Plas Newydd, home of the Marquess of Anglesey, the royals reconvened at Holyhead to board Britannia. Crowds reportedly broke through police cordons to get close to the Queen, the Duke of Edinburgh, the Prince of Wales and Princess Anne as they arrived at Mackenzie Pier.

After this brief visit, the Royal Yacht sailed to Scotland and the creation of the new Prince of Wales had little practical implications in the years that followed. Prayer books were altered with pens in Anglican churches, substituting 'Charles Prince of Wales' for the previously printed 'Charles Duke of Cornwall' in prayers for the royal family until updated copies could be issued. Press speculation rumbled about how and when the Queen may choose to enact her commitment to present Charles to the Welsh at Caernarfon Castle. And behind palace doors a royal spectacle was devised to invest the Prince of Wales, and a plan concocted to try and ingratiate Charles with the Welsh.

2

Sending the Prince to Wales

'Fydda i ddim yn gadael i'r Gymraeg ddiflanu heb ymladd hyd yr eithaf.'

'I will not let the Welsh language die without fighting til the end.'

The murmurations of starlings which flock and float above the autumn waves off Aberystwyth prom had left to nest by the time Charles arrived in town. It was just as well, as his term studying Welsh made him the main attraction – at least with a certain demographic. 'When he left his student halls at Pantycelyn to drive down to the old college, all the little old ladies would come out of their houses to wave at the future Prince of Wales.' I was sitting with Lord Dafydd Elis-Thomas at a pandemic-approved distance in April 2021 as the former culture minister described the appeal of the heir in Aberystwyth. 'They were little grannies, I think they had learned his timetable and would emerge as soon as his blue MG pulled out of Pantycelyn.'

Lord Elis-Thomas was a Welsh nationalist and a chair of Plaid Cymru's youth wing in 1969, but his sensible outlook on life meant he was among the students at Aber, as it's known, who were invited to share seminars with the future King. It was an early interaction with Charles which would flourish into friendship later when Lord Elis-Thomas became the first Presiding Officer – effectively the Speaker – of the new National Assembly for Wales. The role allowed him a regular audience with Charles, and to the disdain of his former Plaid Cymru colleagues Lord Elis-Thomas became so enamoured that he treated the Prince almost as a de facto head of state. So it is perhaps unsurprising that he took an agnostic attitude in Aber in 1969.

The little old ladies may have been putting pressure on Charles, but it was Special Branch causing concern for others in the town. Undercover officers, based out of Shrewsbury, joined local detectives in monitoring potential troublemakers. While Charles was given tailored tuition on the ancient Princes of Wales, the laws of Hywel Dda and a crash course in spoken Welsh, the local Welsh nationalists from Plaid Cymru candidates to hapless vandals were regularly stopped and occasionally rounded up. But not Dafydd Elis-Thomas, who found himself at the Black Lion pub where the local coppers would drink. In another bar you'd share a pint with the Prince's closest companion in Aberystwyth, his equerry David Checketts. He was an ex-RAF squadron leader who had looked after the younger Charles during a brief time studying in Australia in 1966. Having swapped Sydney Harbour for Ceredigion Bay the smart Checketts found time for quiet drinks when the Prince had taken to his student room. Professor Sir Deian Hopkin, who taught at Aberystwyth at the time, recalled bumping into the equerry among the academics. 'Just up from the college, in Laura Place, opposite the church was what was called Staff House. It was a house which was a club for the staff. And Checketts used to come there. He didn't say very much, but we would try him out, and say, "Oh, what is he like?" But we got nothing much!' Hopkin is one of Wales's finest jazz musicians, as well as being a professor of Welsh history and a former Vice Chancellor of South Bank University. But at Aber he was one of the youngest lecturers at the college and found the Prince to be an intriguing student. Deian Hopkin also noted the demographics of Charles's biggest fans – 'all these little old ladies saying "Ooh, lovely boy!"' – but also observed how the young Prince was allowed to settle into a term of tutorials. The lessons would instil in Charles a foundation of knowledge about Wales and the Welsh that would guide his relationship with the country for the next fifty years.

It had been announced in November 1967 that Charles would study at the University of Wales College at Aberystwyth. The student union's president, Roy Widdus, was pleased 'although I cannot really see that one term is long enough for the Prince,' he said at the time. The principal of the college was Sir Thomas Parry, a former librarian of the National Library of Wales and a distinguished figure in Welsh life. Sir Thomas said an education in Aberystwyth would give Charles 'an insight into the history of Wales, its literature and the whole background of present Welsh life.'

Not everybody was as vocal in their welcome. A few days after the announcement, the breadth of feeling among the student population was more adequately reflected in a motion passed by the union representing Welsh-speaking students. 'Don't send Charles here, say students,' the headline in *The Mirror* blared. A motion had been passed 'deploring the decision by the University College of Wales, Aberystwyth, to accept the Prince as a temporary student in 1969,' it said. The committee attacked the principle that a university place should be offered without sitting an exam. It also criticised the decision to offer a special course for Charles, who would study the Welsh language, history and Wales's 'current problems' during his term in the Welsh town. 'The committee in no way feels privileged at welcoming this special student into its midst, and realises that the only person who can feel privileged is the said student,' the students complained.

The decision to send Charles to Aberystwyth was a political one. There was pressure on the royal family from the government, in the form of the Secretary of State for Wales, George Thomas, to strengthen the union of the United Kingdom just as shoots of nationalism began to sprout. In July 1966 the Carmarthen by-election had been won by Gwynfor Evans who became the first Plaid Cymru member of parliament, while Winnie Ewing took the seat of Hamilton for the Scottish National Party in November 1967. In contrast to the singularly joyous press coverage of the creation of the Prince of Wales in 1958, the 1960s had sent a schism through the country's traditional values. The loosening of society's norms had given freedom for nationalism to grow beyond the far fringes of Welsh society. The established political orthodoxy in Wales, where the Labour government could guarantee a hefty return of MPs, faced challenges from an awakened, informed and sometimes rebellious population. The nationalist cause had been bolstered by the reaction to the drowning of the village of Capel Celyn in Gwynedd in 1965 to create a reservoir whose waters would flow to Liverpool and Wirral. Likewise the tragedy at Aberfan in 1966, where a tip of coal waste crushed a school and its pupils, fomented anger at the institutions which had allowed it to happen. The idea that a Prince could learn the language, history and culture of the Welsh during a tailored term was fanciful. For some, it was page-turning royal fodder in their morning paper, but for the politically energised it provided ammunition. His arrival in Aberystwyth provided a high-profile opportunity to rail against the establishment.

While the buds of political nationalism had begun to flower in the 1960s, a more fervent wing of Welsh nationalist extremism posed an immediate, unpredictable threat to the Prince's arrival in Aberystwyth. The Queen had concerns for 'my son's safety', the *Sunday Mirror* reported. It said the monarch had raised them with the prime minister in August 1968. Threats against him, which had been regarded as a joke, were now being treated seriously, the paper said. A Home Office conference of police chiefs had sought to prepare for the Prince's protection during his term at Aberystwyth, following the Queen's reported anxiety about the risks he may face from extremists in the seaside town.

The concern was real. In November 1967 a bomb planted at the Temple of Peace in Cardiff exploded at four o'clock in the morning. It had been timed to avoid injury, but to coincide with the day of a meeting about the Prince of Wales's investiture plans. *Mudiad Amddiffyn Cymru*, MAC, was responsible – the Movement for the Defence of Wales – and this was the latest in a series of similar bombings. In January 1968 a small device exploded at the Snowdonia Country Club, while the tax office in Llanishen in Cardiff was targeted in March of the same year. A month after the *Sunday Mirror*'s report of the Queen's anxiety, an alarm-clock style time-bomb exploded at RAF Pembrey in Carmarthenshire, seriously injuring a soldier. The bombs were all part of the campaign by MAC to draw publicity to their opposition to the British state. Its leader, John Jenkins, wanted to disrupt plans for the investiture. He would go further as the ceremony in Caernarfon approached, but no bombs interrupted the Prince's term at Aberystwyth.

'I expect at Aberystwyth there may be one or two demonstrations, and as long as I don't get covered too much in egg and tomato, I'll be all right,' the Prince said in the spring of 1969. 'But I don't blame people demonstrating like that. They've never seen me before, they don't know what I'm like. I've hardly been to Wales, and you can't really expect people to be over-zealous about the fact of having a so-called English Prince to come amongst them and be frightfully excited.' He was speaking on the radio, having given his first ever interview to the BBC broadcaster Jack de Manio. It was the latest stage in the introduction of Charles to the world, if not just to the Welsh. He lacked the PR polish of a politician, his anxieties hidden only by a realistic degree of concern about choppy waters in Aberystwyth en route to the investiture ceremony that summer. Dragged from happy studies at Cambridge to a history lesson on the Welsh coast, Charles's classes at Aberystwyth would be a prelude to the grand performance at Caernarfon Castle on the first of July.

The eggs did not materialise, let alone the tomatoes. To his surprise, a reassuring number of onlookers cheered Charles's arrival at the Pantycelyn student accommodation when he began his term at Aberystwyth. In correspondence seen by Jonathan Dimbleby, the Prince wrote: 'So far no demonstrations have occurred and in fact the welcome has been incredibly warm and reassuring.' In jacket and tie, the awkward Prince stood out regardless of the cameras and crowds. With him came a team of around a hundred police officers, enacting an elaborate and discreet operation to protect the heir to the throne during an unprecedented era of terrorism. The bombs were the ultimate fear, but there were plenty of small-scale protests for the police to monitor, mostly comprised of placard-wavers and hunger strikers who were seeking to highlight their political opposition to the Prince's presence.

In his public appearances Charles remained cheery if formal. In his biography Jonathan Dimbleby gave examples of the mischievous Prince that broke through in private. 'In a letter to his equerry from the registrar at Aberystwyth which ended with the hope, "I look forward to an uneventful term," the Prince scribbled in the margin "How boring!"... On a memorandum from the university noting that while at Aberystwyth "His Royal Highness... would comply with the College rules and regulations," he added the postscript, "Like hell!".'

For all the attention Charles got, making friends proved difficult. Dafydd Elis-Thomas was in Aberystwyth as a postgraduate student and saw the Prince in the occasional seminar. 'The whole point was that we were told to just treat him as you would any other student. Because that was what he wanted.' The tailor-made course for Charles allowed him to mix with students at seminars that were cherry-picked for him by his tutors. Lessons in Welsh history, as well as the causes of more recent evocations of Welsh nationalism, were delivered by Edward 'Tedi' Millward and Bobi Jones. Both men were committed nationalists and fervent republicans, but their choice was to educate the Prince with as much contemporary and historical Welsh context as could be condensed into his eight-week term.

'I was the chair of the Plaid youth section,' Dafydd Elis-Thomas reminded me. The nationalist party was doing well on the back of Gwynfor Evans's victory in Carmarthen and the debate ahead of the investiture. 'We had produced some cheeky stickers which said, '*Senedd, nid Tywysog*,' or something like that. So I was a sort-of republican.' Some stickers calling for a parliament in place of a Prince were small fry in the pond of opposition to Charles. 'I was on the national executive of Plaid Cymru, and there were very serious discussions as to how we should handle the situation.' While the purely political campaigners for Welsh independence had always condemned the militant few, the risk of being lumped together with violent extremists meant the Aberystwyth students who opposed Charles had to tread carefully. The need for caution came from the top of the party. 'Gwynfor was very keen that we shouldn't do anything that would antagonise the public,' Dafydd Elis-Thomas said.

Innocent nationalists were routinely stopped by police. It felt over-the-top to Dafydd and his friends, who were legitimately campaigning for a political cause that they believed in. Their movement was building, but the wave of Welsh nationalism in Aberystwyth was hitting the rocks of royal security. While some students were irritated by the onerous presence of detectives and checkpoints, it helped to know where the officers drank.

'There was a particular pub called the White Hart,' Dafydd Elis-Thomas grinned. 'It was frequented by police officers after hours. And as a postgraduate mature student, I found my way there quite easily.' The arrangement was helped by Dafydd Elis-Thomas's approach to his postgraduate research, which involved being at the library doors when they opened in the morning and heading to the pub after lunch. 'They were very hospitable, the people who ran the pub. And so [the police officers] would be there, and there would be all sorts of interesting discussions.' Dafydd raised his eyebrows at me and laughed. Some of the officers were local, Welsh-speaking detectives who were part of the team that protected the Prince and looked out for trouble.

Beyond the bar room of the White Hart, the monitoring of Charles's fellow students seemed intense. Dafydd called it 'serious, very in-depth surveillance activity' which targeted people in Aberystwyth and the surrounding area. The Special Branch operation had its basis in the credible threats posed by MAC, and the impact on student life was minimal beyond the politically active cohort. Even among the campaigners treading a straight and narrow path, there was pressure to become more disruptive. Dafydd said he met 'the guy who was allegedly an agent provocateur', a nationalist campaigner who suggested to him that the causes he believed in could be achieved through more dangerous means. 'The way to do it is with political violence, that is what he was trying to say.' Dafydd had nothing to do with him after that, he said, and vowed never to be seen in his presence for fear of the consequences. In later life Dafydd Elis-Thomas would go further, not just avoiding those who advocated violent means for achieving their goals but shopping arsonists to the police. The gelignite bombings by MAC were followed by the burning of holiday cottages in Welsh-speaking heartlands. It was an arson campaign which continued into the 1970s and 1980s. During that time Dafydd Elis-Thomas was elected as an MP and eventually led Plaid Cymru, and saw the torching of the cottages as detrimental to the political campaign to protect rural, Welsh-speaking communities. 'I actually did, personally, shop a few of the people suspected of cottage burning,' he told me. 'Because I thought the best thing I can do is to tell the police everything that I think I know, or may suspect, so that they can deal with it.' This was during the 1970s. He passed people's names to the police? 'Well, yes. Because I thought [the arson campaign] was extremely negative in its impact on the political arguments for housing, and really prevented – for years – any sensible policy on second homes, because it appeared that you were responding to what was, again, terrorism. The burning of property is terrorism.'

The gelignite bombs and the arson campaign against holiday homes were the violent sideshow of an otherwise peaceful, committed and legitimate political movement. Like Dafydd Elis-Thomas, most nationalists shunned violent protest of any kind. Special Branch in Aberystwyth gathered plenty of intelligence, but there were no bombings or burnings during Charles's time in the town. The greatest threats the Prince of Wales faced were some rather benign placards from the small groups who occasionally got in his way. He did get a shout of 'Go home, Charlie!' when he asked one protester what the Welsh slogan meant in English, and he knew the nationalists sang a mocking song about their English Prince of Wales.

'Carlo' by Dafydd Iwan was at the top of the Welsh language music charts; its title was a play on the name given to some pet dogs in Wales, but in this case it referenced the puppy Prince of Wales.

> I have a little friend who lives in Buckingham Palace
> And Carlo Windsor is his name…

Dafydd Iwan, who led the Welsh Language Society, used the song to highlight what he saw as transparent attempts to Welshify this English Prince. The chorus mocks his polo playing with 'dadi', and lampoons the idea that Charles was now a cultured Welshman.

> Every week he reads *Y Cymro* and *Y Faner*
> He reads Dafydd ap Gwilym in bed every night…

Knowing that the protesters were poking fun, Aberystwyth must have been lonely for a Prince who would rather have been with his new friends at Cambridge. Deian Hopkin told me that Charles seemed 'almost bewildered' by the experience, and that those who had met him found him to be 'terribly shy'. Correspondence published by Jonathan Dimbleby in his biography showed Charles was resigned to a degree of isolation. 'No-one can make any real friends in nine weeks,' he wrote in one message, while later in the term he confessed 'I suppose I've had a lonely time'. Opportunities to make friends failed to present themselves, despite the choreographed seminars and occasional common room drinks. In a television interview, broadcast after he had left Aberystwyth and before the investiture that summer, Charles blamed his royal status for putting off prospective friends.

You see, the trouble is that one has to remember that I'm in a slightly different position from several other people, and I think they try and put themselves in my position too much. I think out of certain necessity I have perhaps been more lonely. I mean, I haven't made a lot of friends, if that's what they mean, and I haven't been to a lot of parties or anything – there haven't been very many, and I've had a lot of other things to do. I mean, I've been around Wales a lot, looked at things and visited people, and essentially it is I suppose compared with other people's lives, more lonely, and in this sense I suppose I've had a lonely time.

Charles escaped the confines of the college. 'He didn't obviously immerse himself in college business,' Deian Hopkin recalled. 'He didn't take part in anything like that.' One person heard him practising the cello in his room. Some saw him surfing at Borth beach, the longest stretch of sand along the Ceredigion coast. He travelled around Wales at weekends, staying with friends and fishing on the Glanusk Estate near Abergavenny. In Aberystwyth there was a reticence to approach him, according to Hopkin. 'How do you treat somebody like that? We didn't have the same kind of social media, the same kind of exposures of people. It was an unnatural world, where they were over there, and we were over here.'

Charles's neighbour in his student hall at Pantycelyn did extend the hand of friendship. Like the Prince's tutors, his closest possible companion was also a nationalist and a republican, though it didn't interfere with their cordial, if slightly formal, relationship. Geraint Evans was studying international relations and philosophy at Aberystwyth and was in his final year in the Easter term of 1969. At the beginning of the academic year he had chosen a quiet room on the third floor of Pantycelyn. Evans's room was sandwiched between the Prince and the protection officer. While Geraint slept, Charles was on one side and the police were on the other. Their friendship, if you could call it that, mostly concerned polite smiles and small talk in the corridor, or in the canteen downstairs. Part of Evans's distance stemmed from his own need to concentrate on his academic work; the Prince's arrival at Pantycelyn had coincided with the busiest moment for those approaching the end of their studies.

Despite the busy schedule, there was time for tea. Geraint Evans told the BBC in 2022 that the Prince 'graciously said yes' to an invitation to tea at his parents' home in Talybont, around seven miles north of Aberystwyth. Some of Geraint's university friends also attended, and when Charles arrived they settled down to a spread of cake, trifle and tea prepared by Geraint's mother and father. 'The other thing to say about that occasion,' Geraint told the radio station, 'was that the policeman came as well. I suppose just in case we put something in the tea! But in the end it was a very happy occasion.'

The pleasantries were genuine, the tea was a sincere attempt to entertain Charles during his short stint at Aber. The benefit of Geraint Evans's effort was to expose the Prince to more of the characters and traditions of a Welsh-speaking community. 'One of the points of him being there was to meet Welsh people, to acclimatise him as to what it was like to be in Wales,' Evans told the BBC. As so many seemed to do, Geraint Evans put his personal feelings about monarchy and nationalism to one side in dealing with Charles, the student. Being a prince meant that some kept their distance, but the royal title did not discourage his only neighbour in Aberystwyth from befriending the lonely newcomer.

The developing friendship did, however, concern the Secretary of State for Wales. George Thomas, the Labour MP who would later become the Speaker of the House of Commons, was so concerned about the Prince's friendship with Geraint Evans that he wrote to the prime minister, Harold Wilson. It was a communication that Evans only became aware of when archive papers were released in 1999 under the thirty-year rule. They showed that the student had been vetted, and his nationalist beliefs had prompted George Thomas to write by hand to Wilson. 'He suggested that Harold Wilson should speak to the Queen about the undue influence that the neighbour might be having on Prince Charles. This was absolutely staggering,' Geraint told the BBC. He felt it reflected the mindset of a 'paranoid' Secretary of State who was determined that the Prince's stint in Wales, and the subsequent investiture, should proceed without incident. Thomas's mindset was further revealed in other archive papers, which showed his concern that some of the nationalist discussion was rubbing off on Charles. In another handwritten note to the prime minister after the investiture in July 1969, George Thomas wrote:

> I have no information about who his advisers are, but a dangerous situation is developing. In my presence in Cardiff he referred to the 'cultural and political awakening in Wales'. This is most useful for the nationalists... If the Prince is writing his own speeches he may well be tempted to go further. The enthusiasm of youth is a marvellous spur, but it may lead to speeches that cause difficulty.

Thomas flagged what he felt was 'concentrated attention' on Charles by Welsh nationalists in Aberystwyth. 'His tutor, his neighbour in the next room, and the Principal were all dedicated Nationalists. It has become quite evident to me that the Aberystwyth experience has influenced the Prince to a considerable extent.' Thomas asked Wilson to speak to the Queen about it. The prime minister agreed that one of his officials would have a quiet word with Her Majesty's private secretary.

If Charles had an awakening to the Welsh nationalist perspective, it probably came from his tutors. He did not attend lectures, but instead attended seminars with selected students and individual Welsh tutorials with Tedi Millward and Bobi Jones. He also had a history tutor, E.L. Ellis, or Ted Ellis to his colleagues. 'He wrote the history of Aberystwyth University,' his friend and long-serving colleague Deian Hopkin told me. Ted Ellis was 'a very, very good historian. He was also warden of Pantycelyn at the time.' The fact that Ted Ellis could teach Charles and keep an eye on him in his halls of residence 'tied in very neatly', Hopkin said.

Ted Ellis would also read the future King's essays, though the strength of his student's ability was never shared with other staff. 'We never found out anything about the quality of those essays. It didn't go through our books! I tried very hard to see if it was recorded in any way, but Ted was far too discreet,' Deian laughed. Tedi Millward was Charles's most famous tutor, both because of his reputation as a nationalist at the time, and because of his subsequent dramatisation in an episode of the Netflix series, *The Crown*. Millward wasn't just a nationalist, but – like Dafydd Elis-Thomas – he was also a committed republican. 'It caused quite a bit of a stir,' Deian Hopkin told me. 'Tedi was a well-known Welsh nationalist and was a Plaid Cymru parliamentary candidate.' Deian Hopkin knew Tedi's commitment not through their university friendship, but from the political front-line. Deian's mother, Loti Rees Hughes, had been the Labour candidate for Ceredigion in the 1959 election and had supported the subsequent Labour effort to win the seat from the Liberals, which eventually succeeded in 1966 when Elystan Morgan beat the incumbent Roderic Bowen. Tedi Millward took fourth place for Plaid Cymru that year. Shortly before Charles arrived in his study in 1969 Millward had completed a two-year term as vice president of Plaid Cymru, and earlier in the 1960s he had been instrumental in establishing the pressure group, the Welsh Language Society, whose actions had done much to raise the status of the language and to demand greater rights for Welsh speakers to access services in their native tongue. If his background gave George Thomas a fright, it gave Charles an education.

Tedi Millward found a willing student in the Prince of Wales. The young Charles was sensitive, intelligent and curious. Millward was content to oblige, and placed his political objections to one side in order to coach Charles in language and Welsh life. He committed to teaching the Prince in just the same way as he would instruct any other student, but also accepted privately that refusing to do so would have attracted adverse publicity for both the university and Plaid Cymru. The cultural introduction to Welsh life was shared among the Prince's tutors, but Tedi Millward was principally in charge of Welsh language tuition. A novel approach at Aberystwyth offered Charles the chance to immerse himself in Welsh as the university had invested in technology for a language laboratory in the old college buildings on the seafront. Rows of yellow-painted booths were equipped with headsets and microphones. Students would sit in a booth and listen to Welsh phrases, before repeating them back. Tedi Millward would be at the front, wearing his own headphones, listening to his students' progress as they repeated the recordings into their microphones. Gentle encouragement would help to refine their pronunciations. The scene was a modern take on the instruction of Eliza Doolittle by Professor Henry Higgins in *My Fair Lady*. In the musical, Eliza's progress from cockney flower girl to amateur aristocrat is measured by her performance at an embassy ball. For Charles there would be an equally public, pressured assessment of his language learning. Towards the end of his term at Aberystwyth he would deliver a speech in Welsh at an eisteddfod organised by the Urdd, the Welsh language movement for young people. Beneath the canvas of a hot marquee, Charles would deliver a speech of a couple of hundred words in duration. He would do so at an event filled with singers, dancers and performers of poetry and prose, while knowing that both the Urdd organisation and many of its attendees were torn about the Prince's presence.

The Urdd was one of many Welsh organisations that became conflicted about Charles in 1969. Its council had faced a rebellion from some members after it initially decided to accept an invitation to attend the investiture in Caernarfon, before rejecting the idea. As a compromise, it invited the Prince to the eisteddfod in Aberystwyth on a Saturday at the end of May where he would deliver a short address and present a trophy.

News of the speech broke a few days beforehand, intriguing newspaper readers around Britain. The *Birmingham Daily Post* wrote that Charles would 'make his first public speech in Welsh when he presents the Royal Prize to the winning county at the Urdd (Welsh League of Youth) National Eisteddfod at Aberystwyth on Saturday'. On the day itself the *Aberdeen Evening Express* announced that the future King would 'make history later today – he will be the first member of the Royal Family to make a speech entirely in Welsh'. *The Express* carried a quote from a fellow student, who remarked that 'providing he gets quietness while he delivers his speech, he should do very well indeed. He has plenty of confidence'.

Charles had written the speech himself, in English, before it was translated on his behalf. It was to be three hundred words long, with ten times as many people in the audience to hear him. While they would judge his pronunciation, his appearance and his delivery, Charles was never going to achieve an Eliza Doolittle transformation for the committed nationalist republicans who would make up a proportion of the audience. It was impossible to predict how many there would be, or how they would react.

Charles's big moment would come at the climax of the eisteddfod. Each area of Wales would receive a mark for the achievements of its citizens in all of the categories of performance, arts and crafts at the eisteddfod. Representatives of each district processed through the marquee, beneath great garlands of Welsh flags which had been hung from the wooden posts that held up the canvas roof. On stage, the compere John Garnon slowly announced the scores for each district, save for the final three who had the highest scores of all. As he prepared to call the Prince of Wales to the stage, John Garnon said in Welsh: 'As we heard this afternoon from the president of the day, one of the most glorious things at the Urdd Eisteddfod is hearing competitions for learners. And as Dr Goronwy Daniel said, what greater privilege and honour can a nation have, than having a member of another nation come among us to learn the language and to understand its traditions?' The inference was clear and the audience clapped, some stood to signal the strength of their appreciation for the imminent presence of the Prince. Others remained seated, silent. 'We have, in our midst today, someone who has come to Aberystwyth to do that.' There was more scattered clapping, while others looked around to see where the Prince might be lurking before his arrival on stage. But as John Garnon continued his introduction, a heckler can be heard in the audience. Others try to hush him. In the pictures filmed by ITV a police constable leans into the frame as he peers around the curtain at the back of the stage, checking for trouble in the front rows. The compere's words quickly disappear as John Garnon rushes to announce the arrival of the Prince of Wales before the heckler gains any further momentum.

Charles appeared from a seat near the front and stepped up onto the stage. Around a hundred people at the front of the pavilion rose from their seats as well and began to walk out, their heckles and groans audible above the continued clapping and occasional cheer of the largely supportive crowd. Some of the protestors unrolled pieces of paper with 'Arwisgo '69 – Brad 1282' which means 'Investiture '69 – Betrayal 1282', referring to the year of Llywelyn ap Gruffydd's death. For a few minutes the protesters slowly edge out of the pavilion, helped on their way by security guards and police officers. They are clapped on their way, some in support of their actions while others applauded their departure. The ITV cameras showed Charles standing still on stage in his suit and tie, arms neatly behind his back. He broke into a smile once the protesters had left, and he realised that those who remained had risen to their feet to applaud him. The applause began to settle, but when it was clear that the chants of the protesters were echoing back through the canvas walls of the marquee, it picked up again. Once the situation was calmer, John Garnon returned to the microphone: 'All that I can say is that many more people have chosen to stay inside.' There was a ripple of laughter and, as if the previous few minutes of tension had evaporated, the itinerary on stage kicked in again. The three Welsh districts to have achieved the highest marks of the eisteddfod were called to the stage, but in the short silence before the compere could announce the third-placed county, a repeated thud could be heard. Charles and John Garnon briefly glanced up and to the right. One of the ejected protesters had made some progress up the side of the marquee and was making his objections heard by slapping his hand against the taut canvas. Choosing to ignore the interruption, the compere continued with the schedule and called the winners of small cups and shields for third and second place. Then the winners of the Pantyfedwen Cup were called, the star prize for the highest-achieving area of Wales, who would also receive the Queen's Prize from the Prince. The representatives of Ceredigion walked quickly to the centre of the stage and, wearing sashes bearing the county's name, stood and received a small replica of the cup. The compere announced that the royal prize would be awarded shortly, but only after the Prince of Wales had addressed the audience in Welsh. While the moment had been heavily previewed in the press, it still elicited an excited cheer from those who had opted to remain inside. Charles, having listened to all of the proceedings that were conducted solely in Welsh, cannot have understood every word. On his cue, he walked to the centre of the stage and stood in front of the collection of microphones that fed the public address system and the broadcasters who would share this moment with the world. He reached inside his suit jacket and produced the paper that, with phonetic spelling and only a few hundred words, would complete his first speech in Welsh. Charles looked around the marquee and smiled.

Mister Llywydd ac aelodau'r Urdd...

A collective gasp can be heard on the tape as the room heard Charles's clipped public school accent soften around the Welsh words he had learned during the crash course in Aberystwyth.

Pleser mawr ydy cael bod yn Eisteddfod Genedlaethol yr Urdd ar y diwrnod olaf hwn...

For the next few minutes the Prince spoke confidently and sincerely in a language which he had absorbed in the yellow booths of Tedi Millward's laboratory. He spoke of his great pleasure at being asked to address the Urdd Eisteddfod on its final day. He mentioned the high quality of the singing and joked that the songs were so impressive

that he wished the choir would join him in Caernarfon –
before adding, with a smile, that he knew they would
rather not. In his speech he praised both the events of
the Urdd, which had become a movement of
transformative influence on the fate of the language, and
the cultural heritage which came with it. These weren't
just Tedi Millward's language lessons paying off; the
history had transferred as well. It was the type of
sentiment that would worry George Thomas, but which
thrilled those who found an ally in Charles.

*Fydda i ddim yn gadael i'r Gymraeg ddiflanu heb
ymladd hyd yr eithaf.*

Charles vowed to fight to the last in order to prevent the
Welsh language from disappearing. Each powerful line
brought with it the cheers and applause of those in the
audience who were still processing the reality of a future
English King addressing them in Welsh, let alone the idea
that he might also be on their side in the fight to preserve
their cultural treasures. He told the audience that he was
reading the fourteenth-century poetry of Dafydd ap Gwilym
in bed every night, and quoted a line back to them. This
was 'Carlo' getting the joke. Those who had stayed to
support him, and cheered when the protestors were ejected,
were now presented with more than a speech in Welsh. It
was a commitment to support the Welsh language at a time
when it continued to face opposition from many in Wales,
and an alignment with a cultural battle which had largely
been fought by Welsh nationalists until then.

The Prince was never going to win over his ideological opponents. But he succeeded in making a confident claim to be a supporter of Wales and the Welsh language, and had shown how a visitor from outside the country could learn to love the nation's cultural gems. The verdict of the press was almost unanimous. The *People* said, 'Charles is a Wow in Welsh', and wrote that 'Prince Charles socked it to the people of Wales yesterday. And the people of Wales socked it to a crowd of demonstrators who tried to spoil the wild welcome for the young Prince.' Overlooking much of the cultural significance of the Prince's commitment to the language or his choice of bedtime reading, the paper continued: 'The cool-headed Prince took it all in his stride, and went on to deliver a 300-word speech entirely in Welsh which had the audience roaring with delight.'

Dafydd Elis-Thomas was in the audience that day, and the brief kerfuffle before the speech remained the only moment of open hostility that he witnessed towards the Prince during his time in Aberystwyth. 'I don't remember any situation where people were booing or reacting to him. Even in the Urdd Eisteddfod – it was the only event where I saw him speaking, but there was clearly support for him. I suspect in the majority of the audience at that time,' he told me.

Deian Hopkin said the objections to the Prince were scarce during his term in Aberystwyth. 'There were some people who protested, a few. But I can't recollect much of that,' he told me. 'I didn't actually get the impression that there was a wellspring of objection and complaint about him. At all.'

However well the Prince handled the protest at the Eisteddfod, and however little his opponents achieved in disrupting his time in Aberystwyth, the tense atmosphere made for a tough term.

'The impression he gave me, years later, was that he hated his time in Aberystwyth,' Dafydd Elis-Thomas said. Why? 'Because it was such a disruption. Whatever academic career he actually had, it was an imposition on his time, really, to take him there.' In 1969 it seemed clear to Deian Hopkin that Charles was pleased to see the back of Aberystwyth. 'After he left, he never came back. We never saw him again,' he told me. 'He didn't maintain contact, he didn't come back to visit Pantycelyn that I'm aware of, he showed no real interest. It's a period that I don't think he reflects on very comfortably.' Hopkin spent another twenty-five years teaching at Aberystwyth, but never passed the Prince in the town after that term.

Charles's genuine student experience was at Trinity College Cambridge. The aristocrats kept Charles company, while his experience as an undergraduate came as close as possible to the freedom every young person enjoys at university. But the concoction of his term at Aberystwyth was part of the political performance that the Prince was required to deliver. The benefit to Wales was that Charles grasped the opportunity to learn a little during his time in Aber.

'I think he enjoyed his one-to-one seminars with Bobi Jones and Tedi Millward,' Dafydd Elis-Thomas offered. 'I think that made a lasting impression.' It was the basis of his academic knowledge of Wales, he said, and Dafydd believed that much of it was retained by Charles. By the time the future King had left Aberystwyth he had learned a sufficient degree of Welsh to be able to speak it in public, and had absorbed a doctrine of Welsh history which would become a guiding principle in his dealings with Wales. If George Thomas was concerned that Charles would become a nationalist, he misunderstood the ability of the Welsh to embrace their past with pride. Charles understood the importance of cultural context, and recognised the role the Welsh language had and the threats it faced from the dominance of English. One did not need to be anti-England to be pro-Welsh. It was not a ribbon to be attached only to political nationalists, though Charles recognised in his tutors that their desire for independence from England was intrinsically linked with their ambition to spread the Welsh language more freely among its people. It was an early example of the Prince of Wales embracing what some saw as a quirky, peripheral cause that would become not just fashionable but mainstream. Before climate change and architecture, the Welsh language was Charles's first *cause célèbre*. He aligned himself with a great swathe of Welsh people by speaking those few hundred words at the eisteddfod. A little over a month later, he would speak Welsh to the world as the Queen delivered her promise to present him as Prince of Wales at Caernarfon.

3

The Investiture

*'I look upon it, I think, as a meaningful ceremony.
I shall also be glad when it's over.'*

There were minesweepers in the Menai Strait on the morning of the investiture. The entrance to Caernarfon harbour was guarded by the Royal Navy. Further around the coast of Anglesey, frogmen were aboard Britannia as it remained moored at Holyhead. The men who were guarding the day's key locations were acutely aware of the threats to the ceremonial event, one which would bring crowds to the narrow streets of Caernarfon and millions to their television sets. Overnight, a few violent opponents of the investiture had already made their point, and some had lost their lives. Late editions of *The Times* conveyed the tension facing the royal family and their protection team. 'Royal train is halted after bomb alert', the front page splashed. The picture showed Charles shaking hands with the station manager at Euston the night before. But in the early hours, the paper reported, the carriages of the royal train were kept in a siding after a policeman spotted a suspicious device under a railway bridge near Chester. It was examined and found to be a fake bomb. Later, the telegraph wires running along the track to Caernarfon were found to be cut. The day before, there had been explosions in Cardiff and Abergele. And yet, despite the flashes of violence, the investiture of the Prince of Wales was about to begin, and it would leave an indelible mark on the nation's history.

The precedent for the ceremony was barely historical. As a reference point, everybody in 1969 looked to the investiture of Edward VIII as Prince of Wales in 1911. But when they looked back further, there was no tradition to speak of. The previous Princes of Wales had been created, often celebrated, but never invested with the show that the twentieth century bestowed upon two heirs to the throne at Caernarfon Castle. The only formality in creating a Prince of Wales is in the issuing of letters patent, a royal decree which sets out the monarch's wish to confer the title on their male heir. It is, in essence, a fancy certificate. Anything else is purely ceremonial, and there had never been much of it for Princes of Wales until Edward VIII.

Edward had been created Prince of Wales on 23 June 1910, his sixteenth birthday, by his father, George V, who had only taken the throne a few weeks before. A little over a year later he was in Caernarfon Castle to be invested as Prince of Wales on his very first visit to the country. It would be a ceremony which came at the request of David Lloyd George, the Liberal politician and Chancellor of the Exchequer who was raised in the village of Llanystumdwy in north-west Wales. The village was around sixteen miles south of Caernarfon. Lloyd George would be instrumental in devising the pageant for Edward's investiture in his own political heartland. Caernarfon Castle was symbolic of the conquest of Wales and the expiry of Welsh royalty. Lloyd George, as Constable of Caernarfon Castle, sought to reinvent and reclaim its reputation. He coached Edward to speak a few words of Welsh, though his efforts paled in comparison to the commitment shown by Charles to learn the language and understand its heritage. On the day of his investiture Edward stopped in the square, outside the castle walls, to accept a greeting from local officials. Among the English words of his reply, he was reported to have said in Welsh:

Diolch o waelod fy nghalon i hen wlad fy nhadau.

He thanked 'the land of my fathers' from the bottom of his heart.

The King, dressed in the uniform of an admiral of the fleet, arrived fifteen minutes later and spoke outside the castle walls. 'I believe that the occasion will serve a still deeper purpose in assembling in union and power around his person all the forces of Welsh national life which preserve the fame and the achievements of your historic ancestors, and will sustain in the world of modern times the virtues of the British race and the glories of the British Empire.' Before entering the castle, almost as an after-thought, the King was handed a sword by his equerry with which he rather quickly knighted both the local mayor and the High Sheriff, provoking a cheer from the crowd that 'made the very walls of the houses shake', a local journalist reported.

The castle's inner walls had been cleared of ivy and covered, instead, with banners decorated with coats of arms. Banks of seats circled the large, grassy centre, while a green dais was installed where Edward would be crowned Prince of Wales.

Pathé black-and-white film of the occasion showed the striped gazebo erected on the dais and the rows of standing spectators. The men wore military uniform or top hats, while the women stood in the hot sun in fitted, floor-length frocks and wide-brimmed Edwardian hats. All those around the dais were in royal robes and ceremonial uniform. After kneeling before his father, the teenage Prince had a bright purple cape with ermine trim draped around his shoulders, while a man approached with a velvet cushion that carried the crown.

The painter Christopher Williams was commissioned by George V to paint the scene of his son's investiture. Williams wrote that it was a 'gloriously fine' day. 'I looked on and watched carefully. When the King put the crown on the Prince's head I felt a hush and a sigh. That was the moment to be painted, I thought.' He took a photograph of the scene being played out in front of him, and later incorporated it into a vast panoramic view of the ceremony.

Williams captured the choir of Welsh women in national costume, their tall black hats bobbing with the anthems. There was a glimpse of members of the Gorsedd of the Bards, the Welsh order of writers and poets whose accomplishments at the National Eisteddfod afforded them the right to wear simple robes of white, green or blue. The Archdruid had a white satin robe and a gold chain around his neck. Through it all, David Lloyd George was the showman who appeared to glide slickly between the scenes that played out at the castle entrance and at the dais. Each order of chivalry, every church dignitary and military officer was arranged by Lloyd George to decorate the castle, while the new Prince of Wales was gifted the ornaments of the investiture.

The decorations were a bit much for the young Prince. 'The ceremony I had to go through with, the speech I had to make, and the Welsh I had to speak were, I thought, a sufficient ordeal for anyone,' he wrote forty years later, both his investiture and his accession to the throne a fading memory for the self-exiled Duke of Windsor. 'But when a tailor appeared to measure me for a fantastic costume designed for the occasion, consisting of white satin breeches and a mantle and surcoat of purple velvet edged with ermine, I decided things had gone too far. I had already submitted to the Garter dress and robe, for which there existed a condoning historical precedent; but what would my Navy friends say if they saw me in this preposterous rig? There was a family blow-up that night; but in the end my mother, as always, smoothed things over.'

In the coverage of the event, much was made of Edward's youth. The 'bonnie boy', as the papers called him, was being presented into adulthood with all the trimmings of a pantomime medieval banquet. As he was crowned with the coronet, a ring placed on his finger and a wand – the golden verge – placed in his right hand, Edward, Prince of Wales, paid homage to his father:

I, Edward, Prince of Wales, do become your liege man of life and limb, and of earthly worship; and faith and truth I will bear unto thee, to live and die, against all manner of folks.

It was a form of words, based on medieval oaths of allegiance, which Charles would repeat in 1969. He would also repeat Edward's appearance at Queen Eleanor's gate, the fabled high window where Edward I and his wife supposedly presented the first English prince of Wales, later Edward II, to the people of Caernarfon.

1911 would be the template for 1969, the young Prince would be paraded before his new people, and the part of the pushy Welsh politician would be played by George Thomas. He was the Secretary of State for Wales who passionately supported the investiture. Thomas saw the potential for political gain in delivering a ceremony that accentuated the union of the United Kingdom just as nationalism had been thrust into the mainstream. He loathed nationalists with as much passion as he enthused about monarchy. Thomas's biographers suggested this was largely the result of a long-held inferiority complex, an attempt over the course of several decades to shed his upbringing in Tonypandy and to become an elevated, acceptably pretentious member of society. In his book about George Thomas, *Political Chameleon: In Search of*

George Thomas, the writer Martin Shipton said Thomas was a man who was 'uncomfortable with who he was and who craved acceptance by those further up the social hierarchy'. Shipton painted a picture of George Thomas as a 'servile Welshman' whose 'humble origins provided the essential myth-making ingredients' that were required to ingratiate him with the royal family.

While he was always a Cardiff MP, George Thomas chose to be known as Viscount Tonypandy when he was elevated to the peerage following his period as Speaker of the House of Commons. He spoke with charisma and flourish, but was sharp-tongued and withering to those he despised. The enthusiasm which he showed for the royal family both before and after the investiture paid dividends. In 1981 he was asked by the Archbishop of Canterbury to read the lesson at the wedding of Charles and Diana, and ahead of the ceremony he dined with the family. Martin Shipton described how Thomas made 'cloyingly sycophantic references to the Prince and his fiancée, the Queen and her husband, as well as to the Queen Mother'. He was a controversial figure that the royal family chose to entertain well beyond the requirements of arranging the investiture, and his acceptance into their circle would have meant more than any election victory.

George Thomas became involved in the plans for the investiture when he was appointed Secretary of State for Wales in 1968. His predecessor, the Anglesey MP Cledwyn Hughes, had done much of the preparatory work, but Thomas would be able to take ample credit and the ceremonial spotlight. He sat on the investiture committee alongside Lord Snowdon, the photographer and husband of Princess Margaret who had been made Constable of Caernarfon Castle for the event. The Earl Marshall, the Duke of Norfolk, chaired the investiture committee and was fulfilling the traditional, hereditary role of the Dukes of Norfolk to organise state occasions. The Duke carried the responsibility of arranging the funerals of monarchs and the accession of new ones – the current Earl Marshall, the eighteenth Duke of Norfolk, presided over arrangements and some aspects of King Charles's accession to the throne in 2022. In 1969 the Earl Marshall joined George Thomas and Lord Snowdon in devising and overseeing the second investiture pageant for a Prince of Wales at Caernarfon Castle, and relied heavily on the memory and template of 1911 to deliver it.

The pockets of rebellion that Charles encountered had ensured that the build-up to the investiture would be more divisive and controversial than 1911. While the newspapers put a largely positive spin on the 1969 plans, opposing voices did achieve publicity and support. There was ideological opposition from politicians and campaign groups, and the divide among some Welsh organisations about whether to support or attend the investiture meant the public row rumbled on. Charles's visit to the Urdd Eisteddfod, where he first spoke Welsh, was a compromise by the organisation after its executive was split over whether to attend. Local councils, the Gorsedd of the Bards and famous Welsh choirs had to grapple with members who had a conscientious objection to the investiture.

Plaid Cymru's official stance on the investiture was to ignore it. At its annual conference in 1968 a number of resolutions that wanted to actively distance the party from investiture events did not pass, with one delegate pleading that members would not 'play into the hands of English politicians'. Instead, the conference condemned the ongoing bombing campaign and called for the culprits to be caught. The rejection of violence was clear, and the party would not officially condone other protests. It was up to more radical elements of the nationalist movement to target the investiture. The Welsh Language Society stepped in.

Formed in 1962, the society's aim was to ensure Welsh people could use the language in every aspect of their daily lives. Its creation was driven by a concern that Wales was succumbing to the dominance of the English language, despite the resilience it had shown during times when speaking Welsh had been either frowned upon or forbidden. Various mis-steps and deliberate provocations by the British establishment had spurred a mostly young group of campaigners to instigate direct action to protect their language. This was not a nostalgic effort to save a local dialect from its final breath, but a demand for the right to speak and write in Welsh in their everyday interactions, wherever they lived in Wales. At home, at work, in the shops and on the phone. The goal was to secure official status for the Welsh language. Their call for Welsh language tax returns, birth certificates and post office services made its first big impact in the Prince's university town of Aberystwyth some years before he arrived. In 1963 a group of around seventy protesters sat down on one of the main bridges into the town, Pont Trefechan, and blocked the traffic for several hours. It was an iconic moment in the history of language rights, and an early warning that the 1960s had produced a generation who were prepared to disrupt the established way of running Wales. For years, members of the Welsh language society had targeted road signs that anglicised Welsh place names, painting over some and completely removing others to symbolise the erasure of Welsh local identities. The flooding of the Welsh-speaking village of Capel Celyn near Bala to supply water to Liverpool and Wirral fuelled the campaign. The sight of an English-born Prince being basted in Welsh culture in its aftermath was too much to stomach. But, like Plaid Cymru, the Welsh Language Society objected to violence. For inspiration it looked to Gandhi and Martin Luther King, and it would launch a persistent and targeted non-violent campaign against the investiture.

They hoped that it would pull Wales more strongly into British culture, and the British way of doing things. But that didn't work.

Dafydd Iwan led the Welsh Language Society – *Cymdeithas yr Iaith* – during its formative years and up to the investiture, where his song 'Carlo' became the satirical anthem of a serious movement. I interviewed him in the summer of 2021.

66

The storm that came managed to split many families and organisations in Wales, such as the male voice choirs and so on. But the storm arose because there were tensions, and there were differences of opinion.

While the Welsh Language Society's primary aim was to improve access to Welsh, the arrival of the Prince symbolised a British block on emerging Welsh ambition. 'Sending him to Aberystwyth to learn Welsh – well, that showed us that we needed to use this [moment] to show that *we* support the Welsh language. And that is what I was using, in order to make fun of him, in the song *Carlo*.' Dafydd recalled the lyrics, and explained how the song satirised Charles as 'a little creature who would attend Urdd summer camps, a reader of *Tafod y Ddraig*' – the Welsh Language Society's magazine – 'and Dafydd ap Gwilym, and so on. They tried to make him somebody that he wasn't.'

Leading the revolt against the investiture did not come naturally to Dafydd Iwan, who felt the Welsh Language Society should really have ignored Charles and continued its campaign for prominence for the Welsh language on road signs and on TV. 'I argued that *Cymdeithas yr Iaith* should stick to its core principles, stick with the signs campaign, the education and television campaign,' he told me. 'Announce our opposition to the investiture, that it was a waste of time and meant nothing, and that we did not accept a Prince of Wales – and to leave it there.'

Instead, the Society took to the front line of the emerging culture war. 'What happened, as the propaganda machine in favour of the investiture intensified, I got dragged into it more and more. Against my own principles, really, I was dragged into a more important role of opposing the investiture.' Dafydd Iwan was not alone in his reticence. The writer Meic Stephens, who is credited as being the first to paint '*Cofiwch Dryweryn*' ('Remember Tryweryn') on a roadside wall near Llanrhystyd, sent a letter to Dafydd Iwan to resign his membership of the Welsh Language Society over its stance on the investiture. 'Not because he was in favour of the investiture,' Dafydd Iwan recalled, 'but because he felt we should be concentrating on other things. And reading it now, one can understand his position. I was saying similar things myself. But, on the other hand, we couldn't *not* oppose it.'

If the Welsh Language Society was to be the official opposition to the investiture, Dafydd Iwan would be framed in the press as Charles's nemesis. A figurehead for the campaign also meant far greater attention was paid to the criticism of the plans, allowing newspapers to strike a less deferential tone in its coverage than anything that preceded Edward VIII swearing allegiance to Wales in 1911.

Ahead of the investiture the *Daily Mirror* sent a reporter to tour around Wales for a week, 'during which we talked to hundreds of people in all walks of life, and not once did we hear actual enthusiasm expressed about the event,' it wrote. It surmised that while there may be thousands of supportive Welsh people, most were apathetic about the investiture plans. The paper listed the organised opposition that had been formed by the Welsh Language Society, but it also pointed to 'a darker, more disturbing feeling in some quarters involving dynamite and gelignite and the threat of guns'.

The threat came from *Mudiad Amddiffyn Cymru*, or MAC, a small paramilitary operation which had been responsible for the spate of bombings in the mid-1960s. The group's targeting of water pipelines from Wales to England, and a history of bombing government buildings, meant that detectives from Special Branch and officers at MI5 were concerned about MAC's intentions in the summer of 1969. Newspaper columnists who speculated about the threat from MAC appeared to agree that an assassination attempt was off the cards, primarily because of the greater damage it would do to the nationalist movement. Instead, the concern lay in the potential to disrupt the preparations, and to cause damage and injuries as millions watched the ceremony on television.

MAC's membership, which was small and anonymous at the time, was led by John Jenkins who was a serving member of the British Army. His extreme, violent brand of nationalism was rare, and had been fostered after a troubled childhood and setbacks in securing work in Wales in the years when he wasn't in the forces. He believed that violence was key to highlighting the nationalist cause, and claimed that the response of the British state to the coal-tip disaster at Aberfan was a turning point in his personal campaign. In an era of revolutionaries, MAC were a rag-tag bunch of disruptors who posed a genuine threat to the success of the investiture. They were not assassins or terrorist masterminds, but a group of men who rather clumsily achieved publicity with their bombings, and saw Charles's moment in Caernarfon as their opportunity to get even more attention for the nationalist cause.

The public, especially beyond Wales, were largely nonplussed about the reports of plotting and protest. In Whitehall the Welsh Office authorised 'reasonable' expenditure by local councils on activities to celebrate the investiture. By Christmas 1968 it had led districts across the country to plan village fetes, theatrical performances and even golf competitions to take place around the first of July 1969. In the classified advertising columns, caravan pitch-owners flagged their convenience to Caernarfon Castle.

The money allotted to local councils to celebrate the investiture was not always put to its intended use. In Trawsfynydd in Gwynedd the parish council, having previously been denied enough money from its precept to buy Christmas decorations for the town, went out and spent £23 on coloured lights which sparkled in the street in December. They were not used to celebrate the investiture. Other village councils vowed not to send representatives to the event. The *Daily Mirror* reported that school children in Caernarfon were being invited to enter a peculiar competition organised by anti-investiture campaigners. There would be a prize for whichever child managed to smash a commemorative china mug into the largest number of pieces.

If there was a propaganda war, the Prince was also making his own preparations to improve his image. In

May 1969, around six weeks before the investiture, Charles drove from Aberystwyth to the Wye Valley to be interviewed by David Frost. The film, *A Prince for Wales*, would be released by the Rank Organisation to celebrate the investiture and featured songs by Tom Jones and Harry Secombe. The following month the Prince was at BBC Wales's new broadcasting house in Llandaff, Cardiff, where Cliff Michelmore and Brian Connell would ask the questions for Charles's first television interview. It was a joint production between the BBC and Harlech, the channel three franchise for Wales and the west of England. The three men sat in grey suits on a circular stage, the Prince opposite the BBC's Michelmore and Harlech's Connell. It was the interview which had highlighted his loneliness at Aberystwyth and his progress in studying Welsh. This was half an hour of insight into the Prince's own understanding of Wales, its people and his opponents.

On the protesters: 'It's publicity they want, I suppose, quite naturally.'

On his nationalist tutor, Tedi Millward: 'I have had many interesting discussions with him, particularly. He has enlightened me a great deal about nationalist aims, ideas and policies.'

On protecting Welsh culture: 'They are depressed by what might happen to it if they don't try and preserve the language and the culture, which is very unique and special to Wales. And if something is unique and special, I see it as well worth preserving.'

On representing Wales: 'People seem to want the Prince

of Wales to be more active and exclusive' in working for the Welsh.

The interview showed Charles's youthful enthusiasm, as well as his pragmatism. The arguments of his detractors and opponents were fired at him, but he mostly absorbed their impact and responded sympathetically, and sometimes earnestly, to their criticism. He also denied that he had become a 'political tool'.

> I know I am not exploited by politicians, personally. I mean, perhaps the investiture was encouraged and pushed by certain politicians but not, so far as I can make out, blatantly. I think it is a very convenient cry for people who are anti the investiture, and it is a very convenient one to hang on to because it gives them a jolly good argument. And anything you say, they'll say: 'Oh, you're being exploited,' and there it is. It doesn't matter if you say, 'No, I am not'.

He finished by invoking the Prince of Wales's German motto, *Ich Dien*, and hoped the investiture ceremony the following week would be symbolic of his commitment to serving the Welsh nation.

As the cameras cut away, Charles returned to London. In Caernarfon Lord Snowdon was overseeing the final flourishes inside the historic castle which would be the stage for the investiture. Charles always called him Tony, and this uncle by marriage was a figure who understood the young Prince's sensitive nature. Jonathan Dimbleby described how Tony 'listened with care and offered his own opinions and insights about art and music'. Charles's particular fondness for the aesthetic and the dramatic would be well-catered by Lord Snowdon's modern interpretation of the pomp required to present a new Prince of Wales to the world.

After being appointed Constable of Caernarfon Castle, Lord Snowdon had spent four years working on the project. The early part of that time had involved tidying up the castle grounds and removing some of the relics of the 1911 event. He worked with the Ministry of Public Works to make improvements that would serve the 1969 coronation, and which would also leave a permanent benefit to the visiting public. The ticket offices were smartened up, while the detritus of the 1911 investiture which had lain about the castle was tidied or dumped. Loans from the Tower of London brought new suits of armour to the rooms and hallways along the perimeter. Lord Snowdon asked the Royal College of Art and the Stationery Office to improve the signage and guidebooks for visitors. The artist John Piper, who had painted Welsh hills from Eryri to the Black Mountains in the south, was commissioned to produce ink and watercolour drawings to be sold as official souvenirs.

Once the confines of the castle had been spruced up, Lord Snowdon set to work on designing the film set that would host the investiture. It required a director's eye as the event itself was predicted to become the most watched live broadcast in the short history of television. The centre of the action would be a disc of Welsh slate, twenty-five feet in diameter, where Charles would pay homage to the Queen. Above it, an awning of clear perspex was supported by four steel tubes, inspired by the medieval canopies that sheltered princes from the elements at the edge of the tournament field. Where the awning curled upwards at its front, a fibreglass model of the Prince of Wales's three feathers was fixed to the plastic. The otherwise sparse decoration was as much a consequence of the budget as it was of Lord Snowdon's modernist twist. With £50,000 to spend, the newspapers reported that the cost was far below the unlimited budget enjoyed in 1911 and which *The Times* valued at around two million pounds by the standards of 1969.

On the dais were three thrones designed from slabs of slate, topped with a scarlet cushion. All around this central stage were the scarlet seats of the spectator stands. Designed by John Pound, the principle designer with the supplies division of the Ministry of Public Buildings and Works, they were created from Welsh beech and stained red. The seats were then indented in gilt with the three feathers and were screwed into the stands. After the ceremony each guest was allowed to buy a seat, and the process involved unscrewing it from the stand and sending it to have arms and legs attached by workers at Remploy. A scarlet tweed cushion was included with every seat, and the finished item became a collectible memento. Four-and-a-half thousand chairs were made for the investiture, and all were sold for twelve pounds after the event. First refusal went to the invited guests, before being offered up to everybody else. Lord Snowdon bought six.

The decoration of the castle itself was kept to a minimum. The imposing structure of Caernarfon's fortress hardly needed dressing up. Coats of arms were hung above two gates – Queen Eleanor's and the Water Gate of Eagle Tower. White banners were hung on the walls both inside and outside the castle, with various dragons and supposedly ancient Welsh emblems designed by the College of Arms spread among them.

While the stage was the castle, the centrepiece was the crown. The new Prince of Wales coronet was a gift to the Queen by the Goldsmiths' Company and cost £3,600 to produce, which is around £75,000 today. The silversmith and jeweller Louis Osman made it from gold, with platinum arches, seventy-five diamonds, twelve emeralds and a gold-plated ping-pong ball that was engraved with the Prince's insignia. The finished crown was futuristic, even by the attitudes of the late 1960s.

The Times reported that television coverage of the investiture would be 'the biggest colour outside broadcast and the longest television outside broadcast of a state occasion since the coronation. The programme, introduced by Cliff Michelmore, with Richard Baker and the Welsh actor and playwright, Emlyn Williams, who will speak in both English and Welsh, will begin with the background to the ceremony.'

The stage and the props were ready. The audience was waiting.

*   *   *

At dawn on Tuesday 1 July 1969 the crowds who had camped out in Caernarfon had barely slept. Shops along the narrow streets of the town had remained open all night, with chips and sweets sustaining the hundreds of revellers who wanted to secure the best vantage point. Special Branch officers roamed in plain clothes, their suspicions heightened by overnight reports of trouble.

First, from Cardiff, came news of a bomb inside a Royal Mail postbox the previous day. The steel-plated front of the box blew into Cowbridge Road East as the device detonated, with six nearby Post Office workers narrowly escaping injury. The device was similar to others planted by MAC, and it confirmed the fears of the Queen and the security services that Welsh terrorists would intensify their campaign as the investiture approached. Detectives in the Welsh capital telephoned Chief Superintendent Jock Wilson, the Special Branch officer who had run the operation to protect the Prince from Shrewsbury and was now in Caernarfon to oversee security. The bomb in Cardiff was a shock, but it was hundreds of miles from the investiture.

As night fell before investiture day, the threat edged closer. A policeman in Chester, patrolling the route of the royal train to Caernarfon, found a dummy device under a railway bridge and spotted the snipped telegraph wires alongside the track.

Then, in the early hours of investiture morning, came a deafening blast that was much closer to the ceremony in North Wales. Drinkers inside a hotel in Abergele, some thirty miles from Caernarfon, heard the bang and rushed into the street. The hotel manager could smell phosphorus and returned to get a torch. Just yards from the main road he found the body of one man lying against the wall of an outbuilding. The blast had stripped him of his clothing and blown in the windows all around him. Parts of another man's body were also found, and police believed the pair had been carrying the device towards its destination: the railway line along which the royal train would carry the Prince of Wales to Caernarfon later that day.

Jock Wilson was kept informed. Had the threat been eliminated by clumsy plotters who had blown themselves up? Unknown to Special Branch, and barely anyone else in Caernarfon, the leader of the bombing campaign was alive and right under their noses.

John Jenkins was with the dental corps in a military camp on the edge of Caernarfon. 'The tent flap opened and this captain popped his head in and said: "We got two of the bastards last night!" Then he left... I was distraught, but the trick was that I had to appear delighted,' Jenkins would later say. He knew there were four bombs planned as he had built them himself, but the target of the Abergele device – the royal train – had not been the police's hunch but a newly built social security office in the town. Two more bombs were due to detonate in Caernarfon, timed to coincide with the afternoon's twenty-one-gun salute, while the fourth was due to explode on Llandudno pier where the Royal Yacht Britannia was expected to call.

Dafydd Elis-Thomas was near Caernarfon, too, but had

no intention of watching the investiture that day. 'I was working in the Plaid Cymru office in Bangor, which was a silly thing to do really because I was within five miles of the event. But I wasn't stopped or anything, it was business as usual. I thought the most sensible thing to do was to go to work.' Many of those in the nationalist movement were as tense as Chief Superintendent Jock Wilson about the potential for violent disruption, and there was concern that anything beyond peaceful protest would seriously harm the political objectives of Plaid Cymru and the Welsh Language Society.

'I did feel tense,' Dafydd Elis-Thomas told me. 'It was political terrorism, wasn't it? And if you mess about with that, that has always had a negative political effect. In Wales, anyway.' Conventional politicians, especially a nationalist party gaining traction in the late 1960s, had to condemn the violent acts of the extremists who shared their ambition but not their peaceful principles.

At ten o'clock in the morning the gates to Caernarfon Castle were opened to the invited guests. TV commentators took seats overlooking the dais to convey events to an international audience. In America the investiture was televised by the main networks. With satellite TV links in their infancy, the occasion was as much a test of the technology as it was a global news event.

Richard Nixon had been US President for only six months and did not travel to Wales for the investiture. He had been seen by British TV audiences a few nights before, when the *Royal Family* documentary was broadcast. The slightly twee film of life behind palace walls included the now notorious moment when the Queen was seen preparing a salad at one of the Duke of Edinburgh's loch-side barbecues. It was one of a series of regal mundanities caught by the documentary team which led to the monarchy banning any further broadcasts. The film also showed the awkward small talk when a reigning monarch meets a democratically elected president. The Queen was filmed exchanging framed photographs with Richard Nixon in a gilt-edged room at Buckingham Palace, with her family on hand to move the conversation along. President Nixon was heard observing how his daughters were fans of Charles, with news reports about the royal family being part of the Nixon chat at the dining table.

This set the scene for his eldest daughter to arrive in Caernarfon some three months after the presidential trip to London. Tricia Nixon came on the VIP train alongside prime ministers and ambassadors. Small and blonde, her American twang cut through the stuffy commentary of the television coverage. 'What did you think about your father's remarks, that you take a great deal of interest in the royal family?' Tricia Nixon is comfortable in front of the camera. 'Well, it's true,' she stated. 'I majored in modern European history and I've always had great interest in the royal family. I should say that all our family are great anglophiles.'

Ms Nixon was joined in the VIP seats by the Sultan of Brunei; obscure representatives of European royalty; the prime minister, Harold Wilson; and the leader of the opposition, Edward Heath. A special railway station at the Ferodo automotive works on the edge of Caernarfon was the point at which some dignitaries and royalty alighted to attend the investiture. From Cardiff, an investiture express was bringing invited guests including Sir Norman Lloyd-Edwards, a city councillor who would later become Lord-Lieutenant of South Glamorgan.

'It was so exciting, really.' Sir Norman remembered boarding the train in Swansea with well-dressed invited guests. 'It varied from people in uniform – navy, army, airforce. There were High Sheriffs in their get-up, and then the professors were wearing their wonderful academic gowns and caps. The ladies were wearing the most fantastic clothes and hats – hats were very much in fashion. And I wore morning dress and my councillor's gown,' he said. 'Every employee of British Rail were on the platforms and wore a red carnation. And every bridge we went under, there was a policeman on duty.'

This train of excitement pulled into Caernarfon and unloaded its passengers into the heaving streets of the town. Crowds ten deep filled the pavements. The tired folk pressing at the barriers had held their line since the day before. The smell of fresh paint, and fish and chips filled the noses of those who waited. Yet the crowd of around ten thousand outside the castle was half that of 1911, and the tensions and terrorism of the previous night had deterred some royal supporters and peaceful protesters.

A choir shuffled into the castle, along with every Welsh member of parliament aside from the new Plaid Cymru MP, Gwynfor Evans, who stayed away. Members of the judiciary and sports stars walked across the grass within the castle walls. A Welsh bible from 1588, translated that year by William Morgan, was carried into the ceremony. As in 1911, the enrobed members of the Gorsedd of the Bards, the Welsh chivalric order of poets and writers, joined the council of the National Eisteddfod in attending the investiture. The Archdruid Gwyndaf, along with the former Archdruid Cynan, were totems of the Welsh-speaking establishment and their presence emphasised the split in feelings among the nationalist community about the significance of being seen to endorse the spectacle.

Arriving from Flintshire were two men who hoped to disrupt the events. Ffred Ffransis and Ieuan Bryn had staged a hunger strike at Aberystwyth ahead of Charles's arrival to study by the sea, and now they hoped to leap the barrier and stop the coach carrying the Prince of Wales to his investiture. They took up position, surrounded by a crowd who had no idea of their plan.

Over at the military camp on the edge of Caernarfon, MAC leader John Jenkins watched the clock.

At 1.15 pm the castle was closed to all but those who would be part of the ceremony, and from Caernarfon County Hall a procession of mayors and council members were at the head of a long line of officials who marched into the castle grounds. The Heralds of Arms, in their playing card tabards, moved in unison with High Sheriffs, peers and MPs. Every moment was captured by the cameras.

'There was some nervousness about it all,' Sir Norman Lloyd-Edwards recalled. Two red investiture chairs now guard the entrance at his house in Llandaff, Cardiff. He likes to think that at least one of them was the seat he had at the ceremony that day, from where he watched with excitement and pride as the royals joined the Welsh for a moment of pure British pomp. For all the focus on the tension and the terrorists, much of Wales was in that seat with Sir Norman on 1 July 1969. The majority of Welsh people supported Charles as Prince of Wales and backed the investiture as a means to launch this young Prince into a life of service.

At 2.15 pm the horse-drawn carriage carrying Charles left the Ferodo works with an escort of the Household Cavalry and headed to the castle. Opposite the Prince sat his equerry, Squadron Leader David Checketts, and the Secretary of State for Wales, George Thomas. It must have felt like Thomas's big moment, his great political and personal ambition had been realised. But it was tense. Colour film from the day shows the Prince smiling broadly as the carriage swept into Caernarfon. The crowds cheered his journey, although a patch of boos flowed briefly over the microphones. Within minutes of leaving Ferodo, the carriage was on Bangor Street and nearing the Maes, Caernarfon's town square in the shadow of the castle. Back in the army camp, John Jenkins was still watching the clock. Any moment now.

A bomb, hidden under an oil barrel outside an ironmonger's shop on Bangor Street, failed to detonate. The Prince's carriage sailed, undisturbed, past the device. With Charles edging nearer the castle, the Queen had begun her own journey by carriage from the railway sidings at the Ferodo works. She was joined in the procession by the Duke of Edinburgh, the Queen Mother, Princess Anne and Princess Margaret. In order to signal the Queen's arrival in Caernarfon, a twenty-one-gun salute would be fired. John Jenkins had timed a small device to explode as the salute happened, the idea being that there would be twenty-two blasts filling the air. The bomb was hidden in the back garden of the local police chief on Love Lane, which backed on to the railway sidings where the royal train had pulled in.

The gun salute was a key moment in the pre-prepared script for broadcasters, and on hearing the first blast the radio commentator Emyr Jenkins started explaining to listeners that the first of twenty-one guns had indeed been fired. Except the noise he had heard was the bomb planted by members of MAC on Love Lane, and it was not followed by any other blasts from military guns.

In the Prince's carriage, which was nearing the centre of Caernarfon, Charles leant over to George Thomas. 'What was that, Mr Thomas?' he asked, in a tale recounted later by the former Secretary of State. 'So I said, "Royal salute, Prince Charles". And he looked at me with a question mark in his eyes. And he said: "Peculiar royal salute".' The men released a nervous laugh, and no attempt was made to either divert the route or make further enquiries.

Ffred Ffransis and his companion, who had planned to leap in front of the carriage as it navigated the narrow streets outside the castle, had heard the explosion too. They lost their nerve, helped by the sight of the road being lined with soldiers carrying bayonets shortly before the Prince's carriage arrived. They shouted their disapproval at the passing Prince instead.

As the carriage moved along the perimeter of the castle walls, the microphones picked up a jeer. 'A discordant note, there,' the BBC commentator chipped in. 'Just a few boos among the cheers.' It was barely a bubble in the stream of support shown by the thousands who lined the route, and the Prince's successful arrival at the castle gate meant the ceremony of his investiture could begin.

As the Prince stepped down from the carriage he was greeted by his uncle Tony, Lord Snowdon, in a specially created uniform of the Constable of Caernarfon Castle. 'It looked a bit like a pageboy from a hotel, you know?' Sir Norman Lloyd-Edwards laughed. From his seat, Sir Norman had watched the parades of famous faces and listened to the music. Musicians from the BBC Welsh Orchestra, whose violin cases had been searched by detectives on their way in, provided the ceremonial tunes. Charles would have to walk from one end of the castle to the central slate dais, and as he did so the choir sang 'God Bless the Prince of Wales'. As in 1911, the Prince was surrounded by military uniforms and fancy outfits. But for all the political concoction and sixties design, the parading of the colander-crown and the bell-boy costumes, the moment of the Prince's homage to his mother, the Queen, was blissfully dignified. With the young man's hands clasped between the monarch's, the Prince of Wales pledged:

I, Charles, Prince of Wales, do become your liege man of life and limb, and of earthly worship; and faith and truth I will bear unto thee, to live and die, against all manner of folks.

The commitment was ancient in its tone because it had its roots in medieval investitures, though not necessarily of Princes of Wales. It was the touch of historical credence that the rest of the ceremonial at Caernarfon lacked. It also gave Charles a moment of profound awareness of his fate. Though he had the scars of embarrassment from hearing his mother announce her intention to create him Prince of Wales in 1958 as he sat in his headmaster's study, he now had the reality of a public and televised commitment to serve his country and his Queen.

Wearing his crown and robe, the newly invested Prince of Wales rose to address the invited guests in the castle and his speech was relayed around the world. First, he spoke in Welsh.

Rwy'n bwriadu cysylltu fy hun o ddifrif mewn gair a gweithred a chymaint o fywyd y Dywysogaeth – a'r fath Dywysogaeth ydyw hi! – ag a fydd yn bosibl.

Charles pledged that it was his firm intention 'to associate myself in word and deed with as much of the life of the principality as possible – and what a principality!' He was committing himself to be a Prince for Wales, one who would argue the case of the country and its people. Dispassionate observers had heard him say as much in his interviews, and by his commitment to understanding the causes that ignited Welsh passion while he was at Aberystwyth. But inside the castle, invested publicly and with the might of the British state, he was reaching out to a country that still bubbled with some hostility. The bombs were evidence of that, even if the cheering crowds muffled their impact.

The following day, the papers gushed again with praise for the Prince. The Welsh press issued souvenir editions. A special supplement from the *Western Mail* carried a colour photograph of the moment the Queen placed the coronet on Charles's head, and a headline beneath proclaimed it to be 'the majestic climax — and once again Wales has its Prince'. The presentation of the Prince at Queen Eleanor's Gate was 'a moving moment as Wales greets her Prince', while the Queen's embrace of her son was 'a kiss to set the seal on an historic day'. Page after page of photographs detailed the royal family members in attendance, alongside adverts for Brains beer and the new restaurant at Howells department store in Cardiff.

The London papers were similarly enthused. *The Times* carried a front-page photograph of the Queen placing the coronet on the Prince's head. 'A pledge to Wales from their crowned Prince' was the banner headline above the photograph, which filled the page above the fold of the broadsheet. While its main news article noted that there had been 'bombs and an egg-throwing incident as well as some scattered booing', it rather quickly added that 'nothing marred the solemn grandeur of the occasion'. In a special supplement the coverage was fawning, leaning on the idea that this modern investiture was woven with historical tradition. The Prince's homage to the Queen – his 'liege man' moment – was described by Philip Howard as being delivered in phrases 'that whispered the last enchantments of the Middle Ages'. While Philip Howard had a seat near the royal dais to pen his observations, another *Times* reporter, Trevor Fishlock, was in the crowd outside and his nostrils were twitching. 'There was the sniff of tension in the air. Like every tiny detail here my pass was checked three times,' he wrote, conveying the excitement and nervousness that seemed to come in waves.

The positive coverage of the investiture trumped any critical responses by a factor of a hundred to one. Newspapers and magazines could guarantee a boost in sales with a royal ceremony on the front page, and the prospect of a future King being crowned – albeit with a sparkling coat-hanger – was enough to extend the print runs and puff the special supplements.

There was reporting, too, about the small explosion on Love Lane and a bit more detail about the Abergele bombing from the day before the investiture. But John Jenkins' fourth device, which was on Llandudno Pier, had failed to detonate and this kept his cack-handed terrorism from making further headlines the morning after the investiture.

The unexploded bomb in the ironmonger's yard on Bangor Street remained undetected for several days, but its accidental discovery caused life-changing injuries to a ten-year-old boy, Ian John, who stepped on it as he retrieved his football. He was from the home counties and on summer holiday in Caernarfon with his family. The explosion caused severe burns to his legs and the amputation of his right foot. He would spend many months in hospital over extended periods during a shattered childhood.

John Jenkins was eventually caught and jailed. In later life he expressed regret for the lives lost to the bombing campaign and the injuries to the boy in the Caernarfon blast, though this was heavily caveated by his continuing insistence that all of the blame for MAC's activities lay at the door of the British state. Some in the nationalist movement revered him, but not many. It would be the peaceful actions of Dafydd Iwan and the subsequent political recognition of the campaign for language rights that would have the greatest impact. The spectacular failure of violent nationalist extremism in Wales was a relief to those who used non-violent means to advance the cause of the Welsh language.

The investiture ceremony was a personal success for George Thomas, but politically it failed to achieve the desired result. In 1970 Labour lost the general election to Edward Heath's Conservatives, ending Thomas's stint as a cabinet minister. It did not dent Thomas's ambition, and by 1974 he had become Deputy Speaker of the House of Commons. Two years later he succeeded Selwyn Lloyd to become Speaker and held the role during the terms of three prime ministers. On standing down in 1983 he was elevated to the peerage as Viscount Tonypandy.

The new Prince of Wales appeared keen to remain as far removed from politics as was possible. Having already declared himself neutral and beyond political exploitation, Charles had made a public commitment that required action. The wheels of royal bureaucracy were already turning, with plans afoot for his military service and tours of the Commonwealth. But in the first few years after his investiture in Caernarfon, the Prince would find his feet as an ambassador for Wales and would make a subtle, significant impact on Welsh life.

4

Doing Business

'If you're ever going to open a factory in the UK,
please come and open one in my country: Wales.'

There had been rain showers all morning when the Prince of Wales arrived at the entrance to Expo 70, the world's fair that was held in the Japanese prefecture of Osaka that year. It was April 1970 and the wet welcome for Charles in Japan came during a stop-off on his return to London from a nostalgia-soaked visit to Australia. The Prince, now twenty-one and nearing the end of his time at university, had been with the Queen, the Duke of Edinburgh and Princess Anne on an Australian tour. It had included a return visit to the remote Timbertop boarding school where Charles had spent a term as a sixteen-year-old exploring the forestry of Victoria and embarking on camping trips and woodcutting. He would refer to it as 'by far the best part' of his education, and where he 'had the Pommy bits bashed off me'. If his return to the Antipodes had sparked recollections of youthful happiness, his next stop in Japan would prove to be fundamental in nurturing his skill as a diplomat and an industrial ambassador.

The world's fair was a concept that thrived in the

decades after the war, with the format allowing architects to create display cases filled with national pride. Countries would build elaborate and imposing pavilions, with the structures as important as the exhibits that filled them. The British pavilion at Expo 70 provided a 'progressive' image of Britain, according to *The Times*. Its architectural correspondent wrote that 'even the section on heritage does not depict Britain as a nation wholly wedded to its past, in the manner of too many projections of Britain abroad'. The site of the fair, in the city of Suita, covered an area of just over a square mile. Newsreel from the time shows structures of concrete and mirror, curved metal arches and buildings the shape of golf balls, with interlinking wide plazas dotted with visitors. A Canadian mounted policeman paraded on horseback in his red tunic and pale brown Stetson. Flags of the seventy-eight participating nations were draped along a road which was punctuated by Japanese avant-garde works of art. The host nation had employed its boldest creative minds to reinforce Japan's ambitious attitude. It was an opportunity to welcome the world to a nation that had rebuilt and re-energised after the war.

Charles arrived at the Expo in a white Rolls-Royce, splashing its way along the freshly drenched concrete. The theme of that year's event was 'Progress and Harmony for Mankind', and the exhibits included an early example of a mobile phone and the premiere of the first IMAX film. Colourful cable-cars shuttled between the pavilions. Charles viewed the moon rock samples in the American pavilion alongside a selection of NASA artefacts from the space programme. He met smiling children and a sea of Japanese-made cameras as he strolled between an Expo that seemed to blend futuristic architecture with Jackson Pollock splashes of colour. If the event made an impression on Charles, it may have been to reinforce his desire for Britain to capture some of the Japanese enthusiasm for technology. The Expo attracted millions of visitors and was considered to be a marked improvement on the drab world's fair in Montreal, Canada, a few years earlier. Those who attended Expo 70 were as likely to be impressed by their Japanese hosts as they were by the sprawling exhibitions of the visiting nations. The architect of the Expo's festival plaza, the post-modernist Arata Isozaki, would later win the Royal Gold Medal for Architecture in 1986 for his sometimes brutalist style.

From the Expo, the Prince of Wales went on to tour historic shrines and palaces in western Japan before crossing the country to end his short trip in Tokyo. In his diary was a reception at the British ambassador's residence in the capital city, and a tea party given by Crown Prince Akihito and Princess Michiko at their palace. Japan's hereditary monarchy is older than Britain's, and its royal household – the Chrysanthemum Throne – is an historic institution even more deeply rooted in the nation's consciousness than its British equivalent. In 1970 both Akihito and Charles were heirs to their respective thrones, relatively young men – Akihito is fifteen years older than Charles – who were engaged with the activities of the regal waiting room as their parents held the crown. The status of Japan's royal family had survived the war relatively intact, with the Emperor renouncing any divine right to rule but instead being allowed to continue as a figurehead in a constitutional monarchy. The Emperor and his family continued to command great respect from their people, with a distinct absence of any republican movement. In 1970 the concept of deference to royalty was deeply enshrined in Japanese culture, and Charles was able to capitalise on this as guests mingled at the embassy party.

The ambassador's reception was an opportunity to meet some of those Japanese industrialists whose modern manufacturing techniques shipped new electronic devices from the Pacific to Port Talbot. European markets were export destinations, but they were also being considered as production hubs to help meet the global demand for cameras, washing machines and television sets. One of the companies pioneering the technological essentials of modern life was Sony, a business founded in a bombed-out Tokyo department store in 1946 by two physicists, Masaru Ibuka and Akio Morita. Sony's small, portable transistor radios had been a huge hit in the 1950s, and by the 1960s it had developed television sets. It was a company that was expanding quickly, and as Akio Morita found himself at the British Embassy in April 1970 he was about to have a conversation that would play on his mind and enter Sony's company folklore. 'If you're ever going to open a factory in the UK,' Charles said to him, 'please come and open one in my country: Wales.' Morita's words in response were not recorded, but his actions afterwards have proven the commitment that was made in that Japanese reception.

Sony's official company history states that Morita 'felt that the Prince's interest in promoting direct investments in his country was a sign of his interest in the international business community and of the British royal family's enthusiasm for creating jobs in Britain'. The UK had been the focus for the establishment of a plant in Europe before the embassy event. Wales was one of several areas being considered by the head of Sony's UK operations, Hiroshi Okochi, for a factory to manufacture colour televisions and a site in the town of Bridgend ultimately became his first choice. Morita, according to Sony's records, was 'surprised at the coincidence' and over time the management in Bridgend have placed far more emphasis on Charles's influence than on Sony's own shortlisting operation. Work began on the Sony plant in Bridgend in 1972 with the first television sets being produced in June 1974. Charles visited the factory in December of the same year to officially open the production line and was accompanied by Morita on his tour of the plant. Colour televisions produced in Bridgend would be switched on and watched by families across Europe and further afield. Around half of Bridgend's finished products would be exported to the European continent and Africa, with the Welsh factory accounting for 30% of all colour TV exports from the UK. At its peak it's thought the Bridgend plant was producing around a million analogue TV sets a year.

Was Charles really behind the decision of this

confident, multinational technology company to base its UK operation in Wales? Steve Dalton has heard the story countless times and swears by it. When I met him at Sony's Welsh factory in November 2022 he was preparing to stand down as managing director of the plant where he had worked since starting as an electronics graduate in 1982. Dalton repeated the tale about Charles's involvement in bringing Sony to South Wales, having consulted others to ensure he remained true to the historical narrative which is etched into Sony's relationship with Wales. Dalton refers to the embassy meeting with Sony's founder, Morita. 'Prince Charles asked him, "If you're ever going to open a factory in the UK, please come and open one in my country, Wales," and that's exactly what he did.' Steve Dalton and I were joined by a former senior manager at the Bridgend plant, John Bevan, who was employed when the factory started production in 1974 and also vouched for the gratitude shown to Charles in securing Sony's investment here.

The story is indelible in company history partly due to Charles's habit of repeating it. He has brought it up on his visits to Sony's manufacturing plant in Bridgend and its relocated, newer technology centre in nearby Pencoed. He even recalled the story when he presented Steve Dalton with an honour at Buckingham Palace in 2010. 'He gave me the OBE at the palace, and as he gave me the OBE, those were the words he said to me.' Dalton smiled as he recalled Charles's words. 'He said, "Do you know, I had a hand in starting Sony at the very beginning," and of course I chirped up, "Oh, yes I do, sir.

I know that story very well".' In 2014 Charles visited the renamed Sony Technology Centre to mark forty years since the company first invested in Wales. 'It was supposed to only be an hour-long visit,' Steve Dalton recalled, 'He went everywhere. He talked to everyone. And he recited in the speech he made, standing there in reception before unveiling the plaque, that "I started this"; he used that same story.'

'If you are endorsed by the royal family, then there is some trust and respect about Sony being in the UK,' Steve Dalton said. The royal connections with the new plant were deepened further when a future emperor of Japan came to visit. John Bevan was a manager at the plant when a Japanese teenager required a lift to Atlantic College at St Donat's, an international school on the Welsh coast some nine miles from Bridgend. 'One Saturday morning I was asked to take two Japanese down to Atlantic College, and I did. I didn't query who they were, but it was the young Prince Naruhito, and somebody else.' The future Emperor Naruhito would later undertake postgraduate studies at Oxford University, but his visits to Wales underlined the commitment so many regular Japanese engineers and Sony directors had made to Welsh life. Those who came to Wales from Japan did not live together in company housing but among the broader Welsh population, sending their children to local schools. Some of those children, after returning to Japan, would make the trip back to Wales as Sony employees later in life.

For all the deepening bonds between Wales and its

Sony factory, the investment in Bridgend coincided with many other Japanese companies choosing Wales for their booming manufacturing operations. As Sony's foundations were being dug in Bridgend, Takiron became the first company from Japan to open in Wales in 1972 with its PVC sheeting operation in Bedwas near Caerphilly. The electronics boom brought Sharp and Panasonic, while automotive giants Toyota and a string of Japanese car parts companies in their supply chain made homes on Welsh industrial estates. Sony placed Japanese directors into the business in the 1970s, and John Bevan recalled how they leaned on other companies to follow Sony to Wales. 'Japanese MDs all encouraged other Japanese firms, like Panasonic and Hitachi, to come. At that time there was a growth of Japanese companies.' Sony was, according to Steve Dalton, 'the catalyst' for a deep and long-term business relationship between Wales and Japan.

Dalton also emphasised how useful the royal connection would become when company bosses in Japan reviewed the Welsh operation. Charles's fondness for Sony was a 'comfort point' in the company's history, he said, and which placed an historical bind on Japanese management whenever times got tough in Wales. Plaques commemorating royal visits provide a guard of honour at the entrance to the Welsh factory, while a wall of photographs chart the history of Sony's royal supporter. Dalton identified the power of that pedigree. 'We very proudly talk about our royal connection, about Sony's royal connection,' he said. 'It's a very powerful thing, when talking to Japanese people. And I am talking about business. "We were started by Prince Charles, are you going to mess around with us?" We actually still use it as an endorsing weapon to try and explain things, particularly in Japan where lots of people had no idea the factory existed or how it started. So when we talk about the fact that Prince Naruhito was in St Donat's in Wales, and that connection of ours with Prince Charles, then they start to think, "This is a precious thing, and we should be careful," you know?'

Over the decades Charles kept tabs on what was happening at Sony. He followed the trend in manufacturing, and followed the threats that hovered over the Welsh operation when shopping habits and technological advances put the plant in peril. But even the Japanese respect for monarchy could not trump the economic reality that faced Bridgend's workforce in 2005 when analogue television sets were discarded by consumers in favour of flat-screen products made by Sony in Barcelona. Hundreds of people were laid off in Bridgend and the site was closed, while the newer Sony operation in nearby Pencoed – which had opened as an overflow for the booming Bridgend production line – also saw staff numbers reduced. Bridgend's closure shifted the focus in Pencoed, where workers pivoted from manufacturing TV parts to making smaller circuit boards for the flat-screen market, as well as broadcast cameras. But Steve Dalton's use of royalty as an 'endorsing weapon' may have secured a longer-term future for the Welsh operation despite the existential threat it faced with the demise of the big-box television set.

Charles's pride at getting Sony to come to Wales is rooted in the fact that it was an early and effective victory for his particular brand of royal diplomacy. Lord David Rowe-Beddoe counts Charles as a friend and has worked alongside him in various roles in industry and the arts. He said the Sony experience was Charles's first 'exposure' to industrial diplomacy. 'It was enormous, that was his exposure, as I understand it. The first time that he got involved in business for Wales.' Charles was 'extraordinarily well respected,' by the Japanese, Lord Rowe-Beddoe said, 'and I bet he still is. Because of the links [he encouraged], but royalty – you can't say it too loudly – it was very important.' The strength of those early links with Japanese firms was useful to Lord Rowe-Beddoe when he chaired the Welsh Development Agency in the 1990s. The WDA was a highly effective and sometimes much-missed magnet of industrial spending which succeeded in attracting employment opportunities to Wales at a time when coal mining and steel-making were in decline.

Lord Rowe-Beddoe, who is now in his eighties, maintained a deep affection for Wales while working overseas. At his cottage in the Cotswolds he has the mementoes of a friendship with Richard Burton on his study walls, along with black-and-white public school photos and the decorations of a career in which he has been honoured with peerages, presidencies and patronages. His career took him from the Welsh Development Agency to the Royal Welsh College of Music and Drama and the Wales Millennium Centre, all of which became crucibles of talent on his watch. His appointment to chair the WDA came at a time when it needed reorganising and reinvigorating. In the role, Lord Rowe-Beddoe witnessed how Charles responded to the way Wales was marketed as an investment destination. It was in the mid-1990s that the Royal Yacht Britannia was in Swansea for a function with Charles and invited guests. Lord Rowe-Beddoe was in charge of the invitations and wanted to mix business people with experience of Wales with those they were hoping to attract. 'A sit-down dinner on the Royal Yacht is not a big affair, so I had a very small limit on guests,' he said. 'I think I got four or five chairmen from all over the world who had business in Wales, and three or four chairmen who I wanted to attract. So I brought them together, and let them be themselves.' The Prince of Wales hosted the evening and afterwards Lord Rowe-Beddoe recalled that he said, 'Let me tell you, David, I will always do something for you. An annual event, whatever you want, I will arrange it.' Charles's backing for the WDA began on the boat but extended to dinners at Highgrove and other functions that were adorned with royal patronage. 'That was how it started, my friendship. I call it a friendship, I don't know whether he would, but I do.' Lord Rowe-Beddoe credits Charles's backing with helping to transform the WDA into the most successful inward investment agency in the United Kingdom. 'We tore the pants off them all, eventually!'

Charles had been an 'open door' on matters that were important to the WDA and personally to Lord Rowe-

Beddoe, who said that the Prince had understood the concept of inward investment more clearly than some Welsh politicians. 'I don't want to speak ill of the past, or the dead, but there were one or two Welsh politicians who would throttle the WDA, and I would like to throttle them. Unfortunately they have gone.' Some of the distaste for political attitudes towards the Welsh Development Agency lies in its abolishment in 2006 when its functions were absorbed by the Welsh government. But in its prime the WDA filled trophy cabinets with prized foreign investors, and Charles and his staff were acutely aware of how useful he could be to the process. As well as hosting functions, Charles also had staff monitoring and reporting back on Welsh affairs. Lord David Rowe-Beddoe referred to them as Charles's 'territorials' – his private secretary Elizabeth Buchanan was a key contact in the WDA's heyday, while he would later build relationships with the Prince's new Welsh private secretary Dr Manon Antoniazzi – Manon Williams at that time – in the late 1990s and 2000s. There was also correspondence with the Prince. 'I have lots of letters, as you can imagine. He is a voluminous writer.' Lord Rowe-Beddoe described them as 'proper letters, not just, "Nice to see you, bye-bye!" No, they're proper letters. Well thought-out.' He wanted to follow-up on the important things, not the trivia and social stuff. 'His correspondence is very skilful. I don't think he means it to be skilful, it is him.' He couldn't put it on, it was a genuine interest and understanding.

Having had his fair share of brushes with politicians at

the WDA, and more recently in the House of Lords, Rowe-Beddoe seems content that an unelected Prince should involve themselves in the diplomacy of attracting investment to Wales. 'The weight of what he has done is immeasurable, but you don't see it, you don't think of it, you don't hear of it.' The interactions have confirmed Lord Rowe-Beddoe's credentials as a backer of the institution of monarchy. 'The closer I am to being around politicians, I'm very pleased we *are* a monarchy,' he smiled.

Charles's biggest single impact on the Welsh economy may well have peaked with his first major intervention. Sony's success is a continuing badge of honour for him, and the conversation he held with Akio Morita in the British Embassy in Tokyo remains the most remarkable moment in the diplomatic mission of the Prince of Wales to promote the Welsh workforce. That's probably more than enough for a man whose preferred role in Welsh life was as a convenor of ideas and an accelerator of development and investment. For the day-to-day work of encouraging young people into apprenticeships, and up-skilling the unemployed, he could rely on his charities: The Prince's Trust, PRIME Cymru and Business in the Community. They have done much of the legwork in promoting entrepreneurial spirit among the Welsh population, and have worked with organisations like Sony to place candidates for apprenticeships on the production lines. It was more urgently required in the late 1980s and early 1990s when unemployment rocked communities, such as those in the South Wales valleys, where the pledges of big business to support post-industrial coal towns carried little weight. At that time Helen Mary Jones was managing an employment project for youths with a history of offending, and had got wind of a visit by the Prince of Wales to Aberdare. Charles wanted to meet some of the young people on the scheme, and his visit to the valleys made a lasting impact.

Helen Mary Jones was running the Cynon Valley Crime Prevention Bureau in the early 1990s, though she found there was a far greater fear of any crime compared to recorded offences. 'There were low levels of anti-social behaviour, very little in the way of serious offending apart from the inevitable domestic abuse. But there was lots of fear of crime. We had a community centre on one of the estates where everybody under the age of eighteen was just banned. And that's because of people's stereotypical views of what young people were likely to be like.' One of the objectives of her role was to try and mitigate the impact of cuts to local authority youth services at the time, which largely involved Jones sitting on walls with young people to find out what they would like to do, and then trying to make it happen. 'So on that estate where the young people were banned from the community centre, we went within three years from that situation to having young people sitting on the management committee, and running a youth club twice a week.' It was an experience that pushed Helen Mary Jones into politics, and she later served as a member of the Welsh parliament for Plaid Cymru from its inception in 1999 until 2021. When I met her to discuss her interactions with the Prince of Wales, she had failed to retain her seat at the election and was clutching a folder of job applications as we ordered coffee. The staff at Cafe Brava in Pontcanna knew Helen by name, she is a frequent visitor but also a well-known and forthright politician. Given that Plaid Cymru is a proudly republican party, I had been surprised to hear that Jones had a positive story about the role of monarchy in boosting business and employment in Wales. But her path to politics began with her witnessing the power the Prince could wield.

In 1991 she had already made an impression with her ability to transform attitudes to young people, and had been offered a seat on the local committee of The Prince's Trust. It was essentially a grant-giving committee and included representatives of Business in the Community as well. Without quite being able to recall how, she was given the task of arranging a royal visit. 'Talk about a culture clash,' she said. 'The people coming down from the Prince's office to arrange the visit might as well have been on another planet.' The process began with a young woman with 'a Sloane Ranger name that ended with an "A". It wasn't Serena, but it might as well have been'. The idea of the visit was that the Prince would come with a delegation of national business leaders to meet local traders, and to meet the young people in their natural environment to discuss the issues they faced. 'As you can imagine, I was deeply sceptical about the whole thing, but my management thought it would be a good way of raising awareness of what we were doing.' The person who Helen referred to as Serena arrived at Aberdare railway station, but she may as well have come in the Tardis. 'You can see immediately that she thinks she's on a different planet.' Helen took Serena through the town along the route the organising committee proposed for the Prince's arrival. 'The first thing she spots is this really hideous 1970s Co-op. And she said, "Oh, my God. We can't bring him this way. If he sees that building we will have nothing from him but architecture all day".' Serena wanted to find an alternative route for the Prince to arrive in Aberdare. 'In those days, the Aberdare bypass hadn't been opened and the only way to get into the centre of Aberdare was up that road. So, we had long complex conversations about how else could we get him in. Because he was always going to come from London, so he'd be coming up via Cardiff, and we toyed with all sorts of things like taking him to Swansea and bringing him down the Heads of the Valleys road, and all this kind of nonsense. And all the while I am thinking, "Can he really not concentrate? Can he really not put his Prince's Trust hat on?"'

They decided to bring the Prince to Aberdare by train, where the exit from the station allowed him to be taken across a footbridge and into the middle of town without having to pass the dreaded Co-op. But Serena's crash course in valleys life was about to hit another hairpin bend. 'I mentioned the key people around the project that he would need to meet, but I said I was sure that some of them won't agree to meet him. And she said, "Oh!",' and Helen let out a rather posh and high-pitched exclamation mimicking Serena's shock. 'A lot of them will have political objections, I said, to which she responded, "Are they members of the Labour party?" And I said, no, they're Welsh nationalists.' At this, Serena's pitch jumped an octave higher. Helen had to draw on her own rather posh roots to reassure the Prince's assistant. 'My mother's family are from that kind of background, so when I am speaking English I can be quite Serena-esque, and I said: "It's perfectly all right, I'm one of them, there aren't going to be any bombs. Relax!"' The next stage of planning the trip involved finding a suitable place for the Prince and his delegation to meet the young people. Part of the point of the visit was to underline that there was nowhere in Aberdare for young people to go. There were youth organisations taking space in community halls in the nearby villages, but there wasn't anywhere central in the town. This situation had led to young people hanging out in pubs and an amusement arcade. Young people wanted a youth centre in the middle of the town. 'Part of the point was to see if, as a by-product of the royal visit, could we get some of the business people to support this? I was planning to have conversations around the visit, but it didn't occur to me that the Prince would be much use in that regard. But he was a pull, to get them there.' Helen Mary Jones was hoping to attract support from some of the senior figures from UK business organisations who were coming with the Prince. They included the chairman of the London Stock Exchange and Gerald Ratner, the jewellery shop owner.

The lack of a suitable location meant that only the local fish-and-chip shop was big enough to accommodate the delegation, and did not have the distractions of the pubs and the amusement arcade for the underage youths. Serena released another high-pitched 'Oh!' and agreed that the pub was off limits. 'And we obviously can't go to the amusement arcade because we'd have nothing but problem-gambling talk.' The chip shop also posed its own problems to the organisers, who were concerned that the Prince's fondness for healthy eating and organic production measures would pose a further distraction. 'We settled on the fish-and-chip shop on the strict understanding that the fat friers had to be turned off,' Helen Mary Jones said. 'And Mario, who ran the chip shop, said, "What! What! You're expecting me to serve things other than fried food?" And we said it would be alright, we'd get the bakery to provide some croissants.' As she recalled the story, Helen Mary Jones also dwelled on the patronising tone the Prince's officials took. It was an attitude and an outlook which was not displayed by the Prince when he visited on 22 February 1991.

The court circular for that day, published by *The Times*, stated that 'The Prince of Wales, as President of Business in the Community, will visit the Cynon Valley, Mid Glamorgan, at 11.35 to meet young Welsh business leaders and the Cynon Valley Business Leadership Team.' Charles made a beeline straight for the young people when he arrived in Aberdare. They were six teenagers who wanted a place to go, and who were being steered delicately away from the distractions of drugs and delinquency by people like Helen Mary Jones. Despite the Serenas and the security, the threats of rogue architecture and fruit machines, the Prince was capable of focusing solely on the matter at hand. 'He asked really pertinent questions,' Helen Mary Jones recalled. 'Is that because somebody is very well briefed? Well, if that was the case, that's fine as well, actually.' Briefing documents had been part of the planning process. The organisers had also sent full background information on the young people, and partial backgrounds on the adults 'because if we had sent full backgrounds, for at least two of them, the security people would not have allowed him to meet'. There had also been a 'trauma' on the morning of the visit, she said. 'The security people had turned up to search the building, and Mario would not let them into the attic. And to this day I don't know what Mario had in his attic.' Mario came from an old Italian communist family, and had been rather unimpressed with the prospect of a royal visit from the get-go. 'My colleague asked me, what did I think he had up there? Portraits of Mussolini? But, no, I suspect he just wanted to have some privacy.'

Helen Mary Jones chose teenagers who had something to say to the Prince, not just those who would behave in polite company. 'The kids who were making the most difference were the ones who had been making the most trouble before,' Helen Mary Jones said. 'The young people who are kicking against the traces are often, with the right input, the brightest ones. Because they are the ones looking at their life situation and saying, this is awful. I shouldn't have to live like this.' This meeting allowed them to look at a Prince, who woke up that morning in a London palace, and explain why they deserved better. Of the six, two of them had been in 'low-level trouble' according to Helen Mary Jones. 'I think they had teased police officers, and the officers didn't know how to take it.' They were fifteen or sixteen years old and would end up in deeper trouble if the opportunity arose.

'Then there was Tammy. She was notorious in her school for being an absolute tearaway, but never gave me a moment's trouble.' Confronted with this small gang, Charles listened and encouraged them to share their stories and discuss the solutions which would ease their concerns. Watching this interaction, Helen Mary Jones didn't see the inattentive and distractible Prince that his staff had feared. 'It didn't click with me that he was this kind of fragile ego. I was ready to take no nonsense, both from my politics – I am a republican – but also because on my mother's side, I am a royal Stuart and my brother Martin has probably got more right to the throne than Charlie has. So I wasn't going to take any nonsense from these Hanoverian upstarts. But I was impressed, and I did not expect to be.' The fact that Helen Mary Jones has a family claim to the throne was one of the most surprising moments of the interview. But in Aberdare in 1991, the Prince of Wales continued to impress. 'What was absolutely clear was that he was genuinely interested in what the young people had to say, what their issues were, what they wanted,' Helen Mary Jones added. He was asking 'some really practical questions,' and called on the business leaders to provide some solutions. 'He said, "This is what needs to be done, now what are you going to do for these young people?", and I was like, "Whoa, OK." He was very direct, he said things to them like, "Well, you talk about corporate social responsibility, here's something really practical".'

Television news coverage of the visit showed Helen Mary Jones outside Mario's fish-and-chip shop, the anxieties of the Prince's arrival now replaced by the adrenaline of the moment. She told the reporter how the Prince's visit 'shows the young people that, at the very highest level, the work they are putting in is appreciated'. Charles was seen by the cameras as he sat down to talk to Helen's six teenagers, the chip-shop staff in white coats milled around behind the empty friers. Then, in a short speech at a lectern, Charles outlined his commitment to the principles of Business in the Community. 'By responding to the needs of shareholders, employees, customers and neighbours – all, if you like, stakeholders – companies can open up new marketing opportunities, they can create goodwill and gain more committed, more highly skilled employees. So, ladies and gentlemen, businesses and communities do need each other.' The cameras followed the royal delegation from Aberdare to another stop at Penrhys, an estate that the reporter called 'notorious' and where the business leaders were tasked with reporting back to the Prince about what they saw, and what they were prepared to do to help. Gerald Ratner spoke to the press in the doorway of a housing block, and when asked about Charles's motivation for bringing people to that part of South Wales, Ratner said: 'He is obviously getting people to do it, and he is not giving up.

I understand that he is devoting something like a twelfth of his time towards the business community. He is doing a brilliant job. Unless business really does address the problem, unless businessmen like myself come out and see an estate like this, unless we do something about it we have got problems. Because if somebody doesn't do something about a place like this, it is going to lead to disaster.'

The teenagers who met Charles got their community centre, the presence of the Prince seemingly enough to oil the wheels of local bureaucracy. Whatever the stereotypes of valleys youths, the prominence of a royal visit had shifted perspectives.

As Prince of Wales in the seventies, eighties and nineties, Charles was a useful intermediary for some specific projects and businesses. As a diplomat acting for Welsh interests, he could stitch connections and advance young ambitions. The soaraway success of his Sony intervention provided the template for polite intervention in Wales. The early part of the twenty-first century added depth to Charles's relationship with Wales. This was largely as a result of expanding his team and having appointed Dr Manon Williams as a private secretary with particular responsibility for Wales in the 1990s. During two periods in the royal household until her departure in 2011 her public profile invariably focused on the reported Welsh lessons she gave Prince William. But her astute understanding of Welsh affairs was invaluable to the Prince of Wales. Described unflatteringly by the *Daily Mail* as one of Charles's 'Backroom Boys (And Girls)', Dr

Williams's appointment provided a direct contact for Welsh organisations who wished to develop a relationship with the Prince of Wales and gave Charles a direct line to Welsh affairs. The poet and journalist Dr Grahame Davies would assume a similar role when he joined the royal household from the BBC in 2012. The administration of the relationship with Wales, placed in the hands of two individuals with a deep-rooted understanding of the Welsh people and its language, was key to ensuring the Prince of Wales remained connected and sure-footed in his dealings with the country.

While Charles's diplomacy tended to be soft and publicly unimposing, a far greater impact was made by the organisations he set up and supported – The Prince's Trust, Business in the Community and PRIME Cymru. The former cabinet minister, Alun Cairns, served as Welsh Secretary and was previously a Conservative member of the Senedd in Cardiff and championed Charles's work in Wales. 'One of the great facts that was never repeated or recognised half-often enough,' Mr Cairns told me, 'was that The Prince's Trust had set up more businesses in Wales than the Welsh Development Agency ever did. And I was a fan of what the Welsh Development Agency did. But The Prince's Trust would have had more of an impact on day-to-day communities, on our high streets.' Alun Cairns would become an outspoken supporter of Charles as Prince of Wales, often to the irritation of politicians – largely among his Labour opponents – who would rather keep the royal nose out of Welsh life. He became synonymous with support for monarchy, most notably and most controversially by arranging for the newest bridge across the River Severn to be renamed the Prince of Wales Bridge in 2018. Alun Cairns's council estate upbringing did not dent his royalist tendencies, which was a private passion until he joined the then Welsh Assembly in 1999. Mr Cairns, a fresh member of this new institution, went along to a presentation about The Prince's Trust attended by Charles and a panel of people who had been helped by the Trust.

Cairns was touched by their stories, particularly a bike shop owner from the valleys. 'There was no doubt that the prospects for this young person were pretty challenging and bleak. But The Prince's Trust came in and gave this person the support, the mentoring, the encouragement that very often any family would give, or any parent would give to their child.' The pastoral impact of the Trust made a lasting impact on Mr Cairns. 'As an assembly member, then, I would often refer people to The Prince's Trust. Young people who were looking for support.'

The success of The Prince's Trust is widely known, but Charles faced opposition and indifference at the beginning. 'It was the story of my life really,' he told ITV in 2016. 'We had to overcome all these people who don't see the point.' In Wales, the Trust has provided the mentoring and practical assistance required by thousands of young people to get work or start their own business. While it has famous successes – it backed the Welsh rock band Stereophonics with a grant to buy their first set of speakers – its core work has helped over a million young people to get going. By providing opportunities for teamwork, gaining skills or starting their own business, these pillars of The Prince's Trust have guided its mission since its formal inception in 1976. In one of the milestone celebrations of the Trust's work, Charles said the organisation had been 'inspired by the vision of providing the most vulnerable young people in our society with the opportunities and skills they needed to create a successful future.'

While the success of the Trust became global, other schemes like Business in the Community, which helped the Aberdare teenagers, and PRIME Cymru which encourages older people into business, have delivered the then Prince of Wales's principles. Observers of Welsh public life will have seen umpteen political ambitions come and go, the back-to-work schemes and up-skilling initiatives ebbing and flowing according to ministerial priority. And yet the organisations championed by Charles have been a mainstay of this environment, a toolkit of ambition and ideas which have secured jobs and improved the prospects of thousands of individuals in Wales. While royal patronage was instrumental in establishing these organisations, they are run by professionals.

'Sometimes the call would come, saying that he would quite like to do something around this – maybe climate change, something like that. But very often they would just ask, what's your big project, what can he do to help?' Owen Evans was appointed chief executive of Business in the Community in Wales in 2008, and he always considered it to be among the 'stable' of organisations that Charles supported in Wales alongside The Prince's Trust and PRIME Cymru. 'We all got on fine, but the thing is, everybody was competing,' Owen Evans said. 'The Prince's Trust and Business in the Community compete against each other, they have slightly different markets, but they do compete. There is only so much corporate cash out there, and both are doing the same thing.' Owen Evans said the organisations were encouraged to use the Prince. 'Because whatever you think about monarchy, bloody hell, he is a draw. If you are holding an event and the letters go out with HRH The Prince of Wales on the invitation, they will come. They could be the biggest republicans in the world, but they will be there. I have seen them bow!' Owen Evans said this with some experience of the sceptical and the cynical.

When asked where he sat on the scale of republican to monarchist, he replied: 'Rampant republican. Off with their heads!' For Owen Evans, the idea of unearned privilege grates against everything he was brought up to believe. 'Mam was raised in a council house in Llanelli, and you get what you earn. You're not born with it. Mam was a rampant republican too, Dad wasn't that bothered. But that's where it came from.'

Nevertheless, Evans succeeded in suppressing his own constitutional differences when it came to working with Charles. 'The way I thought of it, he was an asset. Plain and simple. And the more I worked with him, I realised that the bloke was professional. He was quite human. I think he does care, and he is willing to put time in, and you had to divorce that from what he is.' At that point, he was the Prince of Wales and he took a direct interest in how his Welsh organisations were being run. Business in the Community was established to encourage responsible business practices. It is a membership organisation and focuses on developing skills and sustainable business models in the local communities where its members are based. Charles's approach was not to meddle but to engage and encourage the projects that local leadership teams were developing. It might involve a group of businesses gathering to discuss the requirement for IT skills in the valleys, or to encourage sustainable environmental practices among companies operating in the national parks. Events would be arranged with the Prince's presence key to encouraging high numbers of attendees, and cooperation with the organisation's goals.

'I was only there for two years,' Owen Evans said, 'but I must have done four or five high-spec events with him.' This included arranging appearances around his Wales Week of annual visits. 'You had to find something for him to do, but to be fair, it wasn't a challenge. If you wanted to get a group of businesses in to discuss something, he was your man.' Owen Evans discovered he was a man who was 'immaculately briefed', and had a knowledge of business and the issues they faced that extended beyond the remit of any research paper that had been prepared for his visit. As Helen Mary Jones had discovered in Aberdare, the Prince would ask pertinent questions, and chase up decision-makers for solutions.

Despite the relaxed, informed Charles helping to calm any pre-meeting nerves, the question of royal etiquette provided a constant headache for organisers. 'Firstly, there are the small things, like the requirement to find a separate toilet for him.' Owen Evans's mention of the toilet request strikes a similar tone to a tale told about an unnamed Welsh official who, on realising their home would be required for Charles to take a comfort break, arranged for the bathroom to be re-decorated by a team of professionals. 'I am sure he thought every toilet smelled like fresh paint,' Owen confirmed. But there was a respect, earned from this republican, for Charles's ability to do business. Firstly, there was an acknowledgement that this man, at that time in his sixties, had already seen and heard it all before. Few interactions contained new ideas or inspiration, rarely was Charles regaled with an anecdote he hadn't heard before. 'But he was polite, courteous to everybody, he would listen carefully and he would answer them.'

Occasionally, even Charles struggled with the pomposity displayed by some of those he had to meet. Owen Evans recalled a trip on the royal train through Wales, which was used occasionally as an office before the purchase of Charles's home, Llwynywermod, in Carmarthenshire. The train allowed face-to-face discussions, and Owen Evans travelled on the royal express service with 'a very senior figure from West Wales'. Owen and the man were set next to each other, facing Charles across the table. 'The table isn't big at all, we were literally cheek by jowl.' There followed a discussion in which the unnamed west-Walian 'was speaking about something, maybe homelessness, as if it had just been invented and he had the solution. Anyway, I saw Charles a few months later in Portmeirion, and he was being filmed for something and was wearing a microphone. Fair play, he bounded over to me, saying "Oh, how are you Owen? My God, wasn't that man so-and-so awful!" At which point the staff ran out, waving arms, "No, no, you're on camera…!" I think there was some sympathetic editing, if they caught it.' He had a sense of humour, Owen said, as well as the ability to see through the guff and grandstanding that sometimes came with an official appearance.

Protocol around a royal event involved the rather humourless instruction that Charles must have a cup of tea available on arrival at a meeting with business people. 'It wasn't really etiquette, to me, to offer him a mug of tea,' Owen Evans said, 'and it wasn't him who would give you a bollocking! It would be his equerries. But he would have tea in his specific cup.' Choosing a seat during an event on board the royal train came with a helpful piece of protocol. 'You would know exactly where he would be sitting, because somebody had put his cushion there. So that when he walked in, he knew where to sit because his cushion was there. And if you were clever, you knew where to sit if you wanted to be next to him.'

The rigmarole of etiquette and protocol rings as true for Owen Evans in 2008 as it did for Helen Mary Jones in the early 1990s. One of the functions of monarchy is to act as a cultural preservative, to enshrine in the actions of one family the values and traditions that are the

markers of the society they represent. Yet within the firm
there are house rules and creatures of habit, woven with
Victorian formality and routines that have eased the
burdens of glad-handing and ribbon-cutting. In Aberdare
this was exaggerated by the 'Serena' approach to royal
planning, and in Charles's work with business in Wales
the public and private encounters are decorated with
etiquette and officialdom. That is why the greatest impact
the former Prince of Wales could have on Welsh businesses
was done at arm's length and delivered by the
organisations he established to facilitate good work. When
he invested his Royal Navy pension to form The Prince's
Trust in 1976, Charles overcame the doubters. His
regular oversight of his charities has been largely
welcomed by the officers who have run them. And every
now and then, from Tokyo to Aberdare, the direct
intervention of the Prince of Wales made an immeasurable
impact on Welsh communities.

5

'World Class'

I passed a man taking a corgi for a walk as I drove into the centre of Treorchy in the Rhondda Fawr valley. I looked twice, not because I am a particular fan of the corgi – they are notoriously tenacious in temperament for a breed with such little legs – but because it seemed such an old-fashioned omen for what lay ahead. Like polo ponies and marriage breakdowns, the corgi seemed to represent a nineties stereotype of the modern monarchy. They belonged to an era of shoulder pads and pinstripe suits. The new generation of dukes and duchesses were committed to causes as diverse as climate change and mental health support, sustainable fashion and entrepreneurial youths. Surely the corgi was a relic that even Charles would be shaking off? And yet my visit to Treorchy reinforced the traditional foundations that support the modern monarchy. The corgi, as much as the climate, was key to maintaining the popularity of the Crown.

Treorchy would be one of the engagements the then Prince of Wales would undertake with the then Duchess of Cornwall during their final Wales Week in July 2022 before his accession to the throne. The couple's visit to the high street in Treorchy was the fifth engagement of the day. They had started in Cardiff, opening the BBC's new headquarters in Wales and stepping outside to admire a statue of Betty Campbell, Wales's first black headteacher. Charles and Camilla then went to separate engagements: Charles to Cardiff's City Hall to present medals to The Queen's Dragoon Guards, of which he was Colonel-in Chief; Camilla to meet charities for victims of domestic and sexual violence. The couple reconvened at their helicopter after lunch and flew to Treorchy to visit the shops and end up at the local pub.

The Clarence House press office accepted my request to join the royal rota at Treorchy, the system by which a small group of media representatives are allowed to closely observe public engagements by members of the royal family. The royal rota has come in for criticism, most notably from the Duke and Duchess of Sussex who argued that it amounted to an unhealthy relationship of dependency between the press and the palace. Its use in Wales is often staffed entirely by Welsh media, especially on more mundane visits that seem less interesting to the London-based newspapers. I was attending Treorchy as part of my research for writing this book, but I had previously been part of rota engagements for royal visits and the procedure was familiar. In essence, you go where you are told and you don't get in the way. Broadcasters are required to share their material with their rivals, so that no commercial advantage can be gained by getting a slot on the rota. It allows the media to get the pictures they need, as well as to capture any audible reaction from either the royal family or the people they meet. From the palace's perspective, the rota system gives some organisation to the media interest in the royal family's public engagements. From the press perspective, it guarantees front-row access, even if they have to sit on their hands as part of the deal. Throwing questions at the royals is banned and this rule is rarely breached as part of the quid pro quo.

Treorchy was chosen by the palace for a Wales Week visit because, just before the Covid-19 pandemic, it had been named as having the best high street in Britain. Charles and Camilla were natural supporters of small businesses and independent traders, which usually carry traditional attitudes to shopkeeping. The main road had not been hammered too hard by the pandemic, and there was plenty of opportunity to meet young entrepreneurs and family businesses. They included nail bars and shoe shops, cobblers and newsagents, five gift shops and one laundrette. The corgi could be groomed in the dog parlour while his owner would have the pick of the pubs. Of course there were bookies and vape shops, convenience stores and takeaways. But the diversity of outlets along this valleys high street was impressive. Pop over the hill to a similar street in old mining towns and the scene is a more depressing array of shuttered shops and bargain outlets. Few towns in Wales could sustain Treorchy's selection box of businesses, especially after the economic wrecking ball swung by Covid.

Those of us who had secured a spot on the royal rota were given a rendezvous point outside The Lion, a pub at one end of the high street, where we were to assemble and meet members of the palace press office at one o'clock in the afternoon. I planned to get there around half an hour beforehand to check out the much-hyped selection of shops and businesses for myself. After passing the corgi I wondered if the idea of a royal walkabout was a royal relic, an event which could only fail to meet the expectations set by archive footage of flag-waving crowds in less cynical times. But as I turned the corner onto the high street, I could hear the crowd before they came fully into view. Metal barriers along the curb were holding them back, a thousand people were already standing on the pavements waiting for Charles and Camilla to come to their town. Police officers and private security guards, hired by the local council, were controlling a crowd with designated crossing points and areas reserved for local school children. A couple of primary schools had brought their pupils, but what softened my cynicism was the number of people who appeared to have turned up without being cajoled. Treorchy was too far away to have attracted a band of 'royal watchers', the type who turn up at big events bedecked in union flags and with an unhealthy collection of laminated photographs of their favourite member of the firm. Instead, the pavements and the pubs were filled with curious locals, drawn perhaps by the spectacle of a celebrity visit but who were also very supportive of Charles.

I abandoned my plan of popping into the shops before the official visit began, the thronging pavements having the unintended consequence of restricting trade along

Britain's best high street. Instead I found my way to The Lion. The pub was set slightly back from the road, a small front yard had benches for drinkers, while a red telephone box had been turned into an honesty box of second-hand books during the pandemic. For the royal visit the front garden was supporting a male voice choir and an electronic piano, the assembled grey-haired men belting out the Welsh hymn *Gwahoddiad*. It was a rehearsal, but the crowds cheered and shouted out their requests. I thought I was early for the rendezvous, but the broadcast member of the rota was already there. Rob Osborne, the correspondent for ITV Wales, would be covering the visit with a cameraman and sharing the pictures with the other media organisations who pool their resources for these events.

'This is an impressive turnout,' I said. Rob was less surprised. We are both from the valleys, but Rob still lives there, and I confessed that my measure of royal excitement was anchored to childhood memories. This was present-day Wales, the nation whose self-confidence had been boosted by the advent of devolution and Cool Cymru, Grand Slam-winning rugby teams and a men's football squad that was destined for the Qatar World Cup. Why did this town, bustling with its own optimism and pride at the success of its high street, seem so keen to turn up and cheer a royal visit? This was about more than snapping a photo to say 'I was there' – they'd barely get a good look, given the numbers. The people I spoke to seemed to condense it into degrees of admiration and curiosity. They liked Charles, and they've come round to

Camilla, and if their town was going to be on TV that night then they'd want to be there to see it themselves.

As Rob and I spoke, we were joined by print reporters from *WalesOnline* and the *Daily Mail* who had the other slots on the royal rota. More and more members of the public had squeezed on to the pavements on either side of the road, and we discussed what figure might be put on the turnout. Fifteen hundred? Two thousand? We agreed to re-evaluate after the engagement had finished. Two members of the palace press office appeared and, with the clock edging towards the scheduled start time, we followed them to the other end of the high street where the royal tour would begin. While the pavements were packed, there were barriers keeping the crowds away from the shop entrances, giving a clear run down one side of the street for a walkabout by Charles and Camilla. When we were making our way along the street a great cheer came from the school children which was so loud that it drowned out the object of their joy – a burgundy helicopter carrying Treorchy's special guests. It disappeared behind the rows of terraced houses, landing in a field where cars were waiting to bring them to the shops. They didn't hang about. As the press arrived at the top of the street, so did the car carrying the Prince of Wales and the Duchess of Cornwall.

After a handshake with the Lord-Lieutenant and the High Sheriff, some of those who had waited for hours were rewarded with a wave and a 'How are you?' from Charles. While the public were kept behind a barrier, there were still a dozen dignitaries surrounding the couple as they greeted members of the public between the outstretched arms clutching camera phones and flags. Security guards, the media pack, palace staff and the local officials had to navigate the narrow strip of pavement between the shops and the barriers that held back the crowd. One of the photographers ended up on his back, the blinkered perspective of his viewfinder meant his balance was scuppered by another pair of feet. 'I hope we haven't caused too much disruption,' Charles offered, as he breezed between the children and pensioners who were nearest his waving hand. The photographer hoicked himself up with an 'oops-a-daisy' and, along with the rest of the media, we were ushered into a card shop.

As we waited near the back of the little shop with the nervous owner and her daughter, Charles strode in quickly with Camilla. 'You've got a little invasion,' the Prince said, as the woman curtsied and shook his hand. The Duchess spoke to the daughter. 'Have you worked here long? Oh, ten years! And you don't argue?' Aside from the two running the shop, an elderly woman in a wheelchair was positioned near the counter. She had popped in to buy a card shortly before the royal visit and decided to hang on to catch a word. 'So we've interrupted your shopping!' Camilla beamed. They are working royals with decades of small-talk in the tank, yet their interactions, for all the banal pleasantries, are the perfect tonic for the rabbit-in-headlights syndrome that affects so many people when they come into contact with royalty. It softened the elderly woman's nerves to the extent that she asked to have her photograph taken with Charles and Camilla. 'Darling!' the Duchess called to the Prince of Wales across the card shop. 'Darling, we're just going to have a photo.' The Prince, who by now was repeating his wife's interaction with the daughter – 'Oh! Ten years?' – eventually joined the photograph among the Get Well Soons and the Happy Retirements.

Next, the royal couple hopped a few doors down to a boutique clothes and beauty shop. The royal rota had been taken inside as royal hands were being shaken outside the door. In order to squeeze everybody into the shop and leave enough room for the couple to look around, the ITV correspondent, Rob Osborne, had to slink into a small curtained-off area used as a changing room from where he threatened to reappear dressed as the mother of the bride. Other members of the media crouched down to allow the television camera to get as wide a view as possible as Charles and Camilla walked in, though the interaction mirrored that of the previous encounters in the card shop. Once the ice had been broken, small talk flowed about the length of the time the business had been open, and whether online shopping was denting its fortunes.

As they emerged from the shop, a traditional walkabout ensued. When he got close enough to chat, people recalled previous times they had met Charles, reminding him of visits that he must surely have forgotten about. But he smiled warmly, appeared genuinely enthused and engaged in conversation. The sound of the male voice choir grew louder as the walkabout neared The Lion, and by the time the couple entered the pub they could both be forgiven for needing a stiff drink. In keeping with the tradition that no member of the royal family can step foot inside a licensed premises without pulling a pint, Charles found himself behind the bar. For a man who had probably pulled more pints than many publicans, he seemed out of practice as the foamy head of the beer grew ever larger. The photo opportunity was achieved, and of all the images captured in Treorchy that day, the Prince and his pint would be the most popular choice for the press.

As Charles and Camilla departed for their helicopter, I wondered why a royal walkabout still carried so much pulling power in the valleys. Anybody who would predict their demise could take a leaf from my cynical book and reconsider, because time and again the presence of the Prince of Wales, and more recently of the King, succeeded in drawing crowds of genuinely affectionate people to support him. They are not the cheering sycophants and rent-a-crowds that republicans may assume are bused in for these occasions. If there is a degree of organising involved, it is largely to control numbers and to ensure the events can go ahead safely.

'He and the Duchess are always given a huge welcome when they visit,' Dame Shân Legge-Bourke told me when we met to discuss Charles while he was still Prince of Wales. She had been the Lord-Lieutenant of Powys for twenty years until 2018 and remained a lady-in-waiting to the Princess Royal. Dame Shân's home is in the grounds of Glanusk Park on the outskirts of Abergavenny, which she inherited from her father, Wilfred Bailey, the third Baron Glanusk. Most members of the royal family have been chaperoned by Dame Shân on their visits to Wales, and she has an innate understanding of the impact an official visit can have.

'He loves shows, in particular,' she said, meaning the agricultural variety. Having been involved in the organisation of the Royal Welsh Show for years, the arrival of Charles would propel the event into the national press and reinforced the idea that the future King had a deep personal connection with rural life. 'We know the Royal Welsh has got to be one of the most friendly shows in the whole of the United Kingdom. So if he's walking through a crowd – and he's very observant – if he sees a badge like the Welsh Black Cattle Society, somebody is wearing one, he will immediately stop and have a discussion. Because he's recognised it, or he is patron of it,' she said.

Compared to Treorchy, where the small talk was a little bland, on the showground his chat was invariably intelligent and informed. 'I think it gives those farmers who he interacts with enormous pleasure, to be honest,' Dame Shân said. She makes no secret of her admiration for monarchy. Her family's aristocratic credentials are strong, as are her late husband's, Captain William Legge-Bourke, who served as an equerry to the royal household and, as a child, was a pageboy on state occasions. Among the items in the family silver is a sword which was reportedly used by Queen Victoria to knight Sir Edward Elgar. Before his death, Dame Shân's husband 'was trying to find out, from the royal archives, whether she also knighted Clive of India with it. But we definitely know it was Edward Elgar. So all his side of the family have been equerries through the reigns, so to speak. And then they have also been Pages of Honour to the various monarchs.' The boys are given two opportunities to be pageboys at events such as the State Opening of Parliament and the Garter Service at Windsor when they are around eleven or twelve years old. Her son, Harry Legge-Bourke, was a page and most recently Harry's son completed the family tradition. The Legge-Bourkes' most famous claim to the royal household was the position taken by Dame Shân's daughter, Tiggy Legge-Bourke, who was nanny to Princes William and Harry in the 1990s. Glanusk had also been a regular retreat for Charles, where he could fish, swim and lark about with the Legge-Bourkes, safe from prying eyes.

Dame Shân Legge-Bourke placed great value on having Charles turn up to support events in Wales. 'If the Prince of Wales says something, people pick up on it. And there's no doubt about it, it does influence to a certain extent,' she said. 'There is always a headline, isn't there?'

His genuine interest in conserving traditional farming techniques and in preserving the small hill farms, cuts through. 'People actually, suddenly, become aware of what he is doing about something.' Charles has 'feelings for upland farmers, the hill farmers in Wales, particularly now when times are tricky, certainly in the last sort of six, seven years. Whether it is land prices, wool prices, whatever it might be, he has that instant rapport with them, and he knows what he's talking about. He understands how ruddy hard it is.'

There is far less cynicism about Charles backing a campaign compared, say, to a politician's enthusiasm. 'It is rather like when he was pushing for mutton,' Dame Shân offered as an example. 'Nobody else mentioned mutton before he did, or it had just long gone.' But she argued that the backing of the Prince of Wales could make the unpopular mutton a palatable choice once more. 'It had become unfashionable, "Mutton, what are you talking about?", but particularly with Welsh food, he's a great champion. Whether it's yoghurt, whether it's cheese, it doesn't matter what it is' – she reaches for the tea tray in front of us – 'Welsh cakes, for God's sake. I think they really appreciate that he focuses on something, and there is no wavering.'

Dame Shân is unwavering, too, and fantastically blunt at times. 'You know only too well that everybody used to roar with laughter when he said he talked to his flowers or his fish, or what have you. Everybody poo-pooed it and said: "Oh God, he has lost the plot", or something. Oh, how wrong could they be! And look at what has happened now.'

She is right, and his success at backing popular causes at an unfashionably early stage is the praise that is so often offered by his supporters. One gets the feeling that the farming community has not wholly welcomed his interventions over the years, and perhaps the reception at the Royal Welsh Show has become a little warmer since his early adoption of sustainable techniques and organic farming became more mainstream. Indeed, Charles and Camilla have become crowd-pleasers, Dame Shân argued. 'The majority of countryside folk in Wales, the rural population of Wales, really appreciate them coming to visit the show. Because it's not a formal, stuffy, boring event. Over twenty years it has become so much more relaxed. Everybody walks about, everybody chats. And it is a whole different ballgame,' she asserted. 'When I look back at the sixties when the Queen came, it was pretty formal. I remember going and I was thinking, "Oh poor Queen", and Prince Philip, who likes doing his own thing anyway, used to stride off.' Getting around the show was difficult, but the Queen used an open-top Land Rover to view the animals and events. 'So she never got the opportunity, like the Prince of Wales or any other member of the royal family do now, for chatting. To have access to bods.'

His supporters argue that Charles maintained an intense curiosity about the people he met, a genuine eagerness to listen and to understand. 'It's the same with wherever else he goes, it doesn't matter whether it's opening this or that,' Dame Shân chipped in. She believes that Charles has visited more Welsh churches than the Archbishop of Wales, be it to see a rare stained-glass window or to support the campaign to protect yew trees in churchyards. 'His interests are so wide that, when he comes to Wales, he makes the most of it.'

Lord-Lieutenants, who are the monarch's representative in a county, aren't always as close to royalty. Dame Shân's family history means she is better qualified than most who take on this honorary position. Her father was Lord-Lieutenant of Brecknockshire, as was her grandfather and great-grandfather. Brecknockshire was replaced with the Lord-Lieutenant of Powys in 1974, and Dame Shân occupied the role from 1998 until her retirement in 2018. Lord-Lieutenants – or Lord-Loots, as Dame Shân calls them – normally retire from the role when they reach the age of seventy-five. Their years in office give them a remarkable insight into the interactions of royalty with people on their patch. From the stunned silence at meeting some of the most famous people in the world, to those who would rather not meet them at all.

'It is interesting being Lord-Loot, you find out all sorts of things,' Dame Shân told me with a smile. She began to explain how she dealt with people who asked not to be in the line-up when a member of the royal family was making an official visit.

'You will have the usual line-up' – she bobs her index finger – 'da-da-da-da-da, ending up with the chairman, probably, or the CEO, or whatever it might be. And on one or two occasions – not many – I have said: "Would you be happy to greet the Prince of Wales and welcome him?", and: *"Oh I don't want to do that."* And so I, in my usual' – she snorts – 'tactless way, say: "Oh, is there a reason?" – *"No, I just don't want to."* So I have left it, taken them off the list, fine. And then I've said, "You will be here, though, in the room where he is going to meet groups of six people." And I go in and watch the chairman and he takes the Prince round to the first group, the second group, and then the third group with this particular person. And he shook hands with him. And I didn't tip the Prince of Wales off and say, "That one doesn't like you at all", or "the role", you know. Historical stuff. And that's fine, end of visit. Great success. Move on to the next visit. And four days later I get the most *charming* letter from this particular person saying how understanding and very aware the Prince of Wales was. And the awful thing is that I did laugh, and it happened on a couple of occasions. And it is that which I find incredibly encouraging. That somebody who is anti-monarchy, or who is not a monarchist in any sense of the word, they have only got to meet them and' – she raises her hand and twists it in the air – 'Schwooom!'

'It totally twists them around?' I ask.

'Absolutely. It is a complete change of tack, because they are actually human beings, talking to another human being.' Dame Shân subscribes to the late Queen's catchphrase that the royal family need to be seen to be believed. 'I think that is absolutely vital. I think it is the same with any member of the royal family. Young or old. Next generation. If you have that interaction with people – however much they may be – the people they are going to meet may be, shall we say – what's putting it politely? Not very keen! – the minute they meet them, you normally get a little change of heart. They find them approachable and talkative and charming and very well informed. And that does make a difference.'

Over fifty years of interactions with the Welsh had made visits to the country a relaxed affair for Charles by the end of his time as Prince of Wales. In the course of his life as a working royal, he had been to every city and town and toured thousands of miles of farm track, country lane and mountain pass. In the early 1970s he chaired the Welsh Countryside Committee, his first official platform that allowed him to push the rural agenda and begin seriously lobbying for improved conservation methods and to reduce emissions into the rivers and the air. Later that decade he went underground, descending with miners at St John's Colliery in the Llynfi Valley to understand the industry that had fuelled the economy of South Wales but which was in rapid decline. His lobbying for Sony, too, brought him to Bridgend and carried with it the hope of a burgeoning manufacturing sector. He was the young, ambitious Prince who was still seeking to balance his personal mission to do his best for Wales, while acknowledging that not everybody wanted his help. Events in Wales gradually became more formalised around a Wales Week programme, and the appointment of staff to specifically oversee his Welsh diary and contacts meant the Prince of Wales was both more organised and more focused from the late 1990s.

Some persisted with their protests, and the royal family remained an antagonistic presence for nationalist republicans who could use the British establishment to recruit a new generation of Aberystwyth students. In 1996 the Queen's route to open an extension to the National Library of Wales in Aberystwyth was briefly blocked by university students. They had gathered on the road outside Pantycelyn Hall, where Charles had his room for the term in 1969. Two men who jumped a barrier to try and block the Queen's car were arrested. Their photograph was printed on the front page of the next day's *Western Mail* with the headline: 'The shaming of Wales'. This was the only seriously disruptive protest after 1969, and political parties were never keen to support outspoken opposition. Plaid Cymru and republicans in other parties mostly chose to avoid coming into contact with royalty, rather than becoming a republican megaphone for what remained a minority point of view. Rarely would royalty be involved in Welsh politics until the arrival of the devolved administration, the National Assembly for Wales in 1999 and now known as the Senedd, the Welsh Parliament. Members of the royal family attend the opening of each parliamentary session in Cardiff Bay, but the itinerary for other visits to Wales remains largely free of politicians. They rely on both the advice of Dr Grahame Davies, the King's private secretary who has overseen his Welsh interests since joining the office of the Prince of Wales in 2011, and a network of contacts. Lord-Lieutenants are among the friendly correspondents who will send ideas and invitations to Charles's office, while the holders of royal warrants and the causes close to the King's heart were also regular recipients of official visits and private trips.

'I feed Grahame catch-up notes as to what's happening about various things we've done in the past,' Roy Noble told me during a video call. The broadcaster, who was a regular presenter for BBC Radio Wales and S4C and is now semi-retired from the airwaves, was also a Vice Lord-

Lieutenant of Mid Glamorgan. 'I usually try and give them places that might be of interest to Charles to visit during his week in Wales in the summer, and a few days in the autumn as well.'

One of Roy Noble's suggestions was to visit Yr Ysgwrn, the stone farmhouse in Trawsfynydd, Gwynedd, that was home to the shepherd and poet Hedd Wyn, or Ellis Humphrey Evans. Hedd Wyn was his bardic name, and his story symbolised the tragic and futile loss of young lives during the First World War. In 1917 his death in the opening hours of the Battle of Passchendaele denied him the opportunity to discover that his poem had won the main prize, the chair, at the National Eisteddfod. The prize became known as *Y Gadair Ddu*, the Black Chair, as a shroud was draped over it when it was announced to the audience that its winner had died on the front. His story became better known when an S4C biopic was nominated in the foreign language category at the Oscars in 1994. Efforts to create a memorial at the farmhouse where he had lived took a lot longer to come to fruition. When eventually the project was funded and the work completed, the then Prince of Wales visited in the summer of 2019. It was exactly fifty years since his investiture in Caernarfon, and although there was barely a reference to the milestone in the itinerary, the story of Hedd Wyn went around the world once more as the press used the visit to mark the then Prince of Wales's low-key golden anniversary.

Roy Noble was regularly in contact with Charles's office when he was Prince of Wales. While Charles was notorious for his letter-writing, so too were his representatives. The Lord-Lieutenants and their deputies were a reliable cohort, a drip-feed of charity suggestions and future events that the Prince may want to support.

It has led to the Prince of Wales being present at countless launches, official openings and national events. His ethos naturally draws him towards traditional crafts, Welsh produce, the arts and rural life.

'Around the year 2000 a magical thing happened,' Roy Noble told me. I was wondering what moment of recent Welsh mythology he may be referring to, as Roy takes a notoriously romantic, almost evangelical approach to promoting significant moments in the modern history of Wales. 'It happened in Penderyn.' Ah. 'Welsh whisky,' Roy smiled. The distillery at Penderyn in the Brecon Beacons came about when the pub landlord in the Cynon Valley convinced a group of friends to restore the lost art of distilling Welsh whisky. Alun Evans – Alun the Glan – was the landlord of the Glancynon Inn, and one of his potential co-investors was Roy Noble.

'He asked me if I wanted to be a director. And I said: "How much are we talking about?" He said it was £32,000. So I talked to an accountant, and he said: "Welsh whisky? On a risk factor of one to ten, this is a twelve." So I didn't! But now I am a non-executive director, but I don't get paid. I just get whisky.'

When the distillery doors opened in 2004, the Prince of Wales arrived on St David's Day. He returned again to open the visitor centre four years later, where he was seen sampling the product. 'He only took a small swig,' Roy

Noble said, but added with a laugh that afterwards 'Alun was passing the glass around, saying: "Do you want to drink from the glass that Prince Charles drank from?"'

The connection with his network has often been deeply personal. Roy Noble was very unwell in October 2018 and underwent surgery in his local hospital, coincidentally named the Prince Charles Hospital, in Merthyr Tydfil, to remove an abdominal tumour. The operation was a success, though the numerous trips to be scanned led Roy to joke that 'if there was a bluish-green glow in the sky above Aberdare after sunset, it was probably me'. News of Roy's illness reached Charles, who wrote a personal letter. To Roy's amusement, Charles referred to the hospital bearing his name where he had received excellent care, and said that he felt a 'certain personal responsibility' for his welfare knowing that 'Prince Charles' was on the sign above the entrance. The deeply sensitive Charles reached out regularly to his close connections in Wales with a kind word and sometimes a gift. Another of his Welsh contacts described his pleasure at receiving an enamel box in the post from Charles, which had one of the Prince's watercolours on its lid.

Charles also turned to his official organisations in Wales to act as intermediaries and to facilitate private meetings as well as public events. The Prince's Trust and Business in the Community regularly hosted Charles during his Wales Week tours. These occasions allowed the Prince to highlight the good work his charities were facilitating, while also providing the photo opportunity to reinforce the image of Charles the benevolent patron.

Not every ongoing interest that Charles has in Wales is connected to a patronage or an official royal link, but all will be somewhere on the spectrum of causes that he has championed. 'He is a great supporter of social entrepreneurs. People in the community who are trying to make that difference,' Peter Davies told me. His career and connection with Charles began as managing director of Business in the Community in London, before he took on a role managing the Prince of Wales's charities in his native Wales. Inspired by Charles's initiatives to protect rainforests, Peter Davies co-founded the charity Size of Wales in 2010 to protect forestry around the world. 'What he can do, more than anybody, is give voice to those people who have not got a voice,' he said. Peter saw it himself in the 1990s and early 2000s with Business in the Community, where he arranged visits like the one to Aberdare by Gerald Ratner that made such an impact on Helen Mary Jones. 'To take people like Gerald Ratner, and all of these high-flying business people who live in a pretty cloistered environment, out to look at schools and communities that are struggling against the odds – that does have an impact.'

In Wales, Peter Davies took on a part-time role coordinating the Prince's charities in 2005. The flagship was The Prince's Trust, his original vehicle for helping young people to achieve their potential. Davies arrived in his role when Charles was pushing ahead with a stronger, deeper, and better-coordinated relationship with Wales. He was buying his first Welsh home, Llwynywermod, and would use it as a meeting place for his interests in the country.

'At that point, there was a view from the Prince's office that we needed to coordinate some of the Prince's charitable interests a bit more effectively,' Peter Davies recalled. 'There are organisations like the Prince's Foundation for the Built Environment and PRIME Cymru that he was president of, and very engaged with. My role was to support them, help to build their capacity, and also to liaise with the Prince's office in terms of putting princely time into the projects.'

Many of the visits would occur during Wales Week, which would guarantee a flash of publicity. But beyond the photo opportunities, Charles would remain in regular correspondence with the people running his Welsh interests.

'I think people would be surprised how hands-on he is, how engaged he is,' Peter Davies told me. 'I have seen what have become known as those black spider memos,' he added, referring to the sometimes unfair characteristic of Charles's spidery handwriting on his notes to officials. 'His engagement is deeply felt, and that probably even surprised me!' Peter Davies would not class himself as a 'major royalist' when he started working at Business in the Community. 'But over those ten years, I was deeply impressed by the scale of his reach, influence, passion, belief and desire to make a difference in terms of influencing business behaviour.'

The launch of Peter's charity, Size of Wales, was in direct response to Charles's campaign to promote awareness of the need to tackle tropical deforestation. The Prince's Rainforests Project was established in 2007 to seek global solutions to the problem. 'That was the stimulus for conversations in Wales with the Prince, and with people like Heather Stephens' – the philanthropist and co-founder of insurance company Admiral – 'as to what could we do as a nation. If the Prince's own rainforest initiative hadn't been running at that point, I don't think Size of Wales would have been created.'

Twenty years ago Charles was a man who was labelled as either forward-thinking, or on the periphery of the political discussion about sustainability and the environment. Decades spent highlighting the urgency of the climate crisis had only moved him a few rings closer to the centre of the debate. Size of Wales was an endeavour that he could naturally support, and did so without being appointed in any official capacity as a patron or an ambassador.

'He has played a role, continually, through the ten years or so that I was involved. He has been on visits to schools that have run Size of Wales events, he has hosted things for us and has been actively involved in the initiative all the way through,' Peter Davies said. He cited another example where Charles's interest helped secure funding for an ambitious project to build a hydrogen-powered car in Mid Wales. The vehicles being manufactured by Riversimple in Llandrindod Wells were in development at a time when government indecision and broader economic uncertainty was hampering investment in the zero-emissions sector. Charles visited the site in July 2021 'and that had a significant impact on the investment community; it is a small start-up in

Mid Wales. Suddenly the Prince visits it, takes the car out for a drive, gets the media publicity around it and people are aware that the Prince of Wales is taking this small business seriously.'

The public backing of projects has brought investment to some, as well as press exposure. But the true benefit of having Charles on board with any Welsh idea was his convening power. 'It is immense,' Peter Davies declared. He admitted to being 'astounded' that chief executives would respond so quickly and so positively to an invitation from the Prince of Wales to be at a meeting with him, or to visit a project where there would undoubtedly be soft pressure to offer business support. 'It is more than convening power, because he is not happy to simply convene. He wants to see things happen,' Peter Davies said. 'I would get notes from his office to say, "Can you brief the Prince on how that project has gone?" or "Has so-and-so done what he said he was going to do?" It is more than simply convening a meeting and walking away. He expects things to happen as a result of his convening.'

Peter Davies's years of work alongside the Prince of Wales have given him a unique perspective from which to analyse Charles's contribution. Clearly, he feels the new monarch has achieved a great deal in Wales, largely without making waves or getting much public acknowledgement for his efforts. He chose to back projects that are forward-thinking, perhaps on the edges of conventional practice, not because he wanted to appear ahead of the curve but because, very often, he was already there. And yet the perpetual feeling that he had to drag along the unconverted has taken its toll.

'I think there has been an element of frustration within him,' Peter Davies offered as an honest assessment. 'Things keep coming around that he has seen before, and perhaps they have not moved forward. It must be quite a frustrating experience in that sense.'

Charles's longevity may mean that he has seen it all before, but his experiences also give credibility to his occasional public distress at the slow pace of change. He has fine-tuned his ability to get people to pay attention, particularly the decision-makers who could enact change for the causes he supports. It is as true for his conservation work as it is for his backing of Welsh farmers.

'The fact that he is able to host a meeting for Welsh farmers in London to talk to major potential purchasers of Welsh lamb, that is worth a lot,' Peter Davies told me, as he recalled facilitating the event. 'He did that on several occasions, when we were looking to get the premium value for the lamb into premium markets in London. He convened the discussions and the meetings.'

The projects that really caught Charles's eye would benefit from the full force of his personal and organisational support. Perhaps the most visible evidence of the Prince of Wales's influence is passed every day by thousands of motorists heading into Swansea from the M4 motorway. After drivers have descended from the flyover to the dual carriageway that runs into the city, they travel along Fabian Way and pass, on their right, a vast Amazon warehouse and a former Ford car-parts plant which has since been repurposed as a film studio. Opposite, on the side of the road nearest Baglan Bay, is a far more interesting, imposing complex of buildings that arose from the Prince of Wales's ambition that the world's leading design principles should influence its creation.

The site itself is the Swansea University Bay Campus, the £450 million science and innovation centre that formally opened its facilities in 2015 and turned Swansea into a dual-site university. Its original home remained in Singleton, nestled almost on the sand between the city centre and Mumbles. The expansion to a new location, several miles away, made room for five thousand students and the relocation and recruitment of around a thousand staff. Professor Iwan Davies was a Pro-Vice Chancellor at Swansea University and was the project director for the development, which took around ten years to realise.

The geography of Swansea meant there was no room for him to develop a campus within a tolerable distance of Singleton. Two alternative options presented themselves to the design team: the new waterfront development of offices and flats at SA1 on the edge of the city, or a site on the outskirts in an area called Llandarcy that used to house a BP fuel distribution hub, until the oil company pulled out. 'BP wanted to leave a legacy,' Iwan Davies told me. 'Llandarcy was such an important part of BP's history. And they wanted to leave the region with a lasting legacy.' BP still owned the land, and their agreement was required to acquire the site and build the new campus. Professor Davies found a willing partner in the oil company. There was an implicit hope that the redevelopment of the site from one that hosted an extractive industry into an investment in knowledge could become a precedent for how the multinational may withdraw from their various other oil sites around the world. BP was a company in long-term transition, and there was a 'noble ideal', Professor Davies said, in its desire to turn its former Swansea site into a centre of learning and expertise.

With the agreement that Swansea University would build on the land, the broader issues of the area required expert advice. While it had been dominated by heavy industry, the area was yards from the sea and was surrounded by the Crymlyn Burrows, a designated Site of Special Scientific Interest and one of the few places along Swansea Bay that was undeveloped during the city's expansion. BP brought along the Prince's Foundation to become 'involved in advising on this', Professor Davies recalled.

The Prince's Foundation is Charles's vehicle for promoting sustainable development. Its literature says it 'provides holistic solutions to challenges facing the world today', and is inspired by Charles's 'philosophy of harmony: that by understanding the balance, the order and the relationships between ourselves and the natural world we can create a more sustainable future'. It's a phrase, like many other utterings from Charles as Prince of Wales, that could easily have been dismissed as an attempt at regal feng shui just a few years ago. It is now just as likely to be found in the mission statements of house builders and construction giants as it is among Charles's papers. While advising about the site's ecological footprint, the Foundation went further.

'The question then became: "Are you interested in just building a campus? Or are you interested in something that was world class?",' Professor Davies told me. The phrase 'world class' was 'a problem in Wales,' he said. 'I have come across so many people who use the words "world class", and I often say that everything is world class if you are in Cwmllynfell,' he smiled. What it meant was that the development was not solely about the architecture, but about the ecosystem that supported the edifice. Charles would be interested, Professor Davies said, in how the development 'spoke' to the local community, and to the academics who would have to work there. As much attention had to be paid to the design of the bus stops as to the relationship of the entire campus with its local environment.

The Prince of Wales became involved in the discussions about what shape the campus would take, and how it could be developed in harmony with its surroundings. 'It was his insistence on really deconstructing the essential ingredients of what "world class" means, and which kept a focus on the outcomes in a way which, had it just been a building project, would have been lost,' Iwan Davies said.

The assembled team of architects, developers and university staff did not feel that Charles was imposing on their project. If anything, the Prince was seen to step back from initial discussions after getting the ball rolling on the 'world class' concept. 'But I know that he was being briefed the whole time, because the Foundation could have withdrawn their interest at any time,' Professor Davies said.

What the project team appreciated, more than anything else, was the Foundation's methodology. They used a charette system, which brings a team together to design and implement a specific project. Charettes compress the planning process into a relatively short space of time, encouraging participants to brainstorm ideas and quickly fine-tune the design. Professor Davies said the charette was helped to deliver a world-class project. 'It brought together some architects, it brought together planners, it brought together the university academic community – not in an organised way, where the key criteria are often agreed in a consensual, convivial environment,' he said. Instead, it created a focused discussion at a point when nobody had a stake in wanting to protect their fiefdom, or who were already favouring one proposal over another. 'It's a very clever way of doing it,' Professor Davies said.

The Prince's Foundation had a few representatives at meetings, as well as its own architects, while they were joined by other outside professionals including BP. Heads of department at the university were involved, as were senior management and members of the university council. Overall, there were fewer than twenty people in this intensive exercise to distil the meaning of 'world class' for Swansea's new university campus. The Prince of Wales was not at the meetings, but Professor Davies felt his presence.

'What he was able to do – and I think only he is able to do this – was to bring together what I describe as a triple helix of industry, government and the university. And to do so in a non-contentious forum.' While the three members of this triple helix would previously have been confined to their own agendas surrounding a project of this scale, Professor Davies said the Prince's charette enabled 'a genuine meeting of minds for a more noble purpose'.

I pressed Professor Davies for the difference between world class and, well, Welsh class. 'So, one early discussion was: did a campus need two road openings? Because when you think about a campus, what you think about is an entry, and the entry is also the exit. Well, that isn't world class.' The world-class interpretation of the entrance, and exit, from a campus would require a sense of arrival and 'placemaking', Professor Davies said. 'If your architectural vision for the campus is an entry and an exit in the same kind of place, that is not something that will ever get you to a place which will endure for the next hundred years.' Iwan Davies concedes it was 'an understanding which I would not have even thought about'.

On their own, the interpretations of world class seem small, almost petty. Yet the mission of the Foundation was to demonstrate how small details could come together to create a fundamentally better building, and a wider environment which would allow the university to realise the great potential of its new campus.

Charles would host meetings at Llwynywermod as the planning progressed. The university, the architects and the developers would be there to report to the Prince. 'That was hugely persuasive, because what it meant was that he kept an eye on what we were seeking to do, and kept an eye on cost – in the sense that the focus otherwise had been on cost, and not on the ultimate value and place. Ultimately, the Prince was able to appeal to the higher good. Even with the developers.' Iwan Davies was unaware of any resistance to the involvement of the Prince. Part of the reason for that was the use of the charette, which allowed an arm's-length distillation of the design and generated a greater level of commitment from its participants. Charles's team provided the parameters which enabled the project to be enhanced, and those who had taken part believed strongly in supporting its outcome. It wasn't his vision, in a literal sense. But it was his vision that was achieved by encouraging the team to understand what 'world class' meant.

Charles also met once or twice a year with Professor Davies and the architects, where the discussion was more about 'spirit rather than structure'. 'It was about inspiration, about what really inspires you. And the strange thing is, you couldn't have that discussion with anyone other than...' he broke away. 'It's terribly metaphysical, isn't it?' The Prince of Wales provided his own examples of what inspired him, and his indulgences were remarkably disciplined. 'He is an incredible ascetic. Very frugal, actually. Despite the opulence of office, what you came to understand was that the essential quality was ascetic, and that was comforting at one level.' Once construction was underway the meetings reduced, but

Charles continued to write to Professor Davies about the detail of the finished campus, 'to the point where he was also involved in bus stops.' Bus stops. Are they particularly fancy? 'No, they're not,' Iwan Davies laughed. 'But they are elegant.'

The reward for Iwan Davies was the opportunity to think differently about a project which could have easily been designed and constructed according to more functional principles. The Prince's Foundation demonstrated to the university the limitations of conventional practice and promoted the importance of reconciliation in building its new campus. It achieved a 'balance', in the words of the Foundation's remit, which in turn produced a campus that Swansea proudly promotes as being 'world class'.

6

Private Passions

'Sometimes, in a small nation,
you can be more radical.'

It was a wet February evening in 2016 when two disorientated American tourists wandered into the ballroom at Buckingham Palace. Beneath the low glow of crystal chandeliers, the women tiptoed across the deep-pile red carpet. Seemingly lost, one pulled out a mobile phone to try to pinpoint their location.

'Oh my God, this is the coolest place on earth,' the other one said. 'It's like Disney World.'

The one with the phone struggled to get a signal. 'One bar. Two bars. Buffering. Huh?' She was incredulous. 'It thinks we are *exactly* in the middle of Buckingham Palace.' An idea that was quickly dismissed once they glanced around at the rows of people staring back at them.

'Wait, I know where we are,' said the one without a phone. 'Madam Tussauds!' The audience roared with laughter, Charles bobbed in his seat and exchanged a broad grin with Dame Shirley Bassey who sat alongside him.

'Yeah, yeah, you are so right,' the other agreed. 'They

look just like the real thing!' The two women, with their backpacks on, peered at the line of celebrities smiling back at them. 'Oh wait, wait. This one, not so much.' The audience roared again as someone was singled out. 'I mean, that's supposed to be Shirley Bassey?' The other shook her head. 'No, it's nothing like her.' The audience was entertained, and the skit had softened any apprehension ahead of an evening of performances with a royal audience.

Alongside Charles, then Prince of Wales, sat a parade of Welsh showbiz royalty. Dame Shirley was joined by other singers including Sir Bryn Terfel and Amy Wadge. The actors Dame Siân Phillips, Ruth Jones and Michael Sheen were there, too, and behind them sat around 260 invited guests who were all supporters of the Royal Welsh College of Music and Drama. The faces varied from those whose careers had begun at the conservatoire in Cardiff, to the philanthropists whose donations had helped to support the training of its talented cohort of students. Dame Shirley was in the front row because of her super-stardom, but also because of her generosity in supporting young singers. 'Two of them are in the Shirley Bassey Scholarship,' she told me at the time. 'I started off with nobody supporting me. I made it, and I wanted to give that back.'

The purpose of the event was to celebrate five years since the college had opened its striking new building on the edge of Cardiff's Bute Park. While it may have been hundreds of miles away in London, the ballroom of Buckingham Palace provided a lavish stage to celebrate

153

Welsh achievements in the company of some of the donors who had helped to fund it. The new college building was a tall concrete, steel and wooden structure which had been built at a cost of over twenty million pounds to provide a centre of excellence in Wales that could compete with the best *conservatoire* in the world. Wooden panelling surrounds the first purpose-built chamber recital hall in Wales, the Dora Stoutzker Hall. The college's alumni were testament to the power of its teaching; Sir Anthony Hopkins could not attend the palace celebration, but his fondness for his old college caused him to return regularly for unpublicised masterclasses with the acting cohort.

Charles had become patron of the college in 1999, before it was granted royal status during the Queen's Golden Jubilee in 2002. By 2019 he was elevated to become its president, and over two decades he maintained incredibly close ties with the college. The links reflected the intense passion he had for artistic talent, and in nurturing young people's skills. To that end, gala evenings at Buckingham Palace became a hallmark of Charles's support for the talented actors, singers and musicians.

The use of the ballroom was the gold-tier of hospitality that he extended only to his favourite cultural institutions, with Welsh National Opera becoming the only other arts organisation from Wales to enjoy a knees-up at the ultimate royal residence. At the first gala evening for the Royal Welsh College of Music and Drama in 2010 its new building was nearing completion, and the college's supporters were treated to the champagne evening at Buckingham Palace in recognition of the hefty philanthropic effort that funded the construction work. The Queen of Hollywood, Dame Elizabeth Taylor, attended and presented Charles with a bust of her late husband, Richard Burton. Her own attendance at Buckingham Palace, with echoes of her tempestuous love for the Welshman that she married twice, may even have eclipsed the appeal of Charles's hospitality for some of the guests. By 2016 we had lost Elizabeth Taylor, but the glamour of the latest occasion thrilled both the invited guests and the Buckingham Palace staff. A handful of press who attended were taken into the palace through a side entrance, and as the group were chaperoned upstairs, a passing pair of palace waiting staff were in excited discussion about the glamorous presence of Dame Shirley Bassey. Those who watched that evening saw the college's talented students performing an hour of entertainment, and the event itself assisted the college in 'anchoring loyalty' from its most passionate supporters.

'The fundraising had been done,' Lucy Stout told me. 'But, of course, if you're doing your job properly in the development department of the college, you're anchoring loyalty through something like that.' As the college's director of development, Lucy's role included nurturing support and, without sounding too crass, keeping the donors happy. The college walked a delicate path when it came to linking any royal event with an increase in its fundraising totals, and I should be explicit in outlining that the college does not, and would not, tout its supporters for donations alongside their VIP invitations. Gala dinners at Buckingham Palace were not 'cash-for-access' to the future King, but a celebration of the college in the presence of its royal patron and president.

The relationship the college had with Charles extended beyond his position as an honorary figurehead, and it is perhaps because of the depth of that relationship that the college has been quite private, and quite protective, about discussing his role. Charles enjoyed contributing ideas to their management meetings and planting seeds in the heads of attendees at events he hosted in London, Highgrove and Wales. He actively encouraged the college to seek out other examples in his network of charities and organisations who may offer some inspiration. College Principal Helena Gaunt, who I met alongside Lucy Stout to discuss the King's role, said his involvement was useful, positive and productive.

'He is quite radical. He is a radical thinker. You might not always agree, but he is pretty radical, and classical too,' Helena Gaunt said. 'I think that he has an understanding that sometimes, in a small nation, you can be more radical. You can actually get things to happen that are much, much more difficult if you are in the centre of London.'

When Helena Gaunt joined as principal of the Royal Welsh College of Music and Drama in September 2018, one of the first things the then Prince of Wales raised with her was the need to improve young people's access to music. 'He said to me, "We need to do something about this, what shall we do?" And that's not just about what he can do for us in his patronage, that is about a deep passion, it's something that he is concerned about.'

The college had shared some proposals with Charles, who had 'sat there, read every word, and had red-inked' the documents. 'He is engaging full-heartedly with these things, and trying to bring what he can offer. But he won't get behind them if he doesn't fully believe in them,' Helena Gaunt said.

Before the Covid pandemic, Charles attended a meeting of the senior management team and stayed well beyond the time allowed in his schedule. 'It was meant to be twenty minutes. Grahame [the King's man in Wales] was getting up, sitting down again, then getting up,' Lucy Stout said, but Charles was not prepared to abandon the discussion.

Helena Gaunt said other strategic discussions had happened in the midst of official visits or the celebration dinners. 'He just quietly comes up to me and says, "I need to speak to you, I want you to think about this", and that is invaluable. You could see him really thinking as we spoke. He immediately came up with some wonderful offers that we followed up on, so that focused bit of time allows us to brief him and build a sense of trust.' Suggestions include visiting other institutions such as Dumfries House, the country mansion he saved in Scotland, or speaking to colleagues at the Royal Opera House and the Royal Shakespeare Company about specific issues that Charles is aware of. To the college, Charles is a great convenor and connector, a patron who is able to fall on a network of organisations whose mutual trust allows ideas to flow freely and informally. But it is a familiarity that is earned, and a relationship which must be continually nurtured.

'I can remember coming into my very first meeting with him, in my first term,' Helena Gaunt smiled as she recalled the butterflies in her stomach. She was meeting the Prince to discuss a moment to mark his seventieth birthday during a future visit to the college. 'And I tell you, I was extremely nervous about that whole event because I just thought that while it doesn't matter to me personally, there was such a lot at stake. I knew how much he meant to the college, I did not want to get it wrong, and so I was extremely nervous. But as soon as I met him, I thought, "This is fine!" He's a real person, it's very easy, and he wants to connect.' Building that trust is an iterative thing, Helena argued, and that a strong bond existed between the college and Charles. 'It feels incredibly important and powerful.'

Both Helena Gaunt and Lucy Stout described having 'What Can I Do?' moments with Charles, when his open-armed offer of help allowed new connections to be made or for palace gala dinners to be floated. As patron, and lately as president, he gave the college an almost intense level of attention and interaction. 'When we talked about doing something around music education, he was immediately telling us to go and see what's happening at Dumfries House. I did, and I learned about their project. What we then proposed to him was inspired by that, but it wasn't the same.' Taking inspiration, but doing things differently, is a theme in the King's interaction with his Welsh projects.

The college says it benefits from his interest and his suggestions; the ideas he presents are never thrust forward as actions which must be adopted. Rather, they are suggestions backed by knowledge and experience, and are proposals the college feels it would be loath to ignore. And yet I am interested in the hard financial benefits of having Charles as a patron and, since 2019, as a president. The college relies on donors to fund its bursaries, which help to pay the fees for students who are financially disadvantaged, or who meet various other criteria such as a desire to play an endangered instrument (bassoonists, make yourselves known). Other funding is required for specific appeals, refurbishment and replacing equipment, and the work of the development office at the college is to consistently attract and maintain a level of philanthropic support that allows it to offer great teaching, and tremendous prospects, for its seven or eight hundred students. Some of the funding comes from the ultimate beneficiaries of this talent. For example, the TV production company Bad Wolf supports a scholarship which may lure students to work on some of the high-end dramas it makes at its studio in Cardiff. Similarly, the broadcasters ITV and S4C offer bursaries to students who meet certain criteria. Charitable trusts – from the Andrew Lloyd Webber Foundation to the Worshipful Company of Musicians – contribute to the college's activities and bursary funds. On a more personal level, individuals with a desire to support the college are encouraged to do so annually, for special appeals or through a gift in their will after they have died.

Does Charles personally contribute to the fund for scholarships, as Dame Shirley does? Nobody will say. By far the biggest monetary impact of his patronage lies in the events he has attended at their invitation and the galas he has hosted at Buckingham Palace. Discussions about any royal impact on donations are delicate. Lucy Stout goes a little further: 'That is seriously and carefully handled.' I am cautious not to sound too crass again, but how much would one of those gala events raise for the college? The one in 2016, for instance. After checking that the detail had been placed in the public domain among the college's accounts, Ms Stout confirmed: 'We raised nearly £700,000. But there were costs. We netted, probably, just under £600,000.' It is a rare and extraordinary amount for the college to generate from one event. The only similar events to have raised close to that for the college were held in the United States with guests like Catherine Zeta-Jones and were boosted by the more embedded American tradition of arts philanthropy. During the financial year 2015–2016 the college's donations and endowments reached £2,191,000, over a million more than the previous year's total.

The events at Buckingham Palace are infrequent. Six years separated the 2010 gala attended by Dame Elizabeth Taylor and the black-tie night in 2016 with Dame Shirley Bassey. And while the college was at Buckingham Palace at the invitation of the Prince of Wales, there were costs to cover before the night. Was there a hire charge for the world's most famous ballroom? Lucy Stout laughed. 'I wasn't aware of a hire cost for

Buckingham Palace, but Buckingham Palace does things in a certain way. We were informed that "here is the caterer, here is the price list, these are their menus, and this is the calligrapher we work with", and you can quite quickly work out how they want to see it done.' She added: 'That seems completely appropriate.'

'And then the show costs us,' she said. 'We put on a pretty big show, and we involved as many students as possible. He likes to see that.' Luckily for the college, a donor – who wished to remain anonymous – covered many of the upfront costs.

I don't get the impression that Charles's interaction with the college is onerous for its staff. He is almost certainly singing from the same hymn sheet as its tutors when he champions causes such as widening access to music education. He would also have their backs if the college was under pressure. 'He is ready to support us, particularly when things get tough. If we really needed some intervention, I think he would be there, if he felt he could do it,' the principal, Helena Gaunt, said.

Charles understands a lot about Wales. It took him decades of briefings and meetings, but his knowledge of Welsh life has blossomed from the freshly-sown seeds of his tutorials with Tedi Millward. He expressed his desire in Aberystwyth in the 1960s to learn as much about the culture and history of the nation as possible, and his period as Prince of Wales became an era of continuous learning. His more extensive work beyond Wales only served to complement his work here, with his interactions on foreign tours having inspired him to share radical plans with organisations that were being nurtured at home. The power of convening great minds, and sharing big ideas, became a hallmark of Charles's endeavours as heir to the throne and was strengthened by his work in Wales.

'He thinks very strongly about the context here,' Helena Gaunt told me. There is little sign that the King's interest ever flits into interference at the college. 'He understands a lot about Wales – he has got a real, quite deep and intuitive understanding, as well as being simply well informed.'

For every college that embraced Charles, there are countless others who have no connection with monarchy but have every success as an institution. What does royalty give to an organisation whose reputation surely rests on its teaching excellence, its student satisfaction and its graduate employment opportunities? For this particular conservatoire, the King's interest and involvement has grown alongside its own expansion and booming reputation. And yet the close working relationship that the college has nurtured with Charles has existed largely behind closed doors. While the key visits by Charles and Camilla have often been featured in news items, the extent of his involvement in advising on future projects, and even attending meetings of the senior management team, has received no press attention. The absence of media scrutiny can largely be blamed on the shrinking journalistic culture in Wales, where newspaper circulations have declined. Their digital replacements have pivoted towards producing news content that can be more easily sourced, and more quickly consumed, than any in-depth assessments of Charles's Welsh operation. And yet it is an operation that has succeeded in spreading the King's influence into culturally important, politically insignificant areas of Welsh life. For those who have welcomed his interest, he is lauded as an Arthurian assembler of talents where individuals and their ideas are treated equally.

'He brings people together,' Justin Albert told me. Justin is a friend of the King, having met and worked with him on countless projects from the renovation of Hay Castle to tackling the pollution of the River Wye. 'He has the ability to get anybody into a room to have a conversation.'

Justin Albert was the director of the National Trust in Wales until 2022 and was frequently seen at the King's side in his visits, as Prince of Wales, to the projects and events that made up the annual Wales Week.

'He has convened people in Wales around issues that he deeply cares about. So we're talking about rivers, we're talking about pollution, we're talking about the landscape. We are talking about history, we're talking about Welsh identity, the Welsh language,' he told me. Justin Albert's observations of Charles come at incredibly close quarters, and with his own well-furnished Welsh credentials. The men first met around the time of Justin's appointment to run the National Trust in 2011 at Bodnant Gardens, an eighty-acre horticultural wonderland in Conwy in North Wales. Before becoming the Welsh director of the National Trust, Justin Albert had been a documentary film-maker in America. His return to Wales brought him back to his roots, where dinner parties at his home in Powys carried stories of his long-lost relative Lady Charlotte Guest, the original translator of the legendary Welsh language literary work, the Mabinogion. Justin joined the board of the Hay Festival, the leading literary event which draws thousands of visitors to the Welsh border town of Hay-on-Wye every year, and he pioneered efforts to restore the town's castle. But Justin Albert was also well-connected in politics and had been both an external reviewer of the performance of organisations such as S4C and an advisor on environmental projects. No wonder the two men became friends, with closely aligned interests that helped the King with his ambition to continuously learn about Wales and the Welsh.

'I think it comes from that sense that if you're the most privileged person in Britain, he's always felt, it behoves him to do everything you can. I believe that anybody who is born into privilege needs to spend their life – not paying back for it, it's not their fault that they were born into that position – but it is for them to really try and give back. And that's motivating him,' Justin Albert said.

Preserving ancient crafting skills, improving access to higher education, promoting traditional Welsh singing – the King's list of interests in Wales that Justin Albert reels off are all worthy causes. Charles, he says, has become a public voice and a private proponent of issues that can be addressed by an old-fashioned coming together of those who can make a difference. There is an acknowledgement that the King must find it 'frustrating' that the issues he was quite mercilessly ribbed for backing in previous decades are now part of mainstream thinking in conservation and the discussion around climate change. The King has persevered in his mission to improve lives by pushing for problems to be solved, despite the hits he has taken for previously speaking out.

'A few times he has said, "Justin, call me up" or, "Justin, we need to do something about X".' On one occasion it was about improving the profile of unique Welsh interior design and furniture. 'You know, why can't people come and stay in Wales in authentic places, rather than what looks like a plastic Butlin's? And why can't we do it somewhere everybody can stay, not just in a very, very wealthy place?' Justin Albert found himself in a meeting with Charles, alongside designers and representatives from the Welsh Government's historical buildings agency, Cadw. Charles wanted them to 'think – how can we rectify this? How can we make Wales better?' If there was pressure or specific lobbying happening in the meeting, it wasn't obvious. Justin recalled: 'He wasn't pushing us in any which way, but he was convening people to think through the ideas and come up with some solutions, and that's his strength.'

In his intimate gatherings of like-minded experts, the then Prince of Wales would offer his own assessment of the problem and how to fix it. 'In public, he doesn't give his opinion. He just arbitrates in the middle,' Justin Albert said. 'In private, he is very different.'

The private passions which drive Charles are the areas where he can also make the most difference, without making a mess of it. The work of his team is key, particularly the wisdom of Dr Grahame Davies in Wales. 'His advisors are pretty smart,' Justin Albert said. They would spot a good cause that aligned with his philosophy, but also protected the Prince of Wales from potential problems. The most perilous moment for Charles's time as Prince of Wales occurred in his twilight years in the role, when the newest bridge across the River Severn was renamed in his honour. I will address that moment later in this book, but it is a rare example of the public image of the Prince taking a knock beyond the more predictable opposition from committed republicans. He otherwise relied on good advice about the issues he backed here. Some are not particularly Welsh, like his habit for supporting the protection of ancient trees, especially the yews he has campaigned to save in some of our churchyards.

Others are unique to Wales. He is said to be an enthusiastic fan of the music that stemmed from the Christmas tradition of plygain, a service of Welsh carols which traditionally took place in the very early morning in seventeenth-century Wales. The festive hymns, whose themes extend to the crucifixion as well as the birth of Christ, have enjoyed a resurgence in Wales. One visitor to Charles's Welsh home, Llwynywermod, claimed to have seen a CD of plygain music, while – as Prince of Wales – Charles attended a plygain service in Carmarthen in 2012. If anything unites his interests, it is a belief in protecting the culturally significant and distinctively Welsh traditions which have suffered various states of endangerment.

At the National Trust, Justin Albert found the Prince's interest piqued at the renovation work that it had undertaken on a small, dilapidated farm labourer's cottage in West Wales. It was one of the last of its kind that had yet to be bought up and done up with John Lewis furnishings and a prominent slot on AirBnB. Treleddyd Fawr cottage is near St Davids, just inland from the expanse of beach at Whitesands Bay and the quiet, rocky coves where the seal pups learn to catch their supper.

The National Trust found twenty-six layers of wallpaper above the fireplace in the communal area when renovation work began, as the structural integrity of the cottage had finally succumbed to weather damage and the flaws of its basic construction. As a fading link to the history of that corner of Wales, it was as important to the collective memory of its population as any architecturally significant mansion house. It was this desire to save the cottage that drew the National Trust to invest in its renovation, and to attract the attention and support of the Prince of Wales.

'We talked about what to do with the small cottages that, at that time, were being bought by wealthy people. The old *tŷ bach* outside was being turned into somewhere to put their hosepipe,' Justin Albert recalled. 'I would have done it anyway, but it was very nice being so reassured by your future monarch that you are up to the right thing.'

This wasn't some sycophantic act of submission to Charles, not least because it was said with a knowing smile. Charles's record of success for backing conservation projects speaks for itself, and having him as a supporter and advocate can make it much easier to secure further funding and attention. Cash was crucial. 'We could have done the whole thing for £50,000. But it cost about £160,000 to do it up, and it was the right thing to do.' As with the Royal Welsh College of Music and Drama, there is clearly a turbo button applied to fundraising when your project receives royal attention.

The cottage is now the National Trust's second most popular holiday rental in Wales, after the striking house it lets out overlooking Rhossili Bay on the tip of the Gower peninsula.

When he visits Wales, it is the retention of traditions that grabs his interest. The revival of historic skills and crafts, and the pursuit of excellence – especially by young, talented individuals – provide him with hope that others share his own conservation ideals. But there is something about Wales, and the Welsh, which makes him more comfortable here than in other parts of the UK. Justin Albert argued that it was the absence of a Welsh aristocracy which meant that, when he visited, Charles would be greeted by a population that was refreshingly removed from the cultural furniture that constrained him in his role.

'I know I'm biased,' Justin Albert offered, 'but I have seen Prince Charles in London in the winter, in his various houses, and in Scotland. And he is, by far, the happiest in Wales.' His relaxed, informal approach is transmitted to those he meets in village halls and on factory floors. There was a running joke between Justin Albert and Charles's staff that it would take two seconds from eye contact, to shaking hands, to his first words 'and he leaps straight in. The other royals would say, "Ooh, I like your tie, it's got elephants on it, I love elephants". But Charles goes straight in, usually with a question or an observation.' As Prince of Wales, and then as King, Charles would engage in two-way conversations with the people he met, even if the conversation lasted just a minute. It was quite the contrast to the other world leader that Justin Albert had encountered in Wales.

Justin's mother was the film-maker Revel Guest, who chaired the Hay Festival and ended up hosting former US president Bill Clinton at the family home in Powys on one of his visits to the event. Clinton famously labelled the Hay Festival 'the Woodstock of the mind', a tagline which adorned mugs, tote bags and hooded sweatshirts in the Festival shop for a decade after the words were uttered. Justin Albert recalled meeting Clinton 'here at the house, of all places,' and found the encounters to be a little too polished. 'You know, when Bill Clinton's there – and this is me, I will probably never get invited anywhere ever again – but he's a politician, and he is trained in that role. Maybe I am totally wrong, but I don't get the impression that Bill Clinton is actually interested in anything I am saying at all. With Prince Charles, I know he's interested in what everyone is saying. He really is.' One of the first conversations which ignited Justin Albert's friendship with Charles was an animated discussion 'about music, or something, and he followed up right away. And that's what he does, because he is fascinated by people.'

A people person, but a 'crap' politician, Justin Albert asserts. 'I would say he is a *really* crap politician. He's too authentic to be a politician. And that's what kills me, when we hear all these stories from everyone writing about him who don't know him, as if he's a politician. It's not him, you know? He may write letters and things to people which he shouldn't write, but he writes privately to people and says what he feels, and there's nothing wrong with that. They're not public.'

Between official visits and private meetings, Charles would grab opportunities to relax in Wales. Fishing and walking were easy pursuits in the countryside. Long days in Cardiff would be broken by accommodating locals. Former Lord-Lieutenant of South Glamorgan Sir Norman Lloyd-Edwards had Charles and Camilla to tea at his home on the main road through Llandaff. Sir Norman's house was just over the road from the BBC's headquarters in Wales, yet the privacy of his garden wall allowed the royals to dip their toes in his swimming pool without fear of the cameras.

'Charles came here quite often,' Sir Norman told me. 'If he came to Cardiff for the whole day, and there was a gap after the afternoon meeting, before the evening session, he would come here for tea and go for a swim.' The scene sounds more like the South of France than the north of Cardiff. 'We'd sit on deck chairs, just the two of us with some tea and cakes.' The men would chat, 'and he would open his heart,' Sir Norman said. 'I felt very close to him.'

Charles's encounters have led to enduring friendships. He made an immediate connection with the Welsh composer Professor Paul Mealor that began over a search for wedding music. Mealor was born in St Asaph in North Wales and has become one of the world's most-performed living composers. He came to Charles's inner circle when his music was shortlisted and eventually chosen to be performed during the wedding of Prince William to Catherine Middleton at Westminster Abbey in April 2011. Around two and a half billion people who watched the ceremony would have heard his motet, *Ubi caritas*, being performed by the choirs of Westminster Abbey and Her Majesty's Chapel Royal.

The commission led to Mealor's inbox flooding with eighty thousand emails, and he was quickly signed by Decca Records and topped the classical album charts. When I spoke to him he was driving from his home studio on the island of Anglesey to the north-east of Scotland where he has a chair in composition at the University of Aberdeen. His Celtic commute has given him a shared perspective of the Welsh and Scottish nations, while his friendship with Charles has given him insight into the private passions of the King.

'It was definitely the beginning of what became quite an active friendship,' Professor Mealor recalled of the original wedding commission. They have since seen each other in the north-east of Scotland, where, before he was King, Charles would spend around a third of the year based at Birkhall on the Balmoral Estate. When the closest town, Ballater, was flooded, Charles used his convening power to raise morale and money.

'One of the things that was put forward by myself and

a Scottish entertainer called Robert Lovie was to put on a concert for the people of Ballater where all of the proceeds would go to the flood appeal. It was the Duke of Rothesay's flooding appeal, as he was known as the Duke of Rothesay in Scotland,' Paul Mealor recalled.

Tickets sold out as the local population backed the event, which was a Burns Night show of music and poetry, with songs performed by Professor Mealor's choir from the University of Aberdeen. Ahead of the concert, Charles spoke to him. 'He said, "Look, I'd like to come", and both he and the Duchess of Cornwall both came to it. Of course, as soon as they came then all of the media came.' A record of the evening's entertainment was released on CD, which reached number three in the charts and which, for Professor Mealor, confirmed the power of Charles's presence both in arranging to help his closest community and in publicising the outcome. 'Just a small thing like that shows you how much he cares about the community,' he said.

Paul Mealor is popular in royal circles. Even before his deep friendship with Charles, he had been organising music to be performed at Crathie Kirk, the small parish church where the royals worship while in residence on the Balmoral estate. The Welsh musical prodigy, who was a protégé of fellow Welsh choral composer William Mathias, had found a group of superfans among Charles, Camilla and the late Queen which led to him being picked out for projects where the Mealor brand of choral, soulful music was required to set the mood and mark the occasion. Charles 'took a great, active interest in the music that was being performed. He always wants to know what we are doing, and he has a great knowledge of music, and a great passion for music,' Professor Mealor said.

Charles played the cello and sang as a young man. He understands and reads music, and very often his conversations with Paul Mealor naturally convalesce around the topic. If Professor Mealor is in Scotland and sees Charles before a concert, he will discuss the musical repertoire at length, and does so with knowledge and passion. Professor Mealor wrote a piece for the fiftieth anniversary of Charles's investiture as Prince of Wales which was performed during a commemorative event hosted by the Queen in London in 2019. The work was called 'Morwyn Llyn Fan' and was inspired by the legend of the lady of the lake, the lake in question being Llyn y Fan near Charles's home at Llwynywermod. The music was sung by a soprano and accompanied by a harp, and triggered a musical memory for Charles. 'He remarked afterwards how it was very similar to a Welsh folk song that he knew,' Paul Mealor said. 'I had based it on that same Welsh folk song, but I hadn't told him.' Professor Mealor has seen the piles of CDs, at Birkhall and Llwynywermod, which confirm Charles's eclectic and deep-rooted musical tastes.

'Real love of culture – that's important to him,' Paul Mealor reflected. 'If you go to Dumfries House, which he saved for the nation, and see all of the skills, crafts, culture and paintings – they are the things that make us who we are as a society. I don't think any member of any royal family, in any country, has taken on board the extent and importance of culture,' he said.

In a small but determined way, Charles made an impact by supporting specific musical causes in Wales. His greatest achievement in both preserving and highlighting the music of Wales was by reinventing the role of the royal harpist. While Catrin Finch was the first, a succession of women have taken on the role with Alis Huws being the incumbent since 2019. The position is technically called the Official Harpist to the Prince of Wales, though it is based on the role the musician and composer John Thomas undertook as harpist to Queen Victoria in the 1870s. The purpose of resurrecting the role was to encourage new musical talent to take up an instrument that usually required a parent with a Volvo to get you to school concerts. Royal harpists have featured at Senedd openings and special events at Llwynywermod and Buckingham Palace. The instrument, and one of the six women to be royally appointed to play it, become both a function of the Prince of Wales's hospitality and an icon of the culture he both promotes and tries to represent.

At an event to celebrate Wales Week in Charles's Welsh home in 2022, it was Alis Huws's opportunity to perform for her patron and his guests. She chose a work called *Hiraeth* by Grace Williams, and was unintimidated by her audience. 'That's my living, performing,' she told me as the guests mingled around us in Llwynywermod. 'For me I just have to concentrate on the notes, more than taking in my surroundings. You have to keep yourself focused.'

Alis Huws's tenure as royal harpist included the

pandemic restrictions, which decimated the opportunities for her other work, and resulted in a period manning the reception desk at an office in Cardiff city centre. But with the reopening of society came the renewal of Charles's commitment to his harpist, and royal functions in Wales and further afield are a feature of her year. 'It completely depends on what's on the royal calendar. It can vary from performances such as this evening, to being the background music when guests are coming for dinner.' Whether centre stage, or setting the mood music, Alis Huws felt a little weight of history and tradition as she performed. 'It is a huge opportunity and a huge privilege to be in this position. And it is such a unique role to have as well. Catrin Finch had the role in 2000, and she is still an inspiration to me. It is a really amazing opportunity.'

Charles's private passions for the music and culture of Wales very often spilled into his public persona. Welsh visits provided a platform to show off some of the talents he had backed in private. He recorded a Dylan Thomas poem to mark the bard's centenary. Opportunities to support and promote the artistic culture of Wales are grasped with both royal hands. But there is also a more private, enduring relationship with a whole community born not from culture, but from a sense of national loss. Aberfan.

On the morning of Friday 21 October 1966 the Thorn Lighting works in Merthyr Tydfil was producing one lightbulb every second. It was one of the town's largest employers, making thousands of bulbs each day that would glow in homes and offices around the world. In the factory's quality control department, Gloria Davies had just started her shift. She was twenty-three and had been married for two months to her husband, Arnold. When she left the house to travel to work that morning, Arnold was just getting home. He had clocked off his night shift at Merthyr's other big employer – Hoover – and settled down to sleep at their home in Oakfield Street, Aberfan.

At around ten o'clock Gloria went on her break and popped to the canteen. She noticed a colleague was staring at her, giving her a look which said, 'Something's wrong'.

'She said to me, you're from Aberfan, aren't you?' There had been an accident, and the word-of-mouth news coming from the village suggested that a coal tip had slipped down a hill and spilled around the primary school on Moy Road that sat beneath it. Gloria saw some colleagues who had a television switched on. It's not as bad as first thought, they said. And yet she knew it was probably worse. She saw her manager, Dilwyn, who also lived in Aberfan.

'He said, "I'm going home", and I said, "I'm coming too".'

From the comments of her colleagues, Gloria had imagined that small, dry pieces of coal waste had rolled down from the towering heap that overlooked the village. But it was not dry coal on the road as the car pulled into the village, but a thick liquid slurry that had swamped, smashed and smothered the school before spilling across the street and taking out some of the houses opposite. Gloria's cousin, Brian Harris, lived at number 84 Moy

Road. He had been married for three years to Janet, who had brought him to live with her in Aberfan. Brian had been alone in the house recovering from a recent car accident when the coal tip slid down the hillside and engulfed his home after it had soared through the primary school. The disaster killed a hundred and sixteen children and twenty-eight adults, including Brian.

As she told me the story in her living room, Gloria took a deep breath in an attempt to halt a tear. I offered my apologies for bringing it all back, but she stops me. 'No, no. It's OK. It's only that I have loved him, isn't it?' Her husband, Arnold, was asleep at home in Oakfield Street when the disaster happened, far enough away not to be hit by the sliding liquified debris or woken by the rumble.

It had rained for days before the tip slid. 'Oh, it was torrential,' Gloria recalled. 'From the Sunday until the Thursday afternoon. It used to come down from the tip and it used to flood Aberfan, there were protests about it.'

As Gloria had arrived in Aberfan on the morning of the disaster, the weather had cleared. On the road from Merthyr Tydfil, concerned faces peered out from the doorsteps. Emergency services had seeped into the area, and the traffic congestion meant she had to abandon Dilwyn's car to walk the last few streets to see if Arnold was still at home. She woke him, and the two of them went towards the school, seeing rubble still slipping and whole houses edging downhill in the slurried mess that had engulfed the centre of Aberfan.

'You wanted to help, and you felt helpless. Somebody said they had seen Brian being brought out and taken to hospital, so I tried to phone everywhere, but the phones had all been taken over by the emergency services.' It seemed unlikely that he had been rescued, and in the absence of more reassuring news, Gloria's husband Arnold and her father went to help with the rescue effort.

'He was there all night with my father. They couldn't find Brian then,' she said. 'But on Sunday morning they found him. He was quite a way down from where his house was.' Gloria walked along Aberfan Road and saw Brian's wife, Janet, in a desperate state. Her wedding ring, and the clothes she had on, were now her only possessions. 'She was digging her nails into my hands, and I thought, "Oh my God, that's all she's got left".'

Six little girls from Gloria's street died in school that day. Every house had a story of loss, every street suffered the harrowing silence of its missing children. 'You were afraid to laugh for a long time. And, of course, there were no weddings for that generation,' Gloria recalled. That first Christmas there were few decorations in the terraced houses. Before the disaster, two boys, who could see each other's houses across a field, had promised they would light candles in their windows to look out for each other at Christmas. But when only one of them emerged alive from the ruins of the junior school, the mother of the dead boy lit the candle in his memory.

For all of the political upheaval and the public battle to apportion blame and compensate the victims, the community in Aberfan proceeded with a quiet dignity to attempt to overcome the trauma of the disaster. One initiative was the creation of a club called Aberfan Wives, which organised a regular meeting of women in the village where the topic of conversation tended to be anything but the disaster. Over time it has occasionally been assumed, wrongly, that all of the women who attended Aberfan Wives meetings were mothers of children lost to the disaster. Some were, but others – like Gloria – were Aberfan residents who had reason to seek comfort and distraction. Guest speakers were invited, quizzes and day trips were organised. The group's meetings were cathartic and offered an escape in those early years after the disaster. But decades later they continued to meet almost weekly, a few original members were joined by new faces. Membership grew not because of ties to the disaster but because the Aberfan Wives remained one of the few regular social clubs in the village.

Gloria Davies had been secretary of the club when the fortieth anniversary of the disaster arrived in 2006. They had entertained television producers who asked to attend a meeting of the club and pitch their documentary ideas to the wives. Each offer came with strings attached, with the TV contracts requiring archive film and photographs of the dead to be used to pull at the emotions of the audience. 'We didn't want any of that,' Gloria said. 'We just wanted it to be wives, now, in 2006.' For all the normality that the club had offered the wives in the years after the disaster, the attention of the producers had confirmed the group's special bond. 'Yeah, we are special, we told ourselves,' Gloria said, before deciding to gamble on organising a special trip to mark forty years of the club. 'I thought, "Right, I'll write to Her Majesty".'

The Queen's initial reaction to the Aberfan disaster in 1966 was said to have been one of the greatest regrets of her reign. She had waited eight days to visit the village, arriving after a mass funeral and being escorted to family homes to meet the bereaved. The Queen had walked the stretch of Moy Road to the remains of Pantglas Junior School, and images caught on newsreel showed the solemn, rigid face of the monarch. But away from the cameras the emotion of a mother rippled across the surface of the stoic Queen. It was one of precious few occasions when she was seen to shed a tear in public. Sir William Heseltine, who served in the Queen's press team, said in a television documentary that 'I think she felt in hindsight that she might have gone there a little earlier. It was a sort of lesson for us that you need to show sympathy and be there on the spot, which I think people craved from her.'

One of the little boys who was rescued from the crushed remains of the school was Jeff Edwards, who went on to become a local councillor and later the leader of Merthyr Tydfil council. He never saw the Queen's delayed visit to Aberfan as an issue, and nor do others in the village appear to begrudge her waiting for rescue efforts to end before travelling there with all the security and disruption of a royal itinerary. When the Queen died in 2022, Jeff Edwards told the BBC that she had looked emotional during the visit after the disaster, her stern appearance briefly crumpled as she walked from the cemetery to a nearby house. 'When she went into that house she was really upset, and she had to compose herself,' Mr Edwards recalled.

Marilyn Brown lost her ten-year-old daughter Janette in the disaster, and told the BBC: 'You could see that she was quite emotional. You could see that she cared, you know?'

The Queen's ongoing commitment to Aberfan included three return visits after her initial trip in the days following the disaster. While they were visits to offer compassion and to open new facilities in the village, the Queen's presence also had political implications. In the 1990s a visit coincided with wrangling about the repayment of money to the Aberfan Disaster Fund, after money that had been intended to compensate the bereaved had been used to pay for the removal of six similar tips that loomed on the hillside above their shattered homes. The National Coal Board had been found to be responsible for the disaster, but it had refused to pay for the remedial works to prevent a similar landslide. Jeff Edwards claimed the 1997 visit had been 'instrumental' in the £150,000 being returned to the Aberfan fund.

On the fiftieth anniversary of the disaster in 2016 a message from the Queen was read by Charles, who attended the commemoration in Aberfan on her behalf:

> I well remember my own visit with Prince Philip after the disaster, and the posy I was given by a young girl, which bore the heart-breaking inscription, 'From the remaining children of Aberfan'.

> Since then, we have returned on several occasions and have always been deeply impressed by the remarkable

fortitude, dignity and indomitable spirit that characterises the people of this village and the surrounding valleys.

On this saddest of anniversaries, I send my renewed good wishes to you all.

ELIZABETH R.

The Queen's lifelong commitment to the people of Aberfan was clear to Gloria, who would count herself as a traditional valleys monarchist. It was the fortieth anniversary of the disaster, ten years before the message above was delivered, when Gloria attempted to arrange a visit for the Aberfan Wives to London. She had quietly hoped the Aberfan connection would open some golden doors. 'The Queen had visited Aberfan a few times, so why shouldn't we go up there?' Gloria smiled. She recalled her husband's response. 'Arnold said, "Oh, you can leave it there, for goodness sake," but I said, "Look, love, I'll try!"' Through a family connection, Gloria got the name of someone at Buckingham Palace who might help.

On 3 January 2007 Gloria had a letter from the tickets and administration office. 'Nobody knew about this, so I knew it wasn't a send-up. I hadn't told any of my friends, so that if I was unsuccessful, it wouldn't have mattered.' The letter offered a pair of tickets to visit either Buckingham Palace or Windsor Castle, but Gloria decided to channel her inner 'Hyacinth Bucket', she laughed, and picked up the phone to try and secure something better for the women of Aberfan. A short time later the Queen's private secretary wrote to Gloria, and after an exchange with the local Lord-Lieutenant, the Aberfan Wives were issued with twenty-six invitations to attend a garden party at the palace.

'I couldn't believe it,' Gloria said.

Organisations who are nominated for garden parties might secure two or three tickets at most. The decision to invite all of the Aberfan Wives group was highly unusual, and hugely indicative of the significance of Aberfan to the Queen and her staff. Forty years after the disaster, the Queen had maintained her commitment to Aberfan. 'I was trembling when I was telling them,' Gloria said, remembering how the news was delivered at the next meeting of the wives.

The excitement was softened only by the practicalities. How would they get there? A coach was booked and a hotel arranged, and while the women all put down £50 deposits for the bookings, another benefactor stepped in to cover all of the additional costs.

Four decades after the Queen had visited Aberfan, twenty-six of the women who came together in the aftermath of the tragedy to form their club were on a coach to London to visit the Queen themselves. As the coach pulled into the Mall, Gloria broke the news that some of the party would be brought forward among the thousands of garden party guests to meet members of the royal family. In advance of the day, the palace had asked that four of the Aberfan Wives would be presented to the Queen, and four to Prince Charles.

The four who were chosen to meet the Queen included Denise Morgan, who lost her nine-year-old sister Annette in the Aberfan disaster. Denise was eleven at the time, and had shared not just a bedroom but a bed with her younger sister before the rush of coal slurry brought unimaginable tragedy to their home. She would wake in the night, searching for her sister in her bed, and asking again and again why Annette was taken from them.

The reverend June Vaughan was also chosen to meet the Queen. In the grim ruins of Pantglas Junior School she had worked with rescuers to search for survivors and comfort the distraught families of the missing and the dead. Before the disaster she had been involved in running a chapel Sunday school. Seventeen children from her group were killed on that October morning. Guided by her faith and her obligation to the community, she was instrumental in establishing the wives' group after the disaster.

Pat Lee was also chosen to meet the Queen. When her eight-year-old daughter Ann was killed, Pat could not bring herself to enter the chapel where dozens of small bodies were resting after being removed from the school ruins. Pat's husband went in on behalf of the family to identify their little girl.

The three women joined Gloria Davies, as secretary of the Aberfan Wives, to meet the Queen among the crowd of top-hatted guests on the Buckingham Palace lawn. Among the teacups and small talk, the women from Wales shook hands and smiled as the monarch was brought to meet them. The Queen's reaction, caught on camera, is as unremarkable as any other interaction of her reign – a broad smile and a quick chat, a gentle conversation before she was ushered onto the next group of guests. It was exactly what the women wanted, and it remains etched in the group's history as their most successful and enjoyable day out. If it had a more profound meaning, it didn't show on the faces of the Queen or the wives. All of them shared a bond of being touched by the tragedy of the Aberfan disaster in 1966, either personally or as a figurehead of a shocked and grieving population. The garden party meeting forty years later, for all its pomp and formality, was a moment of friendly hospitality and genuine warmth.

The Aberfan disaster was a personal tragedy for the families and friends of those who died. A hundred and forty-four lives taken, a hundred and sixteen of them had barely begun. Every loss was unjust and irreplaceable, and its impact meant that Aberfan became a national tragedy and a moment of intense shame for the institutions that allowed it to happen.

The injustice of Aberfan remained a compelling reason for the late Queen, and now the King, to have maintained the monarchy's close connection with its people. There is an almost unspoken sense of the royal family having an obligation to the community, born perhaps from the occasional reminder of the Queen's regret at delaying her very first visit to the devastated town. It was a regret that Gloria Davies hoped to put to bed in a letter she wrote to Charles shortly after the death of the Duke of Edinburgh in 2021. The letter, a copy of which she shared with me, was a heartfelt expression of sympathy for a man who had lost his father. Recalling how the Duke had visited Aberfan in the immediate days after the disaster, before returning with the Queen on her first visit the following week, Gloria wrote:

> When he came to Aberfan when the disaster happened, he had genuine empathy with all that he saw. Also, when he accompanied the Queen the week after, they could not hide their emotions. I am sure that Her Majesty had been prepared by him of what to expect. It was wiser for them that they left it for a week to return. I know Her Majesty has felt that she should have come to Aberfan sooner, but that would have been unwise as there was so much removal working being done.

In the letter conveying her sympathies, Gloria also sought to gently numb any lingering royal guilt about the response to the Aberfan disaster. It was a personal, private attempt to absolve the monarchy of any feeling of institutional neglect.

Gloria had formed a bond with Charles as Prince of Wales, having met him during the events to mark the fiftieth anniversary of the Aberfan disaster in 2016. 'It was the fiftieth year,' Gloria corrected me. 'In the wives, we never like to say anniversary, because it sounded like an anniversary should be celebrated.' He was coming to the community centre in Aberfan where the Ynysowen Male Choir would perform. Like the Aberfan Wives, the choir had been formed in the months after the disaster.

It brought together men from the community who had lost children and loved ones, and some who had worked to clear the coal tips in order to remove the lingering threat of further slides of waste that hung above the village. It was the moment when Charles forged his own connection with the village, and one which would endure with private correspondence and invitations for the wives to join him at Llwynywermod. Like the outing to Buckingham palace, the coach trip to Charles's home in rural Carmarthenshire was a treat.

The extent of Charles's commitment to the Aberfan community appears as heartfelt as that of his mother's. I asked the broadcaster Roy Noble about the royal embrace of Aberfan, as he had observed Charles on a visit to the village. Noble had been hosting the event in the Aberfan community centre to mark fifty years since the disaster in 2016, and saw the continuing connection between monarchy and Aberfan as an act of public, real-time remembrance.

'I think the fact that the royal family, and more recently Prince Charles going there, was a recognition that it stands as an historical abhorrence that has to be continually returned to, to pay it homage, if you like. Homage and honour. It has to be returned to. "This is what happened here", you know?' Roy Noble has been involved with fundraising for memorials to the Welsh soldiers who died in the First World War, and for the hundreds who died in the Senghenydd coal mining disaster of 1913. He has championed causes where injustice and institutional ineptitude have led to the loss of innocent Welsh lives, and as a result he has little time for a lessons-must-be-learned response to more modern failings.

'Grenfell is a case in point,' Roy Noble told me, turning to the fire at Grenfell Tower in London in 2017 which killed seventy-two residents. 'If you are serious about lessons being learned, why aren't you doing anything about it? Why are there people trapped in those high-rise flats, virtually facing bankruptcy, because they have been told that they have to pay for the replacement cladding? That's an immorality, isn't it?' Roy rails against the lessons-must-be-learned crowd. 'You just find it extraordinary that they would come out with those statements, but it dissipates and gradually diminishes and nothing happens, unless you have people who gnaw at it all the time.'

The closeness of Aberfan to the late Queen was apparent, and its ongoing importance to Charles as Prince of Wales, and now as King, has provided a form of national protection for the memory of the disaster. For as long as the monarch maintains a special connection with the village, the fading impact of the tragedy and its injustice can be slowed. Charles has a real and passionate commitment to upholding the memory and marking it with ceremony and official visits, and has continued to extend the hand of friendship and companionship to the community. And for the Aberfan Wives, the royal interest is both an acknowledgement that they have borne an immense tragedy in their community, while also providing a closeness to the functional end of monarchy.

It has provided genuine warmth and support, as well as the chance to add royal palaces and gardens to their weekly diary of coffee mornings and day trips.

7

A Home in Wales

The ability to rule with conviction and confidence was as essential to the monarchs of the Middle Ages as any claim to territory or conquering armies. Once any arguments about birthright could be set aside, the kings, queens and princes of the darkest centuries would rule 'by the grace of God' in a far more literal sense than recent heads of state. Claiming a connection to the almighty was almost a prerequisite for taking a throne, and the greater the impression of a unique connection to God, the greater the chances of inspiring another loyal battalion to defend their lands or to capture more. And so it was in that spirit of divine devotion that the Welsh king Hywel Dda set off for Rome in the tenth century on the first holy pilgrimage by a Welsh ruler. He returned to Wales with papal blessings, along with a more tangible link to heavenly authority.

The trade in tourist knick-knacks was a more celestial affair in those days, with a visit to the Eternal City presenting the chance to return with a sacred artefact that came with a great backstory and added cachet for its new owner. Hywel Dda selected and brought back to Wales a fragment of wood that he believed to be from the cross on which Christ had died. In the world of Christian relics it is known as the True Cross and its pieces are scattered among cathedrals and royal courts. Some have argued that enough pieces of the True Cross entered circulation to build Noah's ark three times over, but for Hywel Dda it provided a direct link between the dawn of Christianity and his noble court. There are other tales of how this relic came to Wales, and while nobody is quite sure how Hywel Dda got hold of it, he was probably lucky to have avoided returning with a more macabre memento – the finger of St Thomas and the head of St John the Baptist were among the other sacred relics also finding their way to churches and royal courts around Europe. Even a piece of preserved flesh, considered to be the foreskin of Jesus Christ, was widely revered until it was discredited in the eighteenth century.

The piece of wood carried by Hywel Dda was named *Croes Naid*, a term which the scholars at the University of Wales have translated to the Cross of Destiny. It was likely to have been arranged within an ornamental cross and encased in a reliquary, essentially a fancy display box. The *Croes Naid* became part of the Welsh crown jewels, and it remained in the possession of the Princes of Wales. It passed from one to another until it reached the last native Prince, Llywelyn, who had kept it with him during the fighting to defend his lands. But following his death in battle with the English in 1282, the cross was seized by Edward I and became part of the English Crown jewels.

For hundreds of years it remained in the monarch's royal collection, with Edward I considering it his personal property and taking it with him on further conquests of Wales and Scotland. But it later arrived at St George's

Chapel in the grounds of Windsor Castle, where medieval inventories conducted in the fourteenth and fifteenth centuries recorded that the *Croes Naid* was kept in storage alongside more curious relics. These other trophies included a crystal vessel containing the breast milk of the Virgin Mary, two thorns from the crown worn by Christ at his crucifixion, and – perhaps befitting the chapel's namesake – two fingers, part of the heart and a piece of the skull of St George. Around the time of Oliver Cromwell's experiment with republicanism in the seventeenth century, the *Croes Naid* disappeared. An inventory of the crown jewels in 1649 does not record the existence of the sacred Welsh relic at either St George's Chapel or the Tower of London, and neither the piece of wood nor its elaborate display case have ever been found.

There is, though, a reminder of the *Croes Naid* at St George's Chapel today. Crane your neck and peer up above the banners of the Knights of the Garter, between the stone vaulting that extends above the altar, and you may spot a carved and painted image of this Welsh crown jewel. The gold cross is shown standing between the figures of Edward IV and Richard Beauchamp, the Dean of Windsor who oversaw the chapel's renovation under Edward IV in the fifteenth century. This emboss that links Christianity's totem with Wales has perched above countless choir practices, Sunday services and royal weddings. In the past hundred years the chapel beneath it has carried the dresses of more than a dozen royal brides and the coffins of six sovereigns and their spouses.

After arriving at the chapel door on the back of a

specially converted Land Rover, the casket containing the body of Prince Philip, the Duke of Edinburgh, was delivered to the vault of St George's Chapel on a still, sun-speckled Saturday in April 2021. It was a moment captured on television by an overhead camera, giving the same bug's-eye view of the chapel as that which would be afforded to the figures painted beside the *Croes Naid*. If their eyes could have seen, they would have witnessed the only state funeral to happen under pandemic restrictions, as the Queen sat alone on the south side of the quire and with her children scattered sparingly among the gothic stalls. Charles, who had walked with his sons behind the coffin in the castle grounds, now sat in solemn mourning for his father. A month earlier the family had been strained by Harry and Meghan's interview with Oprah, and while the funeral allowed the newspaper columnists to predict a moment of family healing, the public exchanges between Charles and Harry that were captured by long lenses were cool and brief. There is a natural tendency to retreat and to take stock after a moment of great loss and in the midst of family tension. Charles retreated to Wales.

* * *

The Prince's home in Wales is a simple one by the standards of royal residences. Former First Minister Carwyn Jones, who stayed there on official business with the Prince, described it as having 'the feeling of a prosperous farmhouse'. It sits almost halfway across Wales, near the midpoint between the English border to the east and the Irish Sea to the west. Thick woodland and winding country lanes above the market town of Llandovery disguise its exact location, but visitors who navigate the farm track and pass the armed police at the wooden gate find a country home with a distinctively Welsh name: Llwynywermod. It means Wormwood Grove, a nod to the area's reputation for attracting herbalists, and it is thought to be connected to the Physicians of Myddfai, a family who practised herbal medicine in the area from the thirteenth century and for generations after that. Set in almost two hundred acres, the main buildings of the Prince's Welsh home are arranged around a quadrangle. They are the home farm and refurbished coach houses belonging to a long-ruined mansion house next door. Their renovation was overseen by the Prince and the Duchess after the Duchy of Cornwall exchanged contracts on the estate in 2006.

Royal palaces have traditionally been great sprawling buildings of gilt-edged bannisters, velvet curtains and dusty wings. The Prince chose a Welsh home that was designed to be a humbler retreat, yet it remains incredibly upmarket. Decorated with thoughtfulness and taste, local crafters and renowned Welsh designers created a comfortable home and a welcoming venue for entertaining dozens of guests. Anyone visiting from Maesteg or Merthyr Tydfil would recognise a posh person's idea of Welsh interior design. There are no polished miners' lamps or leather recliners, nor has the Prince adopted the paraphernalia of Welsh second-home owners. There are no cushions here embroidered with

'Anyone can hug, but only the Welsh can cwtch'. But you will see an eighteenth-century Welsh dresser, presented to the Queen on her wedding day by the people of Meirionnydd and returned to Wales from the Royal Collection some sixty years after the nuptials. Above a stone fireplace in the dining room is the three feathers crest of the Prince of Wales carved in Welsh slate. A painting of Charles's investiture hangs on the wall in another room. There are comfortable sofas, too, and textiles are displayed around the edges of the room with blankets draped over easy chairs. The fabrics came from local mills including Melin Tregwynt on the west coast near Fishguard, a brand whose designs were the chic embodiment of sophisticated Welsh crafting; by the 1990s every Welsh social climber needed a Melin Tregwynt blanket to arrange ostentatiously beneath their Kyffin Williams oil painting. Oak for the doors was sourced from the Duchy of Cornwall estates, while iron attachments came from local blacksmiths. The Duchess of Cornwall oversaw the outdoor colour scheme which adopts a timeless hue, and both she and the Prince had been involved in transforming the royal residence into a home. During the dusty height of the renovation work the Prince had taken tea and biscuits in a Portakabin, having toured the site in wellies as his vision took shape. When the work was completed, the couple spent their first night at Llwynywermod on 23 June 2008. The Prince gave a speech at Caerphilly Castle a few days later and spoke of his delight at finally getting a home in Wales:

At last I have a base. It is above all a tribute to Welsh craftsmanship which is of a very high order, and that unique rural and industrial craft inheritance that has formed so many equally unique Welsh characters that I have been so proud and privileged to have known during the last fifty years.

Such is the abundance of trees, hedgerows and grassy verges along the undulating B road north of the small village of Myddfai that the farm buildings of Llwynywermod cannot be seen until you arrive at them. Visitors who are allowed through the wooden gates and down the farm track discover a courtyard surrounded on its four sides by buildings of varying shapes: a home farm, outbuildings and a couple of smaller self-catering cottages which have occasionally been let out as holiday homes. Painted off-white, the woodwork and guttering is duck-egg blue while climbing plants cling above the lintels. The buildings surround the quadrangle's formal garden of privet hedges, manicured ilex trees and a gentle, effervescent fountain that froths in the centre of a square, raised pond. Sitting on the western edge of the quadrangle is a barn that was considered to be the largest tithe barn in Carmarthenshire. Beyond the barn lie the ruins of a great country house, and from which the quadrangle and its zig-zag skyline of stone walls and chimney stacks gave the baronets of the Griffies-Williams family the vision of a small bustling village just below their mansion doors.

The only images that depict the ruined country house

in its original condition are watercolours. It was once a great home for the Williams and then the Griffies-Williams families, with its fortunes ebbing and flowing with the economic and political tensions of the centuries. It was at its most prosperous in the hands of Sir George Griffies-Williams who, at the age of twenty-five, had inherited the estate from his uncle in 1785. Eton-educated and studying at Cambridge, Sir George quickly embraced the realities of estate-management and farming life. In the authoritative work on Llwynywermod, *A Royal Home in Wales*, Mark Baker writes that 'farming was an important part of the ethos with which George managed the estates, and by August [1785] he was already negotiating the purchase of hay from Abercothy, together with a wagon and four large black Herefordshire horses'. His first wife and their daughter died tragically young, and it was later that he met the woman with whom he would alter and extend Llwynywermod. Anna Margaretta was the daughter of local landed gentry, and she helped decorate the country house with Sir George. Invoices found by Mark Baker list the curtains, carpets, mattresses and pillows that were sent by coach from London to the Carmarthenshire hills. Silver tea sets and rosewood card tables followed, along with candlesticks and serving forks, and the Griffies-Williams coat of arms was engraved wherever space allowed. The couple had a total of ten children who were all born at Llwynywermod and were baptised down the hill at Myddfai.

By the nineteenth century Sir George's interests were embedded with the crucible of the industrial revolution, where he is recorded as being a director of the South Wales Mining Company. Anna Margaretta died in 1814 and Mark Baker's research suggests it was after this time that Llwynywermod began to appear neglected. Sir George's political and business interests kept him away from the estate, and further family tragedy would derail the ambition for Llwynywermod to remain the traditional seat of the Griffies-Williams line. In the later years of Sir George's life his eldest son and heir, John George, died leaving no surviving children. On the death of Sir George, the estate passed to his second son Erasmus, who had been born at Llwynywermod but would not return there to live and manage the site. Erasmus had been ordained into the Anglican Church and, as he attended to his ecclesiastical duties in England, the mansion house and estate in Wales were leased out. When Erasmus returned in his sixties to a post in St Davids Cathedral he could visit his boyhood home, though the locals were less enamoured with him. He was opposed to the countryside pursuit of hunting with horse and hound, and his devotion to God brought a more formal, professional attitude to the running of church services than the population was prepared to stomach. 'Erasmus must have arrived like St Patrick in pagan Ireland,' Mark Baker wrote in his account of the period. Baker uncovered a letter from Erasmus which complained that the officials of St Davids Cathedral 'were so inbedded [sic] in inherited neglect as to be astonished at being required to do their duty'. His death in 1870 led to decades of debate and dispute over the distribution of the Llwynywermod estate. It was largely leased to various tenants and eventually sold off. The mansion house remained intact but abandoned. The start of the twentieth century was the most perilous moment for the mansion house, its farm buildings, the formal gardens and pastureland that had been a profitable home for Sir George Griffies-Williams. In the 1920s some of the smaller buildings were still being rented out; among the tenants was a founder member of the Farmer's Union of Wales, while the Second World War saw the grounds given over for the Home Guard to prepare themselves should the Nazis have attempted to conquer Carmarthenshire. The mansion house began to crumble, a target for passing vandals that eventually stripped its nineteenth-century eloquence down to a few ruined walls at either end of a gaping void.

The modern saviours of Llwynywermod weren't the royal family but a married couple from Herefordshire. John and Patricia Hegarty bought the estate in 1998 for £352,000 and had hoped to restore some of its best features. The Hegartys had done this kind of thing before, having revived the historic walled garden of Hope End in Herefordshire where they eventually ran a boutique hotel. The ambition in Llwynywermod was to restore the farmhouse building, to buy back parcels of neighbouring land that had previously been sold off, and to landscape the grounds back to their nineteenth-century glory using organic methods. They did not attempt to restore the ruined mansion, but had significantly improved and revived the estate to make it an attractive proposition for a Prince in need of a project.

'After 37 years as Prince of Wales, Charles finally buys a home there.' *The Times* broke the news on 23 November 2006 that HRH would replace the Hegartys at Llwynywermod. The Prince had been forced to sleep in other people's beds on royal visits to Wales, the newspaper said, and the organically farmed isolation of this small estate would end the residential roulette. For his investiture Charles had stayed at the Faenol estate near Bangor, and overnight stays since 1969 had relied on generous hosts, a bed on the royal train or a long drive back to Highgrove or London. Now, after a considerable amount of time searching for a permanent base in Wales, the Prince could develop and revive an estate using the principles of sustainability and traditional skills that he attempted to bring to all of his renovation projects.

Developing the estate into a residence and a retreat could only begin once Charles understood the history of the site. It was important that Llwynywermod's history was examined for two reasons: to appreciate and reinvent the best of its past, and to ensure the site contained no secrets that would come to embarrass or evict the future King. What if the house had harboured a killer, or the grounds had been cursed by pagans? While there was no record of murderous owners, the proximity of the house to Myddfai meant it did have a close link with the herbalists who had previously been the area's best-known residents. The Physicians of Myddfai were a group of doctors who made Carmarthenshire a place of pilgrimage for those in search of a miracle cure. Their practices are now lumbered within the spectrum of complementary therapies that are largely available beyond the National Health Service, but which were the less radical mainstream of medical practice for hundreds of years. The closeness of Llwynywermod to the legends of Myddfai was an attractive proposition for Charles, rather than any deterrent to investing in the estate. The person who studied the records in order to produce a history of the Prince's new Welsh home was the architectural historian Mark Baker, and whose interaction with Charles had begun when Mark was a ten-year-old boy growing up in north-east Wales.

In 1997 Mark Baker had written to the Prince of Wales with a particularly pressing concern. Baker would sit on the school bus every morning as it trundled past the deteriorating glory of Gwrych Castle. When he eventually made a special trip to see the historic fortress for himself, a group of scrap-hunting vandals had moved in and stripped it of its roof, floorboards and anything that could be melted down or sold on. Baker was moved by the injustice of seeing a grand, creaking castle being rendered almost unusable by the passing of time and the absence of any official attention. It was the beginning of a commitment to protecting the heritage of Wales which would forge him a career and a close bond with a Prince who would champion and channel his enthusiasm. In his almost-adolescent desperation, Mark Baker wrote to the Prince of Wales. Given it was the middle of the 1990s, it is easy to imagine that the correspondence secretary at Charles's office admired the rarity of a plea for the Prince to intervene in saving a Welsh castle. There was no automatic, impersonal reply from his office. Instead, a letter of encouragement from Clarence House was sent by return and which gave Mark Baker the confidence and commitment to campaign to save Gwrych Castle from ruin.

'The castle campaign just exploded,' Mark Baker told me. He had agreed to meet me at a Portuguese cafe, tucked across the road from Cardiff Castle. 'It was mentioned on things like *The Big Breakfast*, *Countryfile*, *Newsround*.' The excitement of his boyhood mission to save Gwrych Castle rushed back. He recalled meeting the Prince of Wales – 'at the records office in Ruthin' – to go through the research he had produced as part of his campaign to protect Gwrych from further deterioration. This was 1998 or 1999, as Baker's teenage years became engrossed with studying the history of the castle that he had breezed past on the bus. Rather like Cardiff Castle, which we could see beyond the custard tarts in the cafe, Gwrych Castle was a nineteenth-century creation in the style of a medieval fortress. It was a stately home with battlements, inhabited by Welsh aristocrats until death duties and world wars caught up with the party. Charles's backing of the young Baker was life-affirming, and career-starting. 'When you have got someone who has got a real passion for architecture, buildings and history, it is quite infectious. And as a child, when you have got somebody – literally the next King – telling you this is a great thing to do, you do listen.' Mark Baker was visibly enthused as he recalled making that first connection with the Prince. 'It made me think that there is probably something in it, it's not just a summer project.'

The teenage historian kept in contact with the Prince of Wales, and as he left school and trained in historical architecture, Mark Baker attended receptions and parties whenever Charles was in the country. The Prince's influence popped up more regularly than the man himself. Mark Baker recalled how 'his charities were fantastic'. He had support from the Phoenix Trust, which is concerned with rescuing places like Gwrych. 'All of them got involved, and then the National Trust got a nudge. And the Landmark Trust.' It's clear that Mark Baker credits much of the alignment of support to the Prince, whose convening influence secured wider mentorship, guidance and opportunity for a young and passionate conservationist. Baker will have written to countless other organisations and individuals during his campaign to save Gwrych, but perhaps only the subtle, persuasive influence of the Prince could have ensured that the full gamut of third-sector support would arrive at his desk. Much of the enquiries were done by the Prince's staff, rather than direct lobbying by the Prince. But it was the conviction of the Prince of Wales in Mark Baker's mission that aligned the men. Both of them saw in Gwrych Castle a site that could not be lost either to Wales or to the passing school buses. 'Saving such a cultural asset for the nation is so fundamental to his outlook,' Mark Baker said. I pressed him as to why the Prince would pick a project and throw so much influence at it. 'To help someone who has a similar view is amazing. Having that sort of belief in you is something that I have seen throughout the stories of similar situations. And a lot of it is very low-key. It's not all-singing, all-dancing.' Mark went on: 'For someone that is constantly in the public eye, it is very difficult to show interest in things, because it always gets misconstrued. Because people always want to undermine, all of the time.' If Charles oiled the wheels of Gwrych Castle's rescue, he did so with subtlety and by the proxy of 'his office'. And there was no greater reason than the very basic commitment that Charles had to conservation, according to Mark Baker. 'I think he was just very interested in the history of the place.'

The connection forged between the boy historian and the Prince meant Mark Baker was destined to be entrusted with the work to establish Llwynywermod's suitability to be the first royal home in Wales for hundreds of years. It was a project which Baker began around 2005, before the Prince had committed to buying the estate. The work undertaken by Baker was 'completely confidential', he said, having been commissioned by one of the Prince's charities to research its history. The plan was to present the work to Charles in a commemorative publication that would only run to two editions: one for the Prince, and one for the royal archives. The charity behind the book was the Welsh Historic Gardens Trust, of which the Prince of Wales was its patron. The Trust's mission is to save historic gardens and parks from 'neglect, indifference, insensitive planning and planting' for the benefit of future generations. John Hegarty, who sold Llwynywermod to the Prince, was a member of the Trust and the trinity of historical aficionados was completed with the instruction for Mark Baker to compile the authoritative research.

'It was the seclusion of it that really struck me,' Mark said. 'I could see why he wanted it. I know there were other houses he was looking at, at the time. There was one called Neuadd Fawr near Llandovery, so it was on the other side of Myddfai. But it was too open.' Like Llwynywermod, any purchase of Neuadd Fawr would have concluded with a significant restoration project. While it was a more classically fronted mansion, and in far better shape than the ruined country house at Llwynywermod, it had been derelict for years and sat aside a gently sloping hill which offered beautiful views, and would itself become a destination for walkers and photographers had the Prince moved in. In contrast, Llwynywermod remained remote and discrete. 'With Llwynywermod, you've got the house in the middle, then the farm bit is tucked behind in a little nook. The house is still a ruin, but the farm buildings are really hidden, before you actually get there you can't see them.' Much of the history of the estate was discovered off-site. Paintings and furniture had been sold and spread among stately homes, offices and apartments across the land. Photographs of the mansion house had disappeared entirely, with drawings and watercolours the only visual record of the grand centrepiece of the Llwynywermod estate, which comprises only of its gable ends these days. While Mark Baker sourced the historical records, and located many documents and artefacts associated with its nineteenth-century glory, they would not all be returned to prominence as part of the renovation. Instead, the interior design was delicately considered and chosen by the Prince and the Duchess, while the Duchess's sister Annabel Elliot was employed to achieve a striking, dignified reimagining of Welsh farmhouse chic. The ageing decor of the home farm was stripped out and tastefully replaced with traditional Welsh patterned rugs over flagstone floors. Walls were lime-plastered, with the dining room's timber-framed ceiling now lit by three large wrought-iron candelabras. As the work was carried out, the Prince was updated on a weekly basis with written reports and site photographs. He would make suggestions during his visits, and pointed out any changes which jarred with his aesthetic ambition. Mark Baker recalled: 'I remember at one time being at Llwynywermod and there was something not right with one of the windows. I remember him saying, during the building phase, "That window is in the wrong place". And next time I went there, it had been moved. Little things like that. And it isn't through a third party like an architect or a designer. It is literally him, saying what he wants. And he has got a great mind for buildings, and landscapes as well.'

As the fit-out progressed, the Welsh dresser was sourced from the royal collection. It had been given to the Queen as a wedding present at the time of her marriage to Prince Philip in 1947 from the people of Meirionnydd. Its return to Wales after sixty years was symbolic, just as the Prince's decision to buy a home would allow the estate to resume its role as a small economic engine in rural Carmarthenshire. 'These places were powerhouses on a very local level,' Mark Baker said. The Prince was 'replicating what the family would have done a hundred, or two hundred years ago. The same with Gwrych Castle – it used to employ around two hundred people. We now employ around fifty. So it is getting jobs created again.' The Prince's investment fuelled Welsh craftsmen and engineers, architects and horticulturists. His insistence on using as much local talent as possible ensured that skilled Welsh workers were employed in the reclamation and renovation of the estate. 'It is a bit like a tsunami when it gets going,' Baker said of the Prince's convening power. 'You get all of that regeneration, you get interest from overseas, people coming specifically to the area to see it. It is a good thing, and it is part of our traditions as well.'

In June 2008 the Prince of Wales and the Duchess of Cornwall were ready to open Llwynywermod to guests. Despite the heavy leaning on its isolated, rural location, the estate quickly became a focal point for entertaining and convening the people and organisations that preoccupied the Prince in Wales. Carwyn Jones, who was First Minister at the time of the estate's refurbishment, was one of the first to be invited there for dinner with the royal couple. 'It's not huge, it's a decent size, but it's the sort of farmhouse that would have been quite common in Carmarthenshire at one time, and he did it up. And it's now a home, not a palace.' He repeats the point. 'It's a home, not a stately home.' The informality of Llwynywermod is its distinguishing feature, compared to London palaces and even Balmoral. There are few staff in attendance, and no grand gilded hallways. 'You haven't got somebody in tails waiting to greet you when you arrive, it's not like that. There are staff there, they offer you a cup of tea, and we have had dinner there – my wife and myself – but it's not Downton Abbey. It's far more modest but far more homely, I'd say, as a result.' The lack of formality is conducive to productive meetings. Even heads of state and showbiz stars have been wracked with nerves ahead of a private audience with the heir to the throne. Curtseys are practised for days beforehand. The correct greeting, either Googled or communicated in advance by the palace, is rehearsed with partners over breakfast. Each layer of protocol brings with it a cloak of anxiety that can create smiling idiots of otherwise articulate individuals when they finally meet their royal host. Llwynywermod, while impressive, is the most relaxed residence.

'I've been to St James's Palace, I've been to wherever the other one is – oh, Buckingham Palace! And Windsor Castle. And they're all cold. This wasn't, this was a home.' The actor and producer Stifyn Parri was invited with a group of showbusiness friends to have dinner with the Prince and the Duchess at Llwynywermod quite soon after it was completed. Stifyn owns some renovated barns nearby, and the group assembled in the local pub to be picked up and driven to the royal retreat. At the dinner in Llwynywermod there were no more than a dozen guests, including the actors Ruth Jones and Rob Brydon. It was a quieter affair than the more raucous fundraisers for the Royal Welsh College of Music and Drama which they had helped to promote, and which were designed to entice donations from the wealthy crowd. Instead, the

Prince convened this group for an intimate dinner, which Stifyn Parri recalled with an imaginary stopwatch.

'We had to arrive at 7.45 pm on the dot, not before and not after.' Stifyn raised his eyebrows at me. 'That was so strict by the end that we were told they were going to pick us up from our local pub.' Elegant black cars turned up to collect the group, driven by 'very smart young guys.' Stifyn recalled their prompt arrival. 'Literally, if a bell was chiming, it would have been on the dot.' As appears to happen so often with these encounters, whether with celebrities or factory workers, Charles charmed them. 'At a quarter past eight, himself and Camilla came in,' Stifyn said. 'He had been briefed, and he knew – how he knew this, I do not know – but he seemed to know everybody's CV, even my partner's at the time. Beautifully done.' Despite Stifyn's obvious awe at the situation, he also took on a gentle Miss Marple tone as he looked for clues in the Prince of Wales's strategy when dealing with invited guests. 'I think that the first half hour was for us to get together and relax. And then at a quarter to nine on the dot there was a chime, and one of the drivers, who had miraculously – like Mr Benn – turned into the waiting staff, said, "Dinner is served".' The group was ushered into a 'glorious' dining room, and the twelve guests sat along the length of both sides of the table. Arrangements of flowers from the courtyard garden separated the celebrities as they sat opposite one another, with Charles and Camilla taking their seats at either end of the table. Stifyn found himself sitting nearest to Charles, along with school-friends turned superstars

Brydon and Jones as the food was brought out. 'Apparently he's known for liking a boiled egg in soup,' Stifyn remarked. He had been aware of this culinary quirk before arriving at the future King's rural retreat. 'And in came a soup from the garden with a beautifully perfect, shelled, boiled egg sitting sideways in this soup. And I've done that a lot since, it works, he knows his stuff.' After the soup, in came the fish. As the Mr Benn waiter held the tray at an angle, each celebrity in turn was invited to select their own. It was a 'semi self-silver-service' experience, according to Stifyn. 'Ruth Jones was trying to get a whole piece of fish. I remember that the waiter-stroke-driver-stroke-whatever else – probably bodyguard – said "don't worry madam, you don't need to take the whole fish," and she turned and she said, "But I'm from Port Talbot!" And I remember Charlie laughing his socks off over that.' Further amusement was to come when the Prince enquired about Stifyn's members-only club, SWS, which arranged Cool Cymru gatherings of Welsh celebrities in London, New York and any other exotic spot with sufficient Welsh diaspora to down a case of sparkling wine and a tray of Welsh cakes. The SWS initials stood for Social, Welsh and Sexy. 'He asked me, "Why did you call it that?" And I said it was because I'm all three! And he just burst out laughing. And I said, "Once *you* are all three, maybe I'll allow you to be a member," and he was chuckling in the palm of our hands.' At the other end of the table, Camilla was heard laughing at the anecdotes of her group of performers, though she gave as good as she got. And while this dinner was relaxed, there was a purpose to the gathering. 'What he was trying to do was instigate some more artistic action in that area,' Stifyn suggested, with the underlying ambition to spur creativity in West Wales through the Prince's pick of celebrities. A dinner with a message, subtly conveyed through the gentle guiding of conversation. It was a message which would have to fight for a moment of recollection among the memories of boiled eggs in soup and Ruth Jones's fondness for fish. Nobody recalls if the dinner actually led to a tangible artistic benefit for the community beyond the home farm at Llwynywermod.

The idea that a home was required in Wales for the future King was not something that regularly presented itself in Welsh national life. It was an idea that was championed by his supporters, those like the former Secretary of State for Wales, Alun Cairns, and Lord Dafydd Elis-Thomas who saw an untapped potential in the ambassadorial role the Prince of Wales could offer the country. Mr Cairns put it like this: 'It was an easy hit for an opponent to say, "Oh he doesn't live in Wales, he doesn't have a house in Wales." It almost balanced the equation, or silenced some critics, it's probably fair to say. As well as the fact that Wales would hugely benefit from it, from the global news that he was buying a new property.'

The King's friend, the National Trust's former Welsh director Justin Albert, saw Charles's delight at finding a permanent place in Wales. 'He was very happy, I remember him talking about it, when William was living in Anglesey. Why wouldn't you [be happy]? It's Wales. I am biased, but it is the best country in the world.' Mr Albert is one of the regular attendees at the King's gatherings at Llwynywermod where actors and musicians entertain a gaggle of VIPs in the tithe barn. He has also witnessed the functional side of life in the rural retreat. 'Because it is small, it is intimate, it is totally confidential there, he loves it. He likes the simplicity of things.' It is an oxymoron that a man indulged in the great palaces of Europe should find solace and serenity in a farmhouse. It is a paradox that Justin Albert nails down. 'We have a man who's going to live in vast palaces for the rest of his life, surrounded by flunkies. But actually he's really happy in small places. At Dumfries House [in Scotland] he is also happy, because he's happy there because of the exquisiteness of the work he has done on Chippendale furniture, and it is the most beautiful reconstructed house in Britain. Far more than Buckingham Palace, which is just shiny.' During my conversation with Justin Albert I wanted to pin down the true nature of the place. The photographs and film I have seen are short snippets and from odd angles. And this talk of hosting special guests in a barn – I had imagined a sizeable conversion, bifold doors and underfloor heating. But the man from the National Trust explained the reality of the King's entertainment complex. 'It is a barn! It is a barn with slightly dodgy rugs on the floor. But it really is a barn. And you can fit 50 people sitting in rows. It's very intimate.' For all the frolicking celebrities, garden-gathered ingredients and a more-Habitat-than-Ikea interiors ethic, the greatest charm of Llwynywermod was its ability to spark happiness in the King.

Dame Shân Legge-Bourke, whose family hosted the young Prince of Wales for fishing trips during his time at Aberystwyth, has also been a frequent visitor to Llwynywermod. 'He always wanted to find somewhere in Wales that he could buy that was already organic, that had already been organically farmed. So that shows you how his mind was thinking.'

I wondered if she had seen him there, besides on publicised visits. Others had remarked that he had hosted smaller meetings, or that he would simply retreat to Llwynywermod for a break. But Dame Shân had a better grasp of his itinerary. During the year he was there 'quite a few times', she said. 'And he probably does a couple of visits to wherever, on the Friday or the Monday, and has Saturday and Sunday off to do whatever he wants to do. Whether it is hedging or planting trees. He has lots of receptions there for different sorts of groups and people, that sort of thing,' Dame Shân returned to the subject, and raised the annual event that others had cited as the hottest ticket in Wales Week. 'Because it had a wonderful barn' – there's the barn again – 'which he could then convert into somewhere where he could hold a large dinner. Well, large – I don't mean that large, but you could have fourteen people sitting down or you could have a reception and with what you and I would refer to as a mini concert, you know? And then a drink and some nibblies after. So everybody can mingle.' And the guest list? 'So you have gone from the sublime to the ridiculous, whether it is Bryn Terfel or whether it's – oh for goodness sake, what is our wonderful actor called…' I offer Michael Sheen, Matthew Rhys? 'No, no. He's very tall. Wonderful. Him, reading Dylan Thomas, is just amazing. Oh…!' Might she mean Owen Teale? 'Ah! Thank you so much!' Owen Teale is six foot two inches tall and a star of the TV series Game of Thrones. 'Owen came three years ago and Cerys Matthews. So it is a complete thing of Welsh culture and the arts. And that is what is so nice.'

Anecdote after anecdote extolled the charming appeal of the place, but I had yet to get near the gate for myself. A brief exchange of emails with the Prince of Wales's office enabled me to secure an invitation to what would be Charles's last engagement at his Welsh home as Prince of Wales.

My journey to Llwynywermod began in Treorchy. The palace press office had agreed that I could follow the Prince and the Duchess from their valleys walkabout to their next engagement in rural West Wales. They were to host an evening reception for invited guests, among them a string of ambassadors to the United Kingdom and the First Minister of Wales, Mark Drakeford. Students from the Royal Welsh College of Music and Drama were to serenade them, before the audience had time to mingle afterwards and, I assume, to meet their royal hosts. As I headed up the Rhondda valley I was overtaken in the sky above by the burgundy-coloured helicopter which had earlier delivered Charles and Camilla to the playing field behind Treorchy High Street. The crowd had dispersed by the time the pilot had set a new course for Llwynywermod, zipping above the terraced rows of miners' cottages and disappearing over the hills along the valley's edge. With no helicopter to transport me, I took the mountain road out of the Rhondda and went across country, skirting the edge of the Brecon Beacons and past the meeting point at Storey Arms where climbers begin their hikes up Pen-y-Fan. The countryside evolved from hilltop grassy plains to the tree-lined lanes of Carmarthenshire with its fences and farmyards, the thick greenery making way for bursts of village and town, chapel and church. After driving for over an hour I arrived at Myddfai, knowing I was a mile from the Prince's home but also far too early to turn up at the gate. There was nothing at Llwynywermod to entertain any early arrivals, so I parked in Myddfai where the village hall displayed a plaque above the door: 'Officially opened by Their Royal Highnesses The Prince of Wales and The Duchess of Cornwall, June 30th 2011'. It was a short trip down the hill to cut the ribbon, I supposed, but also a sign of the relationship that existed between neighbours. Attached to the hall was a village noticeboard carrying a babysitter's phone number. Notices from the community council advised passing readers that a tin of red paint had been successfully acquired to refresh the rather tired facade of the village phone box, which stood across the street from the church and was the smallest listed building in that corner of Carmarthenshire. Verges were to be trimmed, the council minutes noted, while a small card carried an advertisement for a carer, required to help an elderly woman with dementia to keep living at home.

Myddfai is the ideal sleepy neighbour for a Prince seeking privacy and discretion. The residents were privately consulted as Charles and Camilla acquired their home in Wales, and their welcoming indifference allowed a comfortable relationship to develop. The heir to the throne and the local population kept a respectful distance, yet there was a warmth between them that extended beyond the occasional ribbon-cutting at the village hall. Neighbouring farmers were invited to social events at Llwynywermod, while the enquiries of visiting journalists were largely shushed or turned away by villagers who were keen to keep schtum about what happened up the road. For a village which lost its pub and post office before the arrival of the Prince, the locals have mostly benefited from higher rental values for their holiday lets and a degree of feudal patronage. My watch told me it was late afternoon on a warm Wednesday, but it may as well have been midnight for all the human life on display in the village. The air was still and the absence of people appeared to be almost total until I drove out towards Llwynywermod, and on his hands and knees a man was applying small strokes of oily red paint to Myddfai's old phone box.

The entrance to the Prince's Welsh estate is so close to Myddfai that I had delayed setting off up the hill until I could arrive only a few minutes ahead of schedule. The pre-agreed rendezvous with the palace press officer was 6 pm, and I followed a discreet temporary sign from the main road that took me down a country lane, bearing right onto a farm track which was marked 'Private'. Thick hedgerows disguised anything that lay beyond the turning, but as my car followed the track around a short bend I saw a large farm outbuilding and four people waiting to meet any visitors: two plain-clothed detectives and two armed policemen, the kind who come with baseball caps and automatic weapons. The detectives, a man and a woman, were studying a phone screen as I pulled up and put my window down. 'I'm sorry,' the male detective warned, 'but I don't think my list is up to date.' I gave my name, and reached for my driving licence when a sigh of relief emerged from the detective scrolling the smartphone. 'I've got you – head round and park in the field.' There was a glow of early evening sun as I followed the track around the farm building and between a gap in the hedge. A slightly sloping meadow had been partly mowed to offer space for cars. It was surrounded by trees which were the last barrier to what sat behind them: Llwynywermod. The palace press officers had arrived just before me, and as I pulled up they asked me politely to stay where I was for half an hour. It would be another hour until the Prince and the Duchess would appear, they explained, and there really wasn't much to see or do before then.

As it happened, the countryside car park provided plenty of opportunities to observe the preparations for a royal event in rural Wales. As I sat in the car with the windows down, I could hear the students of the Royal College of Music and Drama in rehearsal over the hedgerow. An operatic aria drifted over the meadow as a succession of black cars began to arrive. These were the diplomatic limousines carrying ambassadors from Regents Park to rustic Carmarthenshire. A Welsh woman, who had been to Llwynywermod before, emerged from her car: 'It has been great fun watching the Court of St James trying to navigate the lanes of rural Wales!' A short while later a man with a mid-Atlantic drawl was heard opening a car door, before quickly saying, 'Oops, sorry, wrong Mercedes.' The meadow resembled the forecourt of a prestigious used car dealership, with chauffeurs exchanging tales of how long it took to get there from London and sympathising ahead of the long journey home. The absence of any mobile phone signal meant the drivers stood leaning against their gleaming vehicles in the Welsh evening sun, rather than hunched over their iPhones.

While the meadow car park provided its own entertainment, it was time to walk up the sloping path towards a gap in the hedge, and back down a short track on the other side to the doors of the great barn at Llwynywermod. The guests were gathering, and as I descended the path my phone pinged. A BBC News alert flashed across the screen: Boris Johnson's government was beginning to collapse; his Health Secretary and Chancellor had just resigned. As I glanced up, former First Minister Carwyn Jones was striding down the grassy path towards me. 'Have you heard?' he asked. It struck me that we were marooned from the outside world at this rural retreat, a reminder of why Charles chose Wales to escape, as much as to reaffirm his connections at events like these.

At the barn's open side door, Mr Jones was welcomed with a glass of champagne and entered a *Best of Wales* royal selection box. He was joined by the fashion designer Julien MacDonald, whose understated choice of sparkling black suit with its trim of green hexagons was in contrast to the sizzling haute couture that he has sculpted for Beyoncé, Kim Kardashian and Jennifer Lopez. Just behind the fashion designer, in conversation with some of the drama students who would shortly perform, was the tall actor Owen Teale. Welsh newsreader Lucy Owen was there to meet the Prince after shaking hands earlier at the royal opening of the new BBC Wales HQ in Cardiff, as was the chief executive of the Welsh language broadcaster S4C, Siân Doyle. Former Sony boss Howard Stringer stood in the cool shade, while Dame Shân Legge-Bourke helpfully arrived with a change of shoes, switching from driving pumps to party heels at the barn door. Dame Shân, as a former Lord-Lieutenant of Powys, has spent years jumping from farmyard to formalwear. She was once filmed by a BBC documentary crew getting changed in a local lay-by as the busy schedule of official engagements did not allow time to return home to Glanusk Park to switch outfits. In the Prince's barn the guest list leaned heavily towards the Welsh establishment: First Minister Mark Drakeford would sit at the Prince's side during the performance, while the Archbishop of Wales was in a jovial mood. There were other politicians and civil servants from Cardiff Bay.

Glances over shoulders would also reveal the head of the National Trust and a clutch of wealthy supporters of the Prince and the Royal Welsh College of Music and Drama. And then there were the ambassadors, a handful of men talking mostly to each other. In their own fields these guests had acquired seniority, respect and admiration. But in this barn in rural Wales they were in deference to their host, and as the time approached 7 pm there was a buzz of expectation before the Prince and the Duchess made their entrance.

One end of the barn had been arranged to stage the performance, with a piano and a few chairs in position. Coloured lights were shining across a simple backdrop. Small potted trees stood around the edge of the stage. There were seats with red and gold paisley-patterned cushions arranged twelve to a row, split in half by a centre aisle. There was a chair for every guest, with the first few rows reserved for Mark Drakeford and the diplomats. At 6.56 pm the showbiz stars and the ambassadors were seated and hushed, and in the courtyard the host photographer's camera clicked as Charles and Camilla walked the few steps from the farmhouse door at Llwynywermod to the great tithe barn next door. The Duchess had changed her outfit for the evening, while the Prince was guided by Grahame Davies to take his place in the front row alongside the First Minister. Members of the press were kept at the other end of the barn, able to watch the show over the heads of the VIPs.

What followed was a review show of music, comedy and drama; a *Britain's Got Talent* final where all the acts were from the same postcode and everybody won the grand prize. There were no red buzzers for the famous faces in the front row to cast a verdict on the quality of tonight's performance, but their presence and ongoing patronage granted the cast a shot at stardom that would equal any television contest. The acting student Joseph Reynolds was the one to 'begin at the beginning', reciting lines from Dylan Thomas's *Under Milk Wood*; the royal harpist, Alis Huws, performed as a graduate of RWCMD, followed by a trio of musicians on piano and a stunning soprano singing Schubert. At the back of the room there is a late arrival, the Chinese ambassador's chauffeur had presumably had more trouble than his diplomatic colleagues in navigating the lanes to the Prince's Welsh hideaway.

'Shakespeare is another love of our Royal President,' the small, printed programme noted. 'We offer a scene from *A Midsummer Night's Dream* tonight,' and it did so with college students in school uniform, the men becoming shirtless and racing down the aisle between the guests during the raucous crescendo. There was some poking fun at the VIPs as well, with actress Sophie Atherton performing a Victoria Wood monologue in which a team of amateur actors are being given notes on their rehearsal of *Hamlet*. Addressing the Duchess of Cornwall as 'Barbara – you will have to buckle down'. The Archbishop of Wales was next in her sights: 'Where's my ghost of Hamlet's father? Oh yes, what went wrong tonight, Betty?' Somebody in the audience guffawed. And then to focus on the Prince of Wales: 'Hamlet – drop the Geordie, David, it's not coming over. Your characterisation's reasonably good, David, but it's just far too gloomy.' The Prince's shoulders bobbed in the front row as he laughed along. Those around him laughed harder knowing he was amused, but there was little risk that this performance would provoke displeasure. The Prince enjoyed being the focus of the jokes at these little gatherings, and the college had fine-tuned the art of pushing the envelope without breaking boundaries. The press were kept at the back of the hall, so we judged the audience enjoyment by the shaking torsos and chuckles. But the palace's own photographer was allowed a sideways shot of the front row, and photographs released by the palace showed the prince's broad grin and crumpled eyelids as he was absorbed by the merriment of the college's performance.

Around forty minutes after it had begun, the show closed with a performance by the tenor Trystan Llŷr Griffiths, a graduate of the Royal Welsh College who was a Prince of Wales Scholar during his studies. All of the performers lined up along the makeshift stage to receive the Prince and the Duchess. 'It was fantastic,' Camilla utters in her low tone. 'Have you been here before?' The small talk is no more exciting than usual, the impact is just the same – those meeting the royals are fix-grinned, nervous, then gushing in their answers. The First Minister joined them to congratulate the students, as did a few of the diplomats. Behind them, the chairs were cleared and corks popped as the barn was reset for what some guests viewed as the highlight: the mingling.

When they first arrived, the invited crowd were

glancing sideways to assess the fame or fortune of their fellow guest. But now that the royal couple were in the room, each flash of eyes away from a conversation was to gauge the proximity of the Prince and the Duchess and to anticipate their own brief splash of small talk and smiles. Everybody gets a quick word, with Grahame Davies and others ensuring the couple have swept every inch of the barn before departing for the farmhouse.

The press were ushered out while the VIPs could linger in their mingling for another half an hour. During my stroll back to the meadow car park, one of the agency photographers wished aloud that they had been in Westminster chasing cabinet ministers instead.

The event at Llwynywermod, for all its fancy cars and sparkling wine, carried as much depth as a champagne saucer for the outside world and many of those in attendance. What was its purpose, and what tangible benefit was there to the guests and the Prince? The greatest advantage was surely given to those students of the Royal Welsh College of Music and Drama who produced and performed for the Prince, and continued a young tradition of entertaining their royal patron at his home. Much as the minstrels of medieval Wales earned their living among the wealthy and influential, the students get an audience, but also a more tangible benefit for them and their institution: some tuition fees covered by a royal scholarship, and opportunities that only a Prince can help to engineer. The diplomats came, presumably, because diplomatic relations depend on accepting invitations from the heir to the throne. Soft power is an immeasurable concept if there are no tangible outcomes. If the evening drinks and dramatic performances are facilitating new factories being built, or great performers getting agents and West End contracts, there was little public recognition of Charles's hand pulling the strings. And yet the court of the future King decamping to Carmarthenshire allowed Charles to enjoy the company of his closest Welsh friends, while giving a platform to new talent in front of influential eyes.

8

Playing Politics

'If this is the best British artists can produce then British art is lost. It is cold, mechanical, conceptual bullshit.' The Labour MP for Pontypridd, Kim Howells, had just thrown a hand grenade into the art establishment. Writing on a comment card at the end of the Turner Prize 2001 exhibition, Mr Howells returned to add a postscript. 'The attempts at contextualisation are particularly pathetic and symptomatic of a lack of conviction.'

What riled him further was the indignity of the placement of the notorious exhibition along the corridor from the beauty of Henry Moore's sculptures at Tate Britain. While previous Turner Prizes had produced Tracey Emin and Damien Hirst, the unmade bed and pickled animals had made way for an even more brash, awkward and edgy attempt at contemporary art. The shortlist that had infuriated Kim Howells included a billboard printed with the transcription of a porn film, while an actual film from another artist included a segment of retching in the dark. The eventual winner that year, Keith Tyson, produced striking colourful diagrams and already had a reputation for outlandish, radical ideas. Kim Howells conceded Keith could draw, he just wouldn't have crossed the road to get a better look. That 'conceptual bullshit' verdict exploded into the press, with Howells both lambasted for amateur punditry and praised for exposing the emperor's bare bottom.

It could have been awkward for him, as Howells was visiting the Turner Prize Exhibition while employed as a culture minister in Tony Blair's Labour government. Rather than a dressing down, he was allowed to take the credit and the blame for sending the world's best-known modern art prize into a spin. To his surprise, a letter arrived at the Department for Culture from the then Prince of Wales.

'He wrote me a long letter, saying: "Thank God there's somebody who has got a bit of sense, who realises that this stuff that's being produced is rubbish",' Kim Howells told me, paraphrasing the King's letter during a video call from his home in Pontypridd. On the wall over his left shoulder is a painting of an alpine mountain peak, a favourite subject of this trained artist turned minister of state.

Kim Howells studied at Hornsey College of Art where his far-left political inclinations were sharpened by a famous sit-in by students who were annoyed by changes to student union funds. They channelled their frustration into redesigning the art curriculum, and inspired similar sit-ins and protests at other art colleges throughout the United Kingdom in the late 1960s. As a disruptor of groupthink and establishment ideals, Kim Howells had the type of spirit that attracted Charles's sympathy when sections of the press had turned on his Turner Prize review.

If they were kindred spirits, the letter from the palace was still a surprise to Kim. 'Oh yeah, for God's sake. I'm from Penywaun!' Kim chuckled, his upbringing in the small community to the north of Aberdare making him an unusual target for the sympathies of a Prince. 'I had never had anything to do with the royal family.' That wasn't quite true, given the headlines Kim Howells had generated a year before his Turner Prize intervention. In an interview with *The Telegraph* he was reported to have said:

I've never understood the attraction of royalty... They're all a bit bonkers. Think of George III, they even made a film about it. They choose very strange partners, they're not managing the modern world very well.

I had to look up the story after speaking to Kim, but in our video call he remembered saying 'something dreadfully inflammatory like they were all bonkers'. If Charles had been aware of this previous put-down, he didn't let on. 'He never mentioned that,' Kim laughed.

When the letter arrived from Charles he wasn't surprised to read the Prince's views, but he was intrigued that the future King had taken the time to write to him at all. 'And then I heard off somebody else, maybe off Blair, who said to me, "Well, you know he does write letters," and so I wrote back to him.'

The men's correspondence continued, with both finding mutual ground in their distaste for some styles of contemporary art and architecture. Charles, Kim said, had been 'an arch reactionary' in his public comments on buildings, and this had appealed to him. The most famous of Charles's public put-downs came in his criticism of the proposed design of the new Sainsbury wing at the National Gallery in 1984 – 'a monstrous carbuncle on the face of a much-loved and elegant friend' – while he also scuppered a skyscraper planned in the City of London – 'yet another giant glass stump'. As many as three designs by the late Richard Rogers were panned by the Prince of Wales, although Rogers' design for the Senedd building in Cardiff Bay crept through without a critical comment from Charles.

This narrative echoed Kim Howells's approach to art and architecture. As a student, one of his interests had been architecture and building aerodynamics. He had begun to reject the idea that the problems of densely populated cities could be solved by raising mile-high buildings that pierced the clouds, despite having been a sympathetic moderniser until then. Reading Charles's public comments on architecture in the 1980s and 1990s had piqued Kim Howells's interest in the Prince of Wales, and the 'conceptual bullshit' of 2001 had united them. They were an establishment Statler and Waldorf, whose seemingly cantankerous opinions on modern design could be shared privately and written by hand.

'He sits down and he writes with a flourish,' Kim Howells said, defending Charles's notorious spidery hand. The broader criticism of his letter-writing to ministers at the time 'is kind of bullshit,' Kim Howells argues. 'All right, he sits down and he's got strong views about things. Good luck to him.'

Eventually the two men met in person when Howells was appointed a junior minister in the Foreign Office in the mid-2000s. They got on well during their discussions at the grand old buildings off Whitehall, not least because Charles was following the government's actions very closely. 'He would name ministers, and said to me, "I don't think he's right in the head, that guy!"' Kim Howells told me, though the exact target of Charles's criticism remained anonymous. 'I felt that he was somebody you could talk to who wasn't going to blow the gaff up, and so I was able to speak to him quite frankly.' It was a frankness that Charles appreciated, but in the end it was Kim's artistic expertise rather than any political attraction that bound them.

Charles invited Kim Howells to meet him in private at St James's Palace. 'Some army officer took me to this room and left me there. And I suddenly realised that I was sitting underneath a Monet. I wandered around, and there was an Augustus John. There was a Pissarro. This room must have been worth billions,' he told me. When Charles joined him, Kim offered: 'I've never seen that Monet before. "No," he said, "My grandmother bought that in Paris just before the Second World War," and the Queen Mother was a very, very astute collector of art,' Howells said.

Charles took Kim on a tour of some of the rooms at St James's Palace that were beyond the locations used for functions and events, with the Prince of Wales confiding in this Welsh politician the names of the artists and the artworks that he most enjoyed. 'And then he sent somebody in pantaloons off to get his own paintings. And he came back with this portfolio of watercolours and drawings. We spent a couple of sessions looking at those.' And did he tell the future King what he thought of his skill? 'Of course, of course!' There was no deliberate sweetening of the pill, though Kim Howells was treated less as an art advisor than a trusted critic with a shared philosophy.

The 'conceptual bullshit' comment that had first caused Charles to write to Kim Howells could easily have undone many other ministers. The Prince of Wales was writing to offer support and something of a sympathetic ear on a topic that Charles felt was important, though not politically controversial enough to embarrass either party had their correspondence been revealed at the time. Kim Howells's thick skin, and the culture minister's prerogative to have a little fun, meant the Turner Prize retained its reputation for controversy and the two men struck up a friendship that was embedded in their passions for art rather than politics.

The letter itself was not unusual, and touches the surface of a deeper interaction that Charles enjoyed with government ministers. There was a long-running fight by *The Guardian* to obtain the correspondence of the future King with Whitehall departments, and many letters were pulled from the archives and published in 2015. Their contents, on reaching the daylight of public scrutiny, were described as being underwhelming to the point of boredom. They seemed to be lacking in the frankness and political posturing. If anything, the letters to Welsh politicians seem to have been written in support of particular endeavours and issues, and don't appear to stray into overt or awkward lobbying. It was part of a pattern of correspondence that he repeated with another Welsh Labour cabinet minister.

From 2002 until 2010 Lord Peter Hain was a member of the cabinet under the premierships of Tony Blair and Gordon Brown. He was already a veteran activist; known for his anti-apartheid campaigning in the 1970s, he entered parliament as the MP for Neath in 1991 and was a popular and loyal Labour member of the House of Commons. As Secretary of State for Wales, Peter Hain had regular formal meetings with Charles as Prince of Wales which began with an introduction at Highgrove. The usual events followed during Wales Week, while the Welsh Secretary was on duty alongside Charles on official visits to the Senedd. 'You would also send him a report a couple of times a year, and then meet to discuss it,' Lord Hain recalled. But away from the formality of being Secretary of State for Wales, the two men bonded over their fondness for alternative medicines.

'I knew his interest in homeopathy, and so I volunteered that I was also interested,' Peter Hain told me. 'I took homeopathic treatments, not a lot of it, but I found it useful when I did. And I was particularly keen on alternative medicine. Not the kind of cranky stuff,' he added, 'but serious, mainstream alternative medicines. Whether it was nutrition, acupuncture, homeopathy, osteopathy or a chiropractor. The kind of thing which had recognised professional disciplines.'

Peter Hain had told Charles how he had used homeopathic remedies for malaria and yellow fever on ministerial visits to Africa, and how a herbalist had helped cure the shingles experienced by his private secretary when other medicines had been ineffective. Charles's public support for the practical use of alternative medicine stretched back to the early 1980s. In a speech on healthcare in 1982 he told the British Medical Association that 'today's unorthodoxy is probably going to be tomorrow's convention'. Alternative therapies did slowly gain more prominence in the decades that followed, though the medical establishment never properly embraced the possibilities that advocates of complementary medicines would trumpet. As the old-school heads of healthcare refused to give it much of a push beyond suggesting it was a no-harm last resort, there was little political will to drive the debate towards a more widespread promotion and prescription of the alternatives.

'You're the first government minister I have ever found a common identity with on this, a common agreement,' Lord Hain recalled. Their agreement on the need to give a greater push to alternative medicine found a focus when Hain became Northern Ireland secretary in conjunction with his cabinet seat representing Wales.

'This was in 2006 to 2007 when I was in charge of the whole place,' Hain said of his stint at the Northern Ireland office. 'It gave me the great opportunity to try out all sorts of – I thought – radical socialist policies. One of them was to provide half a dozen complementary medicines, medicine alternatives, to those GPs who wanted to participate in a pilot to provide it on the NHS. In other words, you could come to me as a GP with something like irritable bowel, or a bad back. And instead of conventional medical treatment with some sort of drugs or laxatives, in the case of bad digestion, what you could do is go on an entirely different diet with supplements and so on. And with something like homeopathy, too.'

Lord Hain said he allocated around £200,000 to enable GPs on the pilot scheme to offer complementary medicine to their patients, and he remains proud of its success. Charles, too, was impressed. 'He was fascinated by that, and tried to get the Welsh health minister, the Scottish health minister and the Secretary of State for health in my own cabinet to do the same. I suppose he had a champion, for the first time, in government for that kind of thing.'

Lord Hain wrote in his book *Outside In* that the case for complementary medicine was made around the cabinet table after the pilot in Northern Ireland, and that Tony Blair 'was interested and supportive', but another cabinet minister had called it a 'middle-class fetish'.

Charles had a particular soft spot for homeopathy, but over the years he promoted a broad spectrum of complementary therapies and diagnostic techniques. The shrugs of indifference became fewer during Charles's forty years of advocacy, as alternative medicines became easier to research and their proponents better organised in explaining their benefits.

'Neither of us were ever arguing that if you broke your leg, you should take a pill for it,' Lord Hain told me. 'Although arnica' – a diluted herb prescribed by homeopaths – 'can help recovery from a shock like that to your body. So it was always complementary, and certainly at the time we started discussions in 2002 it was pretty fringe stuff.' Homeopathy has had a 'very aggressive campaign against it over the last few years,' Lord Hain lamented. 'It was more benign at that stage. But the other complementary disciplines were seen as a bit whacky.'

Handwritten, personal letters were sent to Lord Hain to acknowledge the work he was doing to promote complementary medicines in Northern Ireland. During that time, both Lord Hain and his wife Elizabeth Haywood were invited to dine with Charles at Clarence House. And when Charles visited Northern Ireland they enjoyed 'a personal drinks session together' as well, Lord Hain said.

But the letter that Lord Hain treasures most is one he received after resigning from the cabinet in 2008. He stepped down from the two roles he had at the time – Welsh Secretary, and Work and Pensions Secretary – after the police were asked to investigate donations to his campaign to become deputy leader of the Labour Party. Twenty donations worth around £100,000 had failed to be properly declared in time, an administrative cock-up that led to no further action other than a period on the back benches. But the publicity had been intense, and Charles stepped in to support him.

'The media went mad about it, and I resigned to clear

my name. Which I did,' Lord Hain said. 'But he wrote me a really nice letter, a long letter over four or five pages, in which he seemed to intuitively understand that this was a lot of nonsense. He somehow saw through it. Perhaps because of his own experiences of being under attack by the media, and by certain politicians. I think he just saw through the fog, and realised that it was a complete Horlicks of a situation.'

Peter Hain told me he had 'never been a monarchist' but found a supporter in the future King. They got on very well, and Charles went out of his way to engage with Peter Hain personally and directly, and in a way which Lord Hain's officials told him had not happened with any of his predecessors.

Dame Shân Legge-Bourke said the King had a legendary reputation for keeping in touch with people. He is particularly thoughtful during difficult times, even to the point of surprising people with his attention. 'He will always make an effort, and take the trouble to either write a letter, or if they are ill he might go and visit them. It is all very private, the world and his wife doesn't know anything about it,' she said. Charles was 'very sensitive', Dame Shân emphasised. 'And very feeling. If the chips are down, then he will do his bit.'

Charles's relationship with Westminster MPs was well-known and well-managed. The mystery surrounding the letters, once revealed in their underwhelming glory, produced the picture of a Prince at ease in pushing the causes he backed, without causing constitutional chaos in the corridors of Whitehall.

If Charles had engineered smooth channels of communication with politicians in London, fresh excavations were required to Cardiff when Wales's new National Assembly was convened in 1999. The opening of a new debating chamber, filled with the representatives of Welsh communities, required not just allegiances with a new cohort of Welsh politicians but also an overt commitment by the monarchy to the new constitutional arrangements of the United Kingdom. How far the late Queen and her heir would go, and how large a role they would play in giving ceremonial dignity to the new institution in Cardiff Bay, was still being worked out. The people of Wales had only narrowly voted in favour of devolving some powers to the new Assembly in 1997, and its establishment in 1999 required the choreography of the state to help it take root.

It would need more than a good luck message. There would need to be a commitment to back the entire ethos of devolved politics. The closeness of the vote to establish devolved government in Cardiff was a concern, with more traditional right-leaning voters – the small-C conservatives – likely to continue to resist its existence and any future attempts at expanding its reach. They were also viewed as the element of the population who would be most supportive of the royal family, and may yield in their opposition to the new political system if the Queen was seen to support it. But that hope had to be balanced with the vocal republicanism that emerged from some of the newly elected members of the National Assembly, who felt this young institution deserved to be free from the medieval pageantry of a Westminster-style state opening.

It required the reformed republican Lord Dafydd Elis-Thomas to negotiate the role of the royals. As the first Llywydd, or Presiding Officer, he was the speaker of the new National Assembly and was consumed with anchoring its legitimacy in Welsh life and in the British constitutional structure.

Lord Elis-Thomas was well-versed in studying Welsh life, particularly the tendencies of those polarised by nationalism and republicanism. His gamble was that the largely younger republican voters would back the new National Assembly despite the Queen being invited to open it, whereas the older, sceptical monarchists would be more likely to accept the institution because it came with the sovereign's blessing. By ensuring that every parliamentary session included a royal opening and ad-hoc visits in the intervening period by the Prince of Wales, the National Assembly and subsequently the Welsh Parliament – Senedd Cymru – could rely on the commitment of the head of state to the newest democratic institution of the United Kingdom.

Lord Elis-Thomas prepared the ground for this commitment in a visit to the then Prince of Wales's Gloucestershire home. More than twenty years on, the political sensitivities of the time still echoed in Lord Elis-Thomas's re-telling of the meeting when I spoke to him about it at his home in Cardiff. Charles had been 'very keen to understand' how the monarchy could support the new National Assembly, he said. 'It was clearly inappropriate to describe either the head of state, or the future head of state, as supporters of devolution. But they were definitely supporters of the constitution. And definitely supporters of being part of a constitutional monarchy, and of believing in the importance of a democratic accountability and the role that the Royal Family, the head of state and future head of state, could have in relation to helping political figures to make constitutional change acceptable to the population because of it being democratically agreed.'

Charles took the Assembly seriously, and it rubbed off. 'Charles knew exactly what he was doing,' Dr Aled Eirug told me. He was a former advisor to the Presiding Officer and said the institution was acutely aware of the 'legitimacy' that the Prince of Wales gave to the institution. 'You've got to be able to appeal to people who might not otherwise have any truck with the Assembly or devolution. And I think the royal family is an important element in that. And I think the royal family understand their role, and their place in that.'

Lord Elis-Thomas knew that the Prince would support the National Assembly because it had received a democratic mandate, albeit a slim one. 'I think he understood very clearly the role of a constitutional monarchy in devolving democracy,' Lord Elis-Thomas said. Charles's interest in political changes within the Commonwealth were evidence that the monarchy could adapt and support the blossoming of new democratic life. Scotland, too, provided a reference point for Charles, where a parliament was being established after a much larger majority voted in favour of devolution. From Birkhall on the Balmoral estate, Charles sent a handwritten note to Lord Elis-Thomas – 'it wasn't one of those handwritten complaining letters' – which was a 'positive contribution' to the discussion about the royal role at the opening of the Assembly.

It was agreed rather quickly that there would be a 'royal' opening, a choice of words that was deliberately different to a 'state' opening. While the Queen would make a speech, it would not be The Queen's Speech, the Westminster event at which the monarch lists the plans of their government. The opening of the new National Assembly for Wales would be treated as a semi-state occasion. For the monarch this meant a day dress instead of ceremonial robes and jewels, and certainly no crown. The Duke of Edinburgh and the then Prince of Wales would wear lounge suits, and even the riders of the horses pulling the carriages would be in particular tunics to match the semi-state protocol surrounding the event. The extravagance of the procession to the new Assembly would be minimal, not least because of the rather drab surroundings of the temporary debating chamber.

The first National Assembly would meet in a red-brick building in Cardiff Bay called Crickhowell House. It had previously been home to the Welsh Combined Health Services Authority and was renovated to provide offices for the new assembly members and their staff. A debating chamber was squeezed into what was known as the computer room by the previous tenants. All around Crickhowell House, Cardiff Bay was a jungle of scaffolding and cement in 1999. The decades-long redevelopment of the docks was still in progress, and had yet to see the arrival of landmark structures such as the Wales Millennium Centre and the new Senedd building. The area was tidied up before the royal opening, and optimistic commentators hoped the cranes and hard-hats reinforced the idea that the Assembly and its surroundings represented a modernising, aspirational Wales.

On 27 May 1999 the Queen, the Duke of Edinburgh and the Prince of Wales arrived on the royal train at Cardiff Central station. With a schedule that seemed designed to dilute the political interaction of the ceremony itself, the royal party first attended a multi-faith celebration at Llandaff Cathedral, a site of religious worship in the Welsh capital for over 1,500 years. This was followed by a private lunch at the National Museum in Cardiff's civic centre. The artist Sir Kyffin Williams was seated to Charles's left for the occasion, his small frame and extra-large moustache visible on the brief glimpse given to photographers before the doors were closed.

Outside the museum's entrance, two rather ornate carriages were waiting, with their grey horses gently tended by their grooms. The carriages had arrived on the back of a lorry from the Royal Mews at Buckingham Palace, and now coachmen were preparing them for the procession from the city centre to Cardiff Bay once lunch was over. The carriages were the extent of the regal pageantry that had been agreed for this first royal opening of the Assembly. The open-top Ascot Landaus would carry the Queen and the Duke along the racecourse at Royal Ascot a month after their trip to Wales. Four of the Queen's favourite grey horses would pull her carriage: Twilight, Windhoek, St Patrick and King's Troop. In a second carriage sat the new Welsh First Secretary, Alun Michael, the Lord-Lieutenant of South Glamorgan, Sir Norman Lloyd-Edwards and the Lord Mayor of Cardiff, Russell Goodway.

It was a working day in Cardiff and crowds were sparse beyond the primary school classes and groups of royal enthusiasts who leant against the barriers. As the royal party trod a temporary red carpet down the museum's front steps, the TV commentator remarked that they were about to travel from 'old' Cardiff to 'new' Cardiff. The day's events until then had been preoccupied with the timeless formalities of religion and culture in block stone surroundings at Llandaff Cathedral and the National Museum. Fresh paint and wet cement awaited them in the Bay.

Crowds thinned almost completely at times during the short journey from Cardiff city centre to the regenerated docks, but in the busier areas they were present in sufficient volume and voice to reassure the politicians and the palace that a royal opening would make a difference. The day's itinerary had included a number of stops around the city, by different routes and modes of transport, to ensure as broad a geographic spread as possible and several opportunities for the average Cardiffian to spot a top-tier member of the royal family, if they had nothing more pressing to attend to.

As the carriages carrying the royal party arrived in the Bay and pulled in front of the new, temporary home of the National Assembly at Crickhowell House, the ITN correspondent Tim Rogers appeared in front of the camera to deliver a few lines to viewers of that night's ITV Evening News:

> Driven through the streets of Cardiff in an open carriage, this has been a day which has not been about ceremonials. It has, in fact, been a day of celebration. The last time the Queen, Prince Philip and Prince Charles attended a state occasion in Wales was for Prince Charles's investiture at Caernarfon Castle.

How different Wales had become by 1999. The biggest change since the investiture of 1969 had not been the Welsh attitude to monarchy, but how the Welsh had begun to see themselves. The population was swimming in self-confidence. The decade had conjured up Cool Cymru, an era that marked the rise of bands like Catatonia and Stereophonics, the resurrection of Tom Jones and the reclamation of what it meant to be Welsh. Even while accounting for lashings of branding behind the pop culture phenomenon, and a slim vote in favour of devolution, the late 1990s had become a time to celebrate Welsh identity. It was Shirley Bassey playing Glastonbury. It was Catherine Zeta-Jones marrying Michael Douglas. In 1999 it was opening the Welsh Assembly, but for some that was simply the warm-up for the Rugby World Cup in Cardiff in the autumn. As the horse-drawn carriages took the royal party down St Mary Street towards their destination, they had driven beneath the flags of all the nations that were sending teams to Cardiff for the rugby tournament. The opening of the Assembly could be considered part of the pre-match build-up.

The presence of the royal family at an era-defining moment in Wales was not a symbol of neo-colonialism or the overbearing arm of the state, but to witness and verify the constitutional development of a confident nation. Thirty years after the investiture of Charles as Prince of Wales there was no campaign to stop the royals turning up to open the Welsh Assembly, but neither was there a great surging desire that the Queen should come and validate this milestone. Instead, the monarch and her heir were in attendance almost as a decoration, one that allowed some grace and gilt-edged dignity to attach itself to the cement of a new political institution. After they were taken inside the converted computer room, the Queen, the Duke of Edinburgh and Charles, Prince of Wales, took their seats before sixty newly elected assembly members in their debating chamber.

The new speaker, the Llywydd, Lord Dafydd Elis-Thomas addressed the room. 'It is with humility and pride that we come together today at a defining moment in the history of Wales,' he said. 'The work has already begun, but it is a day of festivity today. A day to delight in the creation of a new democratic institution.'

The Queen followed him, with a narrative link between the construction site and the firmer foundation the

Assembly would create in Welsh life. 'On the eve of the Millennium this new Assembly extends a bridge into the future. It represents a beginning and an opportunity. It is a forum in which all the people of this ancient and noble land will, in the years to come, have both a more resonant democratic voice and a clearer expression of Welsh society and culture.'

Third to speak was Charles, in Welsh.

Mae hwn yn ddiwrnod hanesyddol i Gymru. Chi, drigain aelod cyntaf y Cynulliad, sy'n cael y fraint o greu hanes.

A translation provided by the palace said:

This is an historic day for Wales. To you, the sixty members of this Assembly, falls the honour of being pioneers.

In Welsh the Prince said they were making history. In English they were pioneers. They may have been fresh-faced in the Assembly, but many of the politicians sitting before him were from an older generation of the Welsh establishment. If Charles's role on opening day was to give this institution support, then it would also mark the cultivation of a new relationship with a political elite.

Some new members weren't too keen on making friends with royalty. 'It just looked so far away from our vision of what we were trying to create, when we were going around and knocking doors.' Leanne Wood watched the opening of the National Assembly in 1999 on television, but joined its ranks as the Plaid Cymru member for South Wales Central following the second Assembly election in 2003. She would later win the Rhondda constituency seat and lead her party, staying in the Senedd until losing her seat to Labour in 2021. She couldn't bear the presence of royalty at official openings in Cardiff Bay, and boycotted most of the events.

'It just felt sickening because, for me, devolution and creating an Assembly was about being able to do things differently. And here we were, copying the same system and doing the same fawning. I wanted no part of that,' Leanne Wood told me. One or two other members sympathised and kept away from the royal openings as well, but other well-known republicans among the Assembly members did not. This can be partly explained by the ambivalent position the political parties tend to take on the royal family, especially Plaid Cymru and Labour. Senedd members and MPs from both parties told me about respecting constituents, particularly older generations, who admired the royal family. It was easier to adopt the position that Plaid Cymru maintained during the investiture and provide no direct opposition to any formalities involving the Queen and the Prince of Wales. But Leanne Wood could not hold back. Around eighteen months after taking her seat in the Assembly, she became the first member to be expelled from the debating chamber after referring to the Queen as 'Mrs Windsor'. After refusing to withdraw the remark, she was ordered by Lord Elis-Thomas to withdraw herself from the day's proceedings.

Her use of the term 'Mrs Windsor' was rather innocuous. Instead of being part of an attack on monarchy, Leanne Wood dropped the wording into criticism of Westminster policy on national security. She had said: 'We are more at risk now than we have ever, ever been before and the measures outlined in Mrs Windsor's speech will not address this issue.' The remark was not immediately noticed by Lord Elis-Thomas, who was chairing the debate. But when a Labour member asked for the matter to be reviewed, Ms Wood was asked if she would withdraw Mrs Windsor from the record 'on grounds of discourtesy'. She was defiant, if a little baffled. 'I dispute the fact that it is discourteous, Presiding Officer,' she said. Lord Elis-Thomas told her it could not be disputed, as he had ruled it was discourteous. She was asked to leave for the rest of the day, and was joined by other Plaid Cymru members as she walked out of the chamber. Whether or not it was discourteous to refer to the Queen as 'Mrs Windsor' was a moot point. In a technical sense it was accurate – on her death certificate the Queen's surname was listed as Windsor. But there was tension in the early years of the Welsh Assembly about the ceremonial aspects of the royal openings that seemed to jar with its otherwise modern image. And for Leanne Wood, it boiled down to a quite fundamental disagreement with the idea that a royal family was required at all.

'I don't understand why a group of people from one family are put on such a pedestal by our society, because it doesn't really make sense,' she told me in an interview conducted before the Queen's death. An ideological opposition to monarchy can be assumed to develop over time, influenced by political ideals about the purity of democracy. But Leanne Wood had an encounter as a teenager which completely shaped her unforgiving attitude to the institution and reinforced her determination to actively resist royalty's grip on the young Welsh Assembly.

'I was fifteen years old, this was in 1987,' she told me, recalling how her local youth club in Penygraig in the Rhondda Valley had just acquired space in a renovated chapel building. 'A small group of us were asked if we could be made available to be involved in the official opening, and that Charles was coming along to do that.'

Leanne Wood had a conversation with one of the youth workers, who told her that she would be boycotting the event because she was a republican. 'I was quite intrigued by this concept. We had a discussion about it, and I agreed with everything she said. She talked about inherited wealth, the hereditary principle, and the unfairness in a democracy because of that. How can you strive for equality and socialist outlook if you supported an unelected monarchy? That made so much sense to me.' When she mentioned her plan to boycott the event at home, her grandmother was 'appalled'.

'I always took my grandmother very seriously and respected what she had to say. So that weighed quite heavily on me, and I had to balance that with the conversation I'd had with the youth worker.'

Leanne Wood eventually decided that she would go to

the event, and it was awkward. 'There were three or four of us who met him. And we just had nothing to say. It felt like a really forced conversation.' The Prince appeared to come from 'another planet', she said. 'At fifteen, we were working-class kids in the valleys. We had never heard of small talk, we didn't know what it was. And here we were, small-talking with this man and his entourage. It was just a really strange, weird experience. And it just confirmed to me that everything the youth worker had discussed with me had been true.'

In the type of environment where so many others claim the Prince excelled in putting people at their ease, it didn't work on Leanne Wood. For every tale told by a Lord-Lieutenant about his ability to win over the most committed critics, there must also be many more like Leanne Wood. It was a formative experience that shaped her decision not to attend any royal openings of the Senedd, though there was one occasion when she felt she had to be there.

'I stood for the leadership of Plaid Cymru in 2012. And I recognised as part of that, that attending that event is something that is the duty of a party leader, and I was representing more than just myself and my position on the monarchy then. I had to represent the party and the country. So I did attend the official opening in 2016. And that's the only time I have.' Through gritted teeth she watched as her colleagues bowed heads and beamed. It reminded her of the experience of watching the royal opening of the first National Assembly on television in 1999. 'Nothing had changed really,' she said. 'And watching people being sycophantic towards royals – it is not a good look.'

Leanne Wood is clear that she feels no personal animosity towards Charles. Her disagreement is with the system he represents. It is a system which Welsh republicans have found difficult to penetrate with arguments that focus on costs and on democratic ideals, when the attachment of the majority of the population is to an institution that cannot be quantified with either an economic benefit or a political value. The danger for republicans was that the more Charles involved himself in Welsh life, the more people liked him. Even those who had previously rebelled against his presence.

'I never thought I would meet him,' Dafydd Iwan told me. The former Plaid Cymru leader, who had sung 'Carlo' to campaign against the investiture in 1969, had been Charles's nemesis in those early days. 'I had avoided meeting him on several occasions,' Dafydd admitted. 'I was almost paranoid at one point because Prince Charles was appearing in places where I had been involved,' he laughed, and cited the official visit the Prince of Wales had made to projects such as the Welsh language learning centre at Nant Gwrtheyrn. 'There were a number of things that I was involved with that Prince Charles was taking an interest in, and turning up at them. But I was careful to make sure I was not there to meet him.' When Dafydd Iwan was a Gwynedd councillor, Charles had been to the area a couple of times and an invitation had been extended. But each time Dafydd declined: 'I managed to be somewhere else.'

Something changed in 2019. Dafydd Iwan was making a programme for the Welsh language broadcaster S4C about the fiftieth anniversary of the investiture of Charles as Prince of Wales. The team was halfway through making the programme when the producer asked Dafydd how he would feel if they asked the Prince if he wanted to meet his old adversary. 'After thinking about it, I thought, "Why not?"' Dafydd told me. Decades had passed since Dafydd was pitched against Charles in the public debate about the crowning of another English Prince of Wales in Caernarfon. Dafydd shared the common republican outlook that the role, rather than the person, was the target of any campaign to end the modern monarchy. But he had also witnessed a more febrile political atmosphere in Britain and America in recent years, and felt that a meeting with Charles may help to illustrate how a political cause can be championed without inflicting hatred on those who may disagree.

'It was a pretty nasty period in British politics,' Dafydd recalled. 'The right wing was strengthening, Brexit was in the air and Jo Cox had been killed in broad daylight by somebody who opposed her politics. I was genuinely sad about the state of British politics because of this hatred that was so obvious. It was very messy in Westminster, with a lot of hatred and shouting across the parties. And I thought that meeting Charles would show that my opposition to the royal family was not an opposition to the person. I have never hated Charles, I had no reason to hate him. I hate the whole organisation that he represents, but over the years I have felt very sympathetic to his position on a number of things. So I thought it was an opportunity to show that I can oppose somebody one hundred per cent, but it is no reason to hate somebody.'

When the question was asked of Charles's office, the answer came almost immediately: he would meet Dafydd Iwan. It would happen at Llwynywermod, and the camera would be allowed to film a brief welcome on the doorstep before Dafydd Iwan and Prince Charles sat down for tea. 'Very few conditions were made,' Dafydd said. 'Only the location, the time, and how long we would have.'

When the programme was broadcast, Dafydd Iwan was shown walking through the courtyard of Llwynywermod with Dr Grahame Davies, the Prince's closest advisor on Welsh affairs. As they reached the open door of the farmhouse, Dr Davies stepped back and out of the shadows of the hallway, Charles emerged with a broad smile. Their brief interaction as they shook hands was audible on the television feed.

Dafydd Iwan: *Shwmai*!
Charles: *Croeso*!
Dafydd: *Ry ni'n cwrdd o'r diwedd*. (We meet at last.)
Charles: *Diolch*.
Dafydd: It has been a long time.
Charles: I know it has, I know it has. You are a very good man to come, if I may say so.
Dafydd: No, no, it's all right.
Charles: I am pleased to see you, it's marvellous. OK, come in.

'We meet at last.' Four words that conveyed the relief that both men must have felt to finally shake hands. If anyone looked apprehensive, it was Prince Charles.

The camera remained outside as both men took comfortable seats. Charles led the discussion, asking Dafydd Iwan about the progress that had been made in strengthening the Welsh language. The subject of music education in schools came up, and 'what he felt passionately about was that the lack of teaching of music was a big loss, and there was not enough teaching of traditional things, such as crafts and music,' Dafydd told me as he recalled the conversation. Fifty years of his own cultural investment in Welsh life had paid off for the Prince, who impressed Dafydd with his knowledge of *Cerdd Dant*, a traditional type of Welsh singing seen at the Eisteddfod, and the strict metre form of poetry known as *cynghanedd*. 'He has made his mark, certainly, and I am not sure to what extent people are aware of that,' Dafydd said. Was the great campaigner, the reluctant adversary, now a fan of the Prince of Wales? 'I do not see the point of the royal family, and monarchy,' Dafydd said as he reinforced his core principle. 'But having someone in the job – well, he is better than many others.'

Some nationalists were disappointed that Dafydd Iwan chose to meet Charles. Perhaps they were worried that, as seems to have happened, the two men might get on well. Dafydd is pragmatic about the consequences. 'There were a lot of people on the extremes of the nationalist movement who felt I had betrayed some big principle, but I didn't see it like that. I saw it as an opportunity to say people are people, and this man is a perfectly pleasant, perfectly interesting person – albeit an eccentric one, and from a completely different background to myself.' Dafydd Iwan's decision to meet the Prince put to bed the pantomime image of one man's dislike of the other. The meeting provided hope for some in the nationalist movement that the Prince had listened and learned a great deal in the fifty years since his investiture. The stories of his understanding of Welsh culture meant that some regarded him, as Dafydd did, as perhaps the best man in a role they'd rather was made redundant. But if the nationalist antagonism was to soften at all, the biggest change in Charles would have to come after he became King. His decision as to whether to pass William the title of Prince of Wales would determine whether anything had changed at all.

The meeting with Dafydd Iwan was significant, but Charles's other interactions with politicians continued. They remained almost entirely uncontroversial, and the lack of gaffes or protests allowed friendships to develop with some of the prominent members of the devolved parliament in Cardiff Bay. One of the greatest relationships was formed between Charles and Dafydd Elis-Thomas, with both men eager to help the other with their shared interests in Welsh culture and traditional crafts. Lord Elis-Thomas had faced criticism from Plaid Cymru members for being so close to Charles, though in private he used the access he had gained to press the Prince about the future. 'I went to Highgrove for tea, and we had a discussion,' Lord Elis-Thomas told me when we met in his garden to discuss the then Prince of Wales. 'I had already told his office that I wanted to talk about...' he hesitated, then picked up again: 'I wanted to have an assurance from him that there wouldn't be another investiture in Caernarfon Castle. Ever. That was the point. So he was quite amused that I wanted to ask him that. "What did you think I would say?" he said, "Do you think that I would want to put William through what I had to go through?" And I said, "Thank you for saying that," and "end of story".'

The two men enjoyed a frankness in their discussions, even though they were very often on the same page. The shared interest came to be particularly useful when Lord Elis-Thomas left Plaid Cymru in 2016 and sat as an independent member of the Senedd during his last term in the Welsh parliament. In purgatory from his party, Lord Elis-Thomas found a home in the Labour government's cabinet the following year. In return for supporting the government's business, he would be the administration's culture minister. It was a job he excelled at, with his professional life having included stints on the Arts Council of Wales as well as interests in other cultural organisations. He was probably the best-informed culture minister of any Welsh government, a fact which instilled varying levels of fear and admiration in the state-sponsored organisations that depended on him for their funding. Soon after embarking on the role of culture minister, Lord Elis-Thomas focused on improving the visitor experience at Welsh castles. 'I even tried to get the slate plinth of the previous investiture removed,' he said, referring to Lord Snowdon's dais installed at Caernarfon in 1969. 'But then it was explained to me that this was now part of the fabric of the castle, and that couldn't happen. But of course [with] the description and presentation of the events that happened in Caernarfon, a lot has changed. And this is why my first action as a culture minister was to promote the castles as those of the Lords and Princes of Wales.'

Charles joined him on part of his efforts to reinterpret Welsh castles. On 5 July 2018 the two men met at Tretower Court and Castle in southern Powys. Although the castle is credited as being built in the twelfth century by the first of the Norman conquerors, the site is believed to have been home to an earlier Prince of Powys.

'Walking around there, we spent at least forty minutes just talking about history, talking about the buildings, talking about the gardens, because a lot of work has gone into the garden at Tretŵr, and he was very enthused by it all,' Lord Elis-Thomas said. Quickly, and without warning, the Prince stopped. 'He turned to me and said, "I want to tell you one thing, Lord Elis-Thomas. It's about this bridge".'

9

Bridging Two Nations

Every summer a field in Wales becomes home for one week to the pinnacle of Welsh culture. Around 150,000 people visit the National Eisteddfod as it sets up a temporary home of marquees and market stalls. It is a travelling showcase of the best traditional Welsh singing, dancing and drama, with a blustery pavilion awarding prizes to the most accomplished competitors. It was a rite of passage for countless Welsh performers, including the opera superstar Sir Bryn Terfel who credits winning first prize as a fifteen-year-old soloist with launching him into the concert halls of the world and collecting Grammy awards on his way around them. Almost everything at the Eisteddfod happens through the medium of Welsh, and the survival of the language owes much to the annual rituals of this cultural movement. Alongside the performance and competition, the Eisteddfod also acts as a stage for the hundreds of bards who, in their pseudo-druidic robes, represent the anointed elite of Welsh life. They congregate for colourful ceremonies to honour the summer's best competitors. These bards are not all poets, but an ever-increasing number of high achievers who are inducted annually into the Gorsedd.

The Gorsedd is the closest Wales has to an order of

chivalry, and it splits its members into three groups who are identifiable by the colour of their robes: white, green or blue. Rather like a form of medieval nobility, they parade around the grounds that surround the main Eisteddfod stage. They are unmissable in their bright robes, parting the deferential crowds and smiling for camera phones and TV crews. In dry weather the Gorsedd ceremonies take place outdoors, with the bards gathering at a stone circle to induct new members. These days the stones are fibreglass and follow the Eisteddfod on its annual August pilgrimage to patches of land in Anglesey, Abergavenny, Llandow or Llanrwst. Until 2005 traditional standing stones had been installed as part of an Eisteddfod visit, though they were often positioned away from the main field in nearby parks where they remain decades after the great festival's visit. Within the stone circles, swathes of Welsh society have been honoured with a colourful robe and a bardic name. While its origins are in the rituals of the ancient druids, the Gorsedd is a relatively modern invention of the eighteenth-century polymath Iolo Morganwg, and its members are more likely to be found sipping tea and eating Welsh cakes than waving joss sticks at Stonehenge.

Accomplished musicians and artists are usually found on this Welsh honours list, but its remit has broadened to those who have contributed to Welsh public life. In Wales, of course, that means rugby players as much as radio presenters. Very occasionally, the British establishment has been given a chance. At the 1946 Eisteddfod in Mountain Ash the Princess Elizabeth, not yet Queen, was inducted into the Gorsedd with green robes. Newsreel footage flashed 'THE PRINCESS: A WELSH BARD' and showed her surrounded by druids beneath a canopy of trees on an uncharacteristically dry day at the Eisteddfod. She is led to the Archdruid who stands atop a flat stone, the future monarch in deference to the Welsh literary elite. The clipped English voice-over explains that the princess will be known in bardic circles as *Elisabeth o Windsor*. 'A national gesture of homage from the people of Wales,' the voice-over purrs. She is given a headdress, helped by another robed member, but in the noisy cinemas of the nation one wonders if the grainy black-and-white film may have led some in Clacton or Cleethorpes to wonder if the future Queen had taken up holy orders instead. *The Times* carried a grainy photo of the occasion, alongside other notable images of the day including a successful atomic bomb test in the Pacific waters of the Bikini Atoll.

The Princess Elizabeth was already enjoying a life of boundless privilege, but being a member of the Gorsedd allowed her one more – the ability to attend future gatherings of the Gorsedd and to nominate new members. Awkwardly, from 2006 until her death, she was in effect excommunicated from the position following a rule change which states that all members of the Gorsedd must speak Welsh. Given his own grasp of the language, it is possible that Charles could yet follow in his mother's green-robed footsteps, although the reported republican leanings of the modern Gorsedd elite would doubtless discourage the idea.

While the Eisteddfod is promoted as a cultural oasis, the festival's site is also occupied with politics and debate. There are organised and ticketed events focused on history, architecture and science. Stalls host charities and public sector organisations with their posters and slogan-covered balloons, dotted among traders selling second-hand books, high-end craft and plastic tat. Lectures and debates occur on small stages dotted here and there. These lines of marquees are the stomping ground for Eisteddfod visitors, with many skipping the pavilion performances altogether for a few days of promenading and exchanging pleasantries with friends who they only ever see at the Eisteddfod. *'Wel, shwd ichi ers talwm?'* and *'lle chi'n aros?'* bounce from the lips of friends, colleagues and cousins as they reunite among the muddy duckboards and flapping canvas of the craft stalls. It is also the chance to discreetly do business, or simply to plant the seed of an idea with a potential collaborator.

In 2016 the Eisteddfod was visiting the market town of Abergavenny, an unusually urban and almost English setting for the event. While an Eisteddfod that is held in a Welsh-speaking heartland of the north or the west would produce a bumper return for the Eisteddfod accountants, its public funding and pastoral ambition to promote the language in less familiar territory sees it reach occasionally into areas where it remains rare to hear Welsh spoken outside the classroom. The site for the Abergavenny Eisteddfod was in the heart of the town, which made it impossible to miss and – the organisers hoped – never to be forgotten. The Secretary of State for

Wales, Alun Cairns, was there to make speeches and to visit some of the stalls. But he also saw a chance to develop an idea he had been mulling ahead of the Prince of Wales's seventieth birthday, which was some three years away. It was not the gift of a place in the Gorsedd, but of something far more tangible, permanent and controversial. Alun Cairns wanted to give the Prince of Wales the naming rights of the motorway bridge spanning the Severn Estuary, the gateway to South Wales and the newest, longest, tallest and widest structure linking the Welsh with the English. From the start of its construction in 1992 until now it had been known as the Second Severn Crossing, but Alun Cairns wanted to call it the Prince of Wales Bridge and he would get the idea rolling at the Eisteddfod.

'I had an informal conversation at the Eisteddfod with Grahame Davies,' Alun Cairns told me when he called for tea. We sat in a patch of sunlight in my back garden, as the pandemic rules prevented us from nipping indoors. I had recently discovered that we were almost neighbours in the rural Vale of Glamorgan. He had come to discuss his side of the story about how the newest crossing over the River Severn came to be named the Prince of Wales Bridge. 'I just said, What do you think would be the Prince's attitude if this suggestion was made?' Alun Cairns bobbed about on his rattan chair as he recalled his conversation with Dr Davies. It was a cautious approach, the questioner clearly apprehensive that his plan – already half formed – would be thwarted at this pivotal point. The caution of his initial approach to Grahame

Davies revealed itself afresh with a nervous chuckle as we spoke in the garden. 'That's how tentatively you sort of explore these things,' he half whispered. 'Because you don't want to embarrass anyone.'

Alun Cairns's first words to Grahame Davies may have been tentatively formed, but he had already done the groundwork. He had been inspired by the decision to rename London's new Crossrail railway line the Elizabeth Line in honour of the Queen, an act of construction so huge, so expensive and so disruptive to Londoners that asking Her Majesty to cut the ribbon on her own stretch of the underground may have lessened the awkward questions about budgets and timescales. The bridge over the River Severn had been open for twenty years, so there were no awkward moments about its construction to be smoothed over with a few ceremonials. Instead, the risk attached to the plan focused on the reaction of the Prince and the public. But at this early stage, the Secretary of State for Wales wanted to know if renaming the Second Severn Crossing for Charles would be possible in both practical and political terms. Mr Cairns's mission was to use the crossing over the Severn estuary as a symbol of what he saw as the Prince's role in bridging two nations, and he used this analogy as he looked for backers of the idea. He had a conversation with the prime minister at the time, Theresa May, and the transport secretary, Lord Patrick McLoughlin. They were 'supportive', Cairns told me. And so, as he spoke to Grahame Davies on the grass of the Eisteddfod in Abergavenny, he had developed a proposal that already had the backing of the UK government. Now it needed the support of the future King. Mr Cairns explained the proposal to Dr Davies, and said how the bridge could not only honour the Prince's service for Wales, but that it would also reinforce the literal link between the nations of the United Kingdom at a moment of acute concern about the small but loud independence movement in Wales.

Grahame Davies was non-committal in his first response, according to Alun Cairns. 'He said, "Mm, let me think about it".' And so their conversation continued on another topic, but as the two men closed their discussion Alun Cairns told me that Dr Davies himself returned to the subject of the bridge. 'At the end of the conversation he said, "Well, no, I think there *is* merit in exploring this".' Mr Cairns said the Prince's man repeated his own catchphrase: 'Bridging two nations'.

While one nation was on board, and the Prince was informed, the Welsh were still to be persuaded. In Cardiff the Labour Welsh government, political opponents of Alun Cairns' Conservatives, would be both suspicious of his motives and nervous of the public reaction to the plan. Mr Cairns was not a distant Westminster figure for ministers in the Welsh cabinet. Before winning his Vale of Glamorgan seat in the House of Commons in 2010, he sat in the Welsh parliament in Cardiff Bay. He was among the first group of members to be elected to the National Assembly for Wales when it was created in 1999. While he was a member he had witnessed the toe-curling reaction from ministers to his previous suggestions that Wales ought to celebrate its Prince with a little more fervour. Mr Cairns was more traditionally Conservative than others in his party, famously keeping a poster of Margaret Thatcher on his office wall. On one occasion it was said to have been swiped and held to ransom by the mischievous staff of his political opponents. His roots were not in the Tory establishment but in the working-class conservatism of a council house in Graigfelen near Swansea in south-west Wales. His first memories of monarchy were of celebrating the Silver Jubilee in 1977 when he was seven years old. The young Alun was so taken by the street parties and games at school that he recalled asking his parents 'When can we do this again?' He was forlorn to discover it would be in twenty-five years' time. 'It was fantastic. It was like Christmas Day in the summer. There were gifts for us children, and there were mugs and all the rest of it.'

His later encounters with the Prince when he was elected to the National Assembly gave him an insight into the impact Charles could have, as an individual and through ventures such as The Prince's Trust. It led him to seek broader recognition for the Prince of Wales in the Assembly chamber, but Mr Cairns said his attempts to encourage celebrations of the Prince's milestone anniversaries had been met with dismissive shrugs from Welsh Government ministers. What hope of gaining their support to rename the main bridge between England and Wales? By all accounts, it was a surprising suggestion from the Secretary of State.

At its most basic level the bridge was considered a reliable road route for trade and tourism, and on a symbolic level it was used regularly in marketing and TV ads to represent the gateway to Wales. Prince Charles had officially opened it in 1996, though he has cut ribbons on countless structures with no suggestion they would eventually be endowed with his title, and – in the case of the bridge – on a signpost and in letters so large that even the thickest fog would leave drivers in little doubt about which bridge they were driving over. Alun Cairns's idea was presented as an opportunity to offer a humble gift to an under-appreciated Prince, but the symbolism was almost too much for some in the Welsh Government. Almost.

'It was designed to lay a trap for me, I think,' Carwyn Jones told me. A trap that he 'didn't want to blunder into.' Mr Jones was First Minister and Leader of the Labour Party in Wales when Alun Cairns asked for his view on naming the bridge after the Prince of Wales. Ownership of the bridge was pretty clear – it remained the responsibility of the UK government in Westminster, and it could call the bridge whatever it liked. But unity between governments about the plan to rename the bridge was crucial if the idea would attract public support. The backing of Carwyn Jones would need to be secured before the plan was announced, because even the most optimistic royalist was anticipating a certain amount of push back, and not just from republicans. Grahame Davies knew this too, having agreed with Alun Cairns that any progress on the plan would require the Welsh Government's approval. The act of persuasion did not involve any deep constitutional or historical argument, this was not a barrister compelling a jury to make a decision based on the weight of the complex evidence presented to them. There was no killer argument to win over the doubters, nor was it a case of recruiting enough key characters to back the plan to trigger a tidal wave of approval. Instead, it was a means of persuasion which, Alun Cairns suggested, relied on the favourable light in which the Prince of Wales is generally held and the enjoyment which public officials take at being invited to ribbon-cutting royal events. It was a time for massaging egos, for leaning heavily on any fondness for cameras and canapés, for dangling a prize still pursued by so many: the company of the future King. But Alun Cairns knew that the trimmings may not be enough to persuade Carwyn Jones to stomach the main course, and so he personally lobbied the First Minister at the crucible of Welsh culture: the international rugby stadium.

'I raised it with Carwyn at the rugby,' Alun Cairns recalled. 'I was sitting next to him at the Principality Stadium and he sort of, yes, showed a bit of sympathy towards it.' Sympathy, but not yet the support the project required. Mr Cairns referred to his conversation at the Eisteddfod with Grahame Davies, 'clearly the First Minister will have to agree'. After the rugby match, a letter from the Wales Office was dispatched by the Secretary of State to the First Minister seeking his explicit approval for the anointment of the Prince of Wales Bridge. It was sent on 8 March 2017.

Dear Carwyn,

I have long been of the opinion that title [sic] of 'Second Severn Crossing' is not fitting for the main gateway to Wales from the South West.

You will be aware that the Severn River Crossings will be returning to public ownership in 2018, once the current operating concession comes to an end. The Crossings are vital pieces of the UK's infrastructure and together have united the people of Wales and England for 50 years.

At this time the Prince of Wales will also be celebrating 50 years [sic] since the title was bestowed on him by Her Majesty the Queen. To mark this occasion the UK Government therefore intends to rename the Second Severn Crossing the 'Prince of Wales Bridge' in honour of the significant contribution that the Prince of Wales has made to our nation.

I am sure you'll join me in welcoming this positive announcement.

Yours,

Alun

Rt Hon Alun Cairns MP

Secretary of State for Wales

Time passed, and the First Minister had not replied. Carwyn Jones remembered feeling uneasy. 'Well, it was the UK Government's idea,' he told me during a video call, 'particularly Alun Cairns, the Secretary of State.' Mr Jones moves about in his office chair, mimicking an excited Alun Cairns. 'You know, *"Let's call it the Prince of*

Wales Bridge!" And I was asked my view.' That it was Alun Cairns's original idea is not disputed, least of all by Mr Cairns. But the development of the idea into the bare minimum of an official ceremony and new signposts on the gantries above the carriageway required the full agreement of his political opponents in Cardiff Bay. And these men agreed on little. Mr Jones hadn't just been the political opposite of Alun Cairns but had been his electoral rival. Mr Jones's constituency seat of Bridgend sat within the South Wales West region, which Mr Cairns had represented on the benches of the National Assembly until his departure for the House of Commons. Both men had been among the first crop elected to the new Assembly after Wales's referendum to devolve some powers from Westminster in 1997. They had both matured into statesmen, Carwyn Jones becoming First Minister of Wales in 2009, and Alun Cairns securing a seat at the cabinet in Westminster as David Cameron's Secretary of State for Wales in 2016. The relationship between Jones and Cairns had developed from the day-to-day debate across the benches in Cardiff Bay to a sometimes bristling interaction as governments at either end of the M4 found reasons to poke and provoke the other. So, when I speak to Carwyn Jones, his answers about the bridge are initially short, shunting the responsibility back across the border. 'I said, It's your bridge, you can call it...' He stops himself. Then he continued by way of explanation: 'Because the bridge is actually owned and run by the UK government, not by us. It's your bridge, at the end of the day, it's up to you to name it.' On a matter of political responsibilities, Mr Jones is right. Even culturally, this may be true. As a proud Welshman driving home from England I don't feel I have reached Wales when I drive onto the bridge but, rather, when I have left it. And yet its gateway symbolism, and the potential push back from those who'd rather not use it to honour the Prince, meant this was a decision that always required Carwyn Jones's approval. And it had to come in writing.

On 24 September 2017 the Secretary of State wrote to the First Minister for a second time.

Dear Carwyn

Second Severn Crossing

You will recall that I wrote to you in February informing you of the UK Government's intention to rename the 'Second Severn Crossing' after it returns to public ownership in 2018.

Since then, my officials have been in close discussion with officials at St James' Palace to complete the necessary processes that will lead to the bridge being renamed the 'Prince of Wales Bridge'. I am confident that these are close to being completed.

As you know, I have long been of the opinion that the title of 'Second Severn Crossing' is not fitting for the main gateway to Wales from the South West and when we discussed that you were in agreement with the plans.

Our intention is to make the announcement early next year, the timing is significant because the Prince of Wales will be celebrating 60 years since the title was bestowed on him by Her Majesty the Queen.

Naturally, I want to ensure that the announcement has the full support of Welsh Government when it is made and that you will be involved in the formal renaming ceremony. My officials are happy to work with yours around handling.

I would be grateful if you could reply confirming that this decision has the full support of the Welsh government and indicate that you are content.

Yours,

Alun

Rt Hon Alun Cairns MP

Secretary of State for Wales

I put it to Alun Cairns that Carwyn Jones felt the letters, asking for his support, were a trap. 'Nonsense,' said Mr Cairns. 'He went for it, big-time. Even if he is saying that he couldn't say "no" now, that is almost a tacit apology for naming it the Prince of Wales Bridge, that wasn't his position.' Following the chat at the rugby match, and the letters, there was a second rugby match where the men had discussed the bridge. 'I spoke to him informally at two rugby occasions,' Mr Cairns told me, 'because he hadn't responded to the letter in the first instance. And I raised it at the second one, and I said Are you content? and he said, Well, I am not going to say no to that, am I? And I remember that. And it was warm.'

On 6 December 2017 there was a third letter from the Secretary of State to the First Minister of Wales.

Dear Carwyn,

SECOND SEVERN CROSSING

Earlier this year, I wrote outlining my plans to rename the 'Second Severn Crossing' as the 'Prince of Wales Bridge', in honour of the significant contribution that the Prince of Wales has made to our nation.

Following our informal discussion, when you expressed your support, we have been working with Palace officials on the details. Before we can take the next step, the Palace has asked for clarity that the Welsh Government supports this initiative. Your office was kind enough to signal that you had seen my earlier letter. However, I am now in a position where I need to be able to let the Palace have a clear steer. I do hope you will feel able to write back in supportive terms.

Yours,

Alun

Rt Hon Alun Cairns MP

Secretary of State for Wales

The first official response to renaming the bridge came from the First Minister later that day.

Dear Alun,

Thank you for your letter of 24 September regarding the renaming of the Second Severn Crossing as it passes into public ownership.

I welcome the idea to rename the crossing the Prince of Wales Bridge.

The Welsh Government will support the proposal and

I stand by to be involved in the formal renaming ceremony.

Yours sincerely
CARWYN JONES
Rt Hon Carwyn Jones AM
First Minister of Wales

Three letters, two rugby matches and months of quiet pestering had delivered the result that Alun Cairns desperately needed. The official backing of the Welsh Government meant his plan to rename the bridge could proceed beyond a grand ambition. Now that Carwyn Jones had not just consented but had 'welcomed' the idea, and encouraged a formal renaming ceremony, work could begin to prepare an announcement and stage a royal opening of the renamed bridge. Until this point, the very idea of renaming the bridge had remained secret. Or, as Alun Cairns put it to me: 'This was obviously highly, very private. There was just no public discussion or consideration over this at all.' But the long-awaited letter from the First Minister encouraged him. 'The letter smiles,' he told me, amused by Mr Jones's willingness to take part in the renaming event. 'The letter came back and it made me smile so much. Yes, I stand ready for any ceremonial event or occasion...' He breaks off, laughing.

While the Welsh Government's approval allowed the plan to go ahead, there was very little work to be done on any practical level. Even the most burdensome of bureaucracies would struggle to fill a filing cabinet with the paperwork needed to rename a bridge. 'I forget what the formalities were,' Alun Cairns said, pointedly. They certainly included asking the Queen for permission, a request which required only one letter and received a prompt reply from her private secretary to state that she was content with the idea. The focus quickly moved to the preparations to announce the plans to an unwitting public, and to prepare an event befitting the magnitude of the gesture. A simple unveiling of a plaque would not be enough. Baptising a royal name across the great span of the Second Severn Crossing would not be adequately accomplished by a sharp yank on a short length of golden rope and the parting of a set of miniature velvet curtains.

A person who was familiar with the early discussions in government about the ceremony said a 'potential option' was for the Prince of Wales to drive his Aston Martin sports car over the bridge from England to Wales to confirm the change of name. Aston Martin had announced in 2016 that it would open a new manufacturing centre in South Wales, and the government foresaw a golden photo opportunity as the vintage car sped along the tarmac above the Severn estuary. The source said the sight of the Prince driving his own car over the bridge would have achieved global attention for Wales, and an additional PR moment for the car manufacturer as it prepared to start building its cars on the Welsh side of the bridge. The idea was floated with Clarence House officials who 'were really up for it', the source said.

Work also took place to select the most appropriate symbol, an image representing the Prince of Wales, that would accompany the publicity around the opening ceremony. It would eventually be printed on the signposts which hang from gantries above either end of the bridge, and so the delicate work of choosing a royal symbol befitting the renamed structure began. Attention did not focus on the existing banner of Wales, with its proud dragon marching over green grass beneath a pure white sky. Nor were the Prince's three feathers deemed appropriate. Instead, officials descended a rabbit hole of ancient royal heraldry and emerged with a peculiar choice.

The official coat of arms of the Prince of Wales was designed for Charles in 1958. It is a grand and mostly golden motif, decorated with the picture-book animals that adorn so many official crests: lions, dragons, unicorns. They are the tools of ancient storytellers which have become the symbols of embedded power and hereditary mythology. Every ribbon and raised claw on the coat of arms carries meaning, the shape and colour all chosen by the College of Arms as a means of distinguishing who a person is and where they came from. In the great hereditary chain that spans the generations, the coats of arms are another link that binds the present-day royal family to their ancestors. Those who marry the Prince of Wales are also given their own coats of arms. These keep many of the characteristics of the Prince's badge on the left-hand side, with the wife's own ancestry illustrated on the right. Diana's coat of arms had the Prince's lion and crown alongside a griffin, while Camilla's keeps the lion and crown but has a blue boar on the right-hand side instead. All are flashy without being naff, detailed but dignified. Each coat of arms is new, yet the component parts are pulled from the vault of history. It is a form of medieval validation for modern changes to monarchy, be it a new wife or a new bridge. Every symbol links back to those who have gone before, and the ability to tie the symbolism of the renamed bridge to the ancient princes of Wales would become one of the only ways the current Prince could stomach the plan.

Choosing which of the Prince of Wales's symbols to stick on the bridge involved a trip to the College of Arms for one official from the Wales Office. There was a strong desire to choose a dragon, but the catalogue of princely dragons produced a surprisingly limited result. The only proper choice, the official was told, would thankfully bear a striking resemblance to the red dragon that flutters on the flag of Wales. But with one glaring difference: this ancient dragon must have a blue tongue. As the heraldry expert Peter O'Donoghue would later tell *WalesOnline*: 'It is the badge of the Prince of Wales. The blue tongue is just a contrasting colour so it stands out.' It was certainly prominent, and an unusual change to the traditional red dragon which surprised almost all except keen students of the College of Arms.

As well as the blue tongue, the dragon had a white collar around its neck. It represented the white label which the Prince of Wales would have worn around his arm, a heraldic symbol to state that he was heir to the throne. It is unfortunate that the pursuit of an historically accurate motif to represent the Prince of Wales would

274

result in the jarring image of a dragon, collared and blue-tongued. One cannot escape the impression that this is a Welsh dragon dominated by a greater power, tagged and choked. The blue-blooded applying a tourniquet to still the tongue of ancient Wales. And yet, in the way that cock-up rather than conspiracy lies behind countless calamities, the government officials believed that the choice was correct because they were acting on the advice of the College of Arms. Any dealings with royalty seem to provoke a chill of formality that freezes other considerations of taste and public perception.

The blue-tongued dragon had been chosen, and it would be unmissable at both the formal renaming of the bridge, and on the overhead signposts that would eventually be installed above the carriageway. A new name for the bridge, and a new dragon to perch above it, had now been selected and approved by the UK Government. It was time to tell the public.

'Severn Crossing to be named The Prince of Wales Bridge,' the press release announced in its headline. 'Welsh Secretary confirms renaming to mark the 60th anniversary of The Queen "creating" the Prince of Wales,' ran the sub-heading. It was Thursday 5 April 2018 and every news organisation in Wales had received the announcement from the UK Government, with its wording leaving no doubt that this was a unique honour being bestowed upon the current Prince of Wales. A point that was hammered home a few lines later: 'The renaming of the Second Severn Crossing, opened by Prince Charles in 1996, will mark The Prince of Wales' 70th birthday year, and will also mark the 60th anniversary of The Queen "creating" him The Prince of Wales at the closing ceremony of the British Empire and Commonwealth Games in Cardiff in 1958.' The press release's celebratory tone was dampened only by some awkward absences – there were no supportive quotes from the Welsh Government's First Minister, Carwyn Jones, and no official line from the palace to back the announcement, either. Were their remarks kept out by the dusty hand of protocol? In any event, their absence was not immediately noticeable as journalists turned to canvas opinion from another voice which had so far remained silent: the public.

At the national broadcaster, BBC Radio Wales, a producer fired out a tweet:

@BBCRadioWales
'What do you think of the new name?'
It was 6.36 am and the dawn scrollers quickly chipped back a reply.
'Total disgrace.'
'Has April Fools Day moved?'
'You don't allow swearing on the air, do you?'
It continued in a singular vein.
'Fawning colonial nonsense!'
'Terrible. The worst possible reflection of what modern Wales is supposed to be about. Horrendous.'

There were meme images too – a cat shaking its head, and a defecating rhinoceros. There must have been some supportive remarks, but they were not to be found among the gush of prickly posts on social media. The animosity seeped into other corners of the internet, with a petition against renaming the bridge attracting over 38,000 signatures in the days after the announcement.

In the mainstream media, morning radio discussed the plan with a mix of head-scratching and bemused analysis. Royal watchers joined Welsh cultural historians to discuss the new name, while presenters asked listeners to come up with better suggestions. There was palpable anger from the online public, in the comment sections below news articles and in social media reactions. But there was also an air of the ridiculous. The *Western Mail* columnist Carolyn Hitt appeared on Radio Wales that morning, and wrote in the paper a few days later that renaming the bridge had been an 'establishment fait-accompli', questioning what it said about 'how we perceive ourselves and how others perceive us, either side of the bridge'. The act of renaming the bridge was 'culturally tone-deaf', she wrote, while the lack of a public consultation with the Welsh people was 'utterly gobsmacking'. Ms Hitt was excoriating. 'They got the "agreement" of the Queen and Theresa May... and, we later discovered, the Welsh Government, but not us. What an insult.' Wales has a small professional media, certainly by comparison with Celtic neighbours. What are referred to as 'London papers' are more widely read in Wales than anything printed here, and the response of the *Western Mail* to the initial announcement is curious. It splashed the story on its front page on 5 April when the government's announcement was published, but its reporting was matter-of-fact and without controversy. It repeated the quotes from the UK government press release, contained no comment from either the Welsh Government or the palace, and nor did it state whether it had asked for any. Other than the main article that regurgitated the press release, no other mention was made in that edition. The leader article was about a shortfall in lottery money for good causes.

There was a noticeable silence from ministers in Cardiff Bay in the hours after the UK government's announcement. When pressed for a comment, a Welsh Government spokesman stated: 'Alun Cairns wrote to the FM about the naming of the bridge last year and we didn't raise any objections.' The FM, Carwyn Jones, hadn't just reserved his objections but had, eventually, offered his support. However, the letters between the First Minister and Alun Cairns that led to Mr Jones supporting the decision had yet to enter the public domain.

Alun Cairns had been worried about the social media response, and had expected a stream of negativity on Twitter. But he was disappointed that the media appeared to amplify those critical voices. 'We knew there was going to be a backlash,' he told me. The radio programmes punting for reaction touched a nerve. He disliked the 'tongue-in-cheek banter', which he said 'undermined the Prince's contribution to Wales, and support of Wales'.

He becomes animated, reminded of his anger at the time. 'It was after Boaty McBoatface. What would you call it? Phone in and tell us what you think, text in, which then became a bit silly,' he said. This approach 'perpetuated' the idea that it was a joke story, and undermined what Mr Cairns had hoped would be seen as a noble gesture for a benevolent prince. Broadcasters, notably the BBC and ITV, were behaving like 'campaigning groups', he said. While Mr Cairns attempted to ride out the negative publicity, some in the Welsh Government and among the Prince's staff couldn't help but squirm. I put it to Alun Cairns that the public and media reaction to the plan had derailed his planned narrative. How much did social media contribute to that? 'Oh, hugely. Hugely.' He cited the end of tolls on the bridge as being part of a broader celebration. 'All of these things coming together, bringing two nations together that the Prince has stood for. So this was the perfect solution. But it was completely undermined by political campaigners, by the First Minister's statement, and by broadcasters.'

If the Secretary of State hoped the negativity would subside after the first day, all expectation was dashed come the weekend. By Saturday the *Western Mail* had tapped the rich seam of online reaction. It filled its pages with commentary on the new name for the bridge. Carolyn Hitt's column took prominence, lamenting the short-sightedness of officials who, she felt, had been forewarned of the potential reaction when Cardiff's Millennium Stadium had been renamed the Principality Stadium. The sponsorship deal had prompted its own outburst of anger on social media from those who twitch at the use of the P-word in Wales. 'Public opinion had already been tested on the potential unpopularity of saddling a large Welsh architectural icon with an imperialist label,' she wrote. While the prose of its senior columnist caught the mood, the paper's letters page was devoted to the topic. Idris Rowlands from Llandeilo was 'disgusted'. Gwyn Hopkins from Llanelli said the 'English Establishment's... intention of ramming the Royal Family down our throats continues unabated'. Huw Beynon decried the 'addictive madness of wanting to name inanimate structures after people'. There were supporters among the correspondents, including Harry Thomas from Neath who said it was 'a dignified name for a magnificent structure which joins two nations with a longstanding "love-hate" relationship'. Margaret Sullivan was annoyed at the negative reaction. 'What on earth is wrong with people? They make a fuss about nothing. It's good for the bridge to have a name. He is our prince of Wales,' she wrote.

On page five, a more ominous headline gave a new angle. *Human rights expert finds bridge renaming 'troubling'*. This was not an argument in favour of protecting the Prince from being exposed to lingering resentment over the bridge's new name. Rather, the Reverend Canon Aled Edwards was calling for a consultation on whether the plan complied with equalities legislation in protecting the public 'from an overbearing state'. The Reverend was a former member of the Commission for Racial Equality and the Equalities and Human Rights Commission, the *Western Mail* reported, and it quoted a Facebook post from the Reverend Canon which outlined why he felt the renaming required an assessment, to ensure it would not cause offence under the 'race provision' of the UK's equalities legislation. 'Whatever our views concerning the appropriateness of calling it the Prince of Wales Bridge, the way in which the policy was announced should trouble all of us,' he wrote. 'Social media comments indicate an offence to individuals based overwhelmingly on their sense of national identity. Governments would do well to remember that "national origins" fall under the race provision in equalities legislation. This matter should have been put out to consultation and subjected to the appropriate equality assessments.' Reverend Edwards is highly regarded in Wales, a modern and compassionate churchman whose embracing of other faiths has seen him earn respect across political and cultural divides. Doubtless to some in favour of the plan, his words were reactive and over-egged. But, along with Carolyn Hitt, he gave a considered and thought through critique that pierced the social media squall.

The argument was fodder for columnists in the London press as well, whose commentary was more reductive. The journalist provocateur Rod Liddle, whose career began in South Wales, chose to rant in the *Sunday Times* at Welsh opponents of the renaming of the bridge. They'd 'prefer it to be called something indecipherable with no real vowels,' he wrote, and likened the bridge to an escape route that was 'linking their rain-sodden valleys with the First World'. The remarks did little to ease the perception that opponents in ivory towers had little concept of the clanger that had been dropped in the Severn Estuary.

Four days had passed since the renaming had been announced. Alun Cairns had given interviews in which he had been grilled about the conception, agreement and delivery of the plan (Carolyn Hitt said BBC presenter Felicity Evans 'couldn't have put Alun Cairns under more pressure if she'd held him by his ankles over the Severn Estuary'), and the Welsh Government had faced calls to explain its involvement. Signatories to the petition against the renaming climbed, and the opposition was picked up by the Press Association and syndicated to news websites and papers across the UK. And yet one voice remained conspicuous by its absence from the reaction: that of the Prince of Wales. It would be eighty-five days until the public heard his official response.

On 2 July 2018 the Prince of Wales began his annual Wales Week tour, and his first stop was just a few yards over the Welsh side of the border. He and the Duchess of Cornwall arrived at the bridge, not in his Aston Martin blazing along the fast lane, but driven cheerfully to the toll plaza on the Welsh side of the water. Grahame Davies was shadowing the couple as they were introduced to Alun Cairns, and were led to a line-up of highway workers. The workmen in their luminous jackets stood in the shade alongside the wall of a small office building at the edge of the carriageway. It was a warm, sunny day and the handful of reporters covering the visit were kept at the usual respectable distance from the Prince. A mocked-up version of a new road sign had been created, with the unusual blue-tongued dragon placed above the bold-type new name for the bridge. The Prince was not photographed with the sign, and there were no speeches at the roadside. Instead, the royal party and Alun Cairns took the road west to the city of Newport, where a ceremony to mark the renaming of the bridge was held in a marquee at the Celtic Manor Hotel. 'It is probably fair to say it took a lower key than it could have,' Alun Cairns recalled. And yet it still made quite an impression on those who turned up.

'It was a big ceremony,' Rob Osborne told me. He has seen a few. As ITV Wales's national correspondent, Rob Osborne has been part of the press pack on plenty of royal visits. 'It was at the Celtic Manor. But it wasn't in the main building, and it was absolutely boiling in there.' In photographs shared by the Wales Office, Rob is seen in suit and blue tie. Behind him is a rather posh marquee, the kind that is lined with cream curtains and adorned with chintzy lights. It has metal doors and a tarpaulin roof, gleaming white. It is a semi-permanent structure attached to one of the buildings set further away from the main hotel that dominates the hillside above the motorway. Journalists had been instructed to meet at the golf club. Some were nursing sore heads, having seen each other the night before at the Welsh language Tafwyl festival in Cardiff Castle.

And the guest list? 'All of the great and the good of Wales. It was him and her (the Prince and the Duchess),

Alun Cairns, Carwyn too. And that was where they unveiled the plaque,' Rob Osborne recalled. The unveiling was almost by-the-by. What the journalists wanted to hear were the Prince's remarks about the structure's new name, which stood twenty-five miles from where this official renaming ceremony was taking place. A senior UK civil servant involved in the renaming of the bridge, who spoke to me on condition of anonymity, said the geographic positioning of the event spoke for itself. 'He unveiled a new name for a bridge twenty-five miles from the bridge. And that says it all.'

Others agreed. 'I think it was pretty self-evident to anybody in that room that this was not his request,' Rob Osborne said. 'He didn't ask for this bridge to be renamed the Prince of Wales Bridge. He had to go along with it, he had no choice in the matter.'

The Prince and the Duchess stood patiently as children performed for them in the marquee. The Duchess cooled herself with a folding fan, the Prince's face reddened as the hospitality tent slowly cooked its guests. Alongside them were Alun Cairns and Carwyn Jones while, on stage, the event was being compered by the Reverend Canon Aled Edwards. He was the human rights expert who the *Western Mail* said had found the renaming 'troubling' just two months earlier. Reverend Edwards has a long tradition of being a moderator of debate, and a driver of consensus on controversial and polarising areas of public life. He told me he was at the bridge renaming ceremony in his role as a 'peacemaker'.

On stage, the Reverend's introductory remarks focused

on the Prince: 'It is my great privilege to invite you, sir, to come and to give your address. And I am sure we will all wait with anticipation for your words on this very special day.' The Prince's face visibly breaks into an exasperated half-smile, his head bows and shakes a little, before striding slowly to a lectern at the side of the stage.

'Secretary of State. First Minister. Ladies and gentlemen, *foneddigion a boneddigesau*.' The Prince glanced at the small, slightly sticky audience. The first of his seven hundred words were expressions of gratitude for the gathering, and a joke that the contingent from the west of England had helped boost the coffers of the Department of Transport by crossing the toll bridge to hear him speak. But the tone became serious, and the Prince's decades of diplomacy took hold of a script that was designed to change the narrative around the naming of the bridge. How does a Prince, so clearly uncomfortable with the occasion, ride this one out? The royal family have a reliable ally to turn to whenever modern discomforts arise: the past. In this case, he took his audience on a trip through history that began with the role of the River Severn as an ancient convenor of trade and ideas, and diverted to the impact Wales has had on him – and the princely footprints he feels he has followed.

Over all these years, whenever I have been in Wales, my soul has never ceased to be stirred, and moved, by the majesty of her landscapes, by the richness and poignancy of her history, by the beauty of her ancient and precious language – *yr Iaith Gymraeg*.

He spoke about Aberystwyth and Tedi Millward. He described the passion, tenacity and humour of the Welsh. And he laboured on the pride he felt at carrying the title of Prince of Wales.

> Wherever I go, I am acutely aware that to bear this name is the greatest possible honour.

And he turned to those who had gone before him, attempting to grip the discourse around the renaming ceremony to the degree that the melting spectators and those listening beyond the marquee could understand his interpretation of a situation where a bridge will now carry his title.

> I am mindful of how the title of Prince of Wales goes back to those great Welsh rulers, such as Llywelyn ap Gruffudd, whose memory is still rightly honoured by all who value a true understanding of our past.

'Those great Welsh rulers.' This was Charles, current Prince of Wales, placing himself in lineage but also in deference to Llywelyn *Ein Llyw Olaf,* the last native Prince. He also used the speech to discuss a passion project, the restoration of historic buildings around the ruined abbey at Strata Florida where Welsh princes are buried. If the imagery was not enough, the last two lines of the speech hammered the historical message.

> It is, therefore, my particular hope that the Crossing's new name will bring to mind all those who, over these

long centuries, have borne that ancient title 'Tywysogion Cymru' and the different traditions and heritages that they represent. Like the tributaries of the Severn, our different pasts meet in a shared present. In such a coming together, while never forgetting where we have come from, we can, I hope, each in our own way, contribute to a better future for all.

'*Tywysogion*' is the plural for Prince, and Charles was bringing all of them with him. Those in the audience got the message. Then – First Minister Carwyn Jones said his political opponents in Westminster had their grand plans scuppered by the Prince's speech. 'I think that they expected some kind of big event where he would accept the bridge being named after him,' Mr Jones told me. 'But he didn't see it that way. He had been well advised. And he saw it as, and accepted it as, the bridge being named after several princes. Not him particularly, not him as an individual, but several princes both post-Edward the first, and pre-Edward the first. Which was, I thought, a neat way of neutralising the controversy while at the same time not appearing to be, you know, unhappy at the bridge being named the Prince of Wales Bridge. It was a neat bit of diplomacy, I thought.' It was neat, and certainly neutralising.

The Reverend Edwards, listening from the side of the small stage, watched the Prince take the role of peacemaker. 'You sense that this was an individual who could understand a context and deliver to it. And what forces were at play to make that happen. It was noticeable. And I think somebody like me who is a first-language Welsh-speaker from Gwynedd with a deep sense of the wrong that was inflicted on Llywelyn Ein Llyw Olaf, it was significant.'

Rob Osborne got the message, too. 'He's clearly at pains to say, not literally these words, but this bridge is not named after me, Prince Charles.' Like the former First Minister, Rob also felt the neutralising force. 'This bridge is reflecting all of the Princes of Wales, that ancient name that goes back centuries, and I hope this is about all of those people, men – it will always be men – who came before me. Thereby acknowledging to everybody, whatever your view: please, guys, this ain't about me, this is about history.'

The Prince mentioned Tedi Millward by name, and those in the audience who knew the Prince's passions could hear those Aberystwyth tutorials emanating from the lectern. It was as if the radiation was seeping out following a 1960s experiment where a band of Aberystwyth intellectuals injected an English boy-prince with Welsh cultural values. I was told that the Prince had to be persuaded to lay it on thick in the speech, that there was some concern that the oozing Welsh context in which he placed himself would seem, well, a bit much. Yet this was a moment when words really mattered, when the public discourse around renaming the bridge had focused on colonial totems and establishment stitch-ups. The surge in the popularity of movements such as Yes Cymru meant discussions about modern Wales inevitably questioned our association with an ancient English monarchy. Despite the media hullaballoo and online abuse, this was the Prince's only public opportunity to place himself in an historical context, where he sits alongside all those centuries-old men who have held the same title: this isn't my bridge, it's ours.

Small-scale and neutralising, Alun Cairns knew the event would be different to what he had envisaged. Yet it must have been a moment of relief. The social media trolling of his plan had stung, the media focus on the backlash had scarred. His hopes for a more glamorous renaming ceremony had been dashed, yet the hot marquee had proved quite adequate for encouraging the royal guest's Welsh spirit to bubble. The Prince's words soothed some of the wounds that the past few months had inflicted and exposed, not just for Alun Cairns but for those close to him who had squirmed at the adverse reaction to his plan. When the Prince's speech had finished, the doors to the marquee were flung open and the cool air swept guests out onto the block paving. It was where Alun Cairns found himself being lined up to speak to Rob Osborne. The relief that the Secretary of State may have felt was in danger of being punctured again by the press.

That morning, ITV had published the results of an opinion poll which asked the public if they supported changing the name. Only 27% supported renaming it the Prince of Wales Bridge; 38% wanted it to keep the rather functional 'Second Severn Crossing'; 16% wanted it to be given another name and the rest didn't know. Rob Osborne had the results to hand when he began his interview with Alun Cairns. 'Sometimes you tell them what the poll results are in advance, but I thought, no, I'll tell him on the spot. See how he reacts.' Alun Cairns had a stock response which he deployed on several occasions when challenged about public attitudes to the bridge. He referred to an international study by the Welsh Government about Wales's brand, and 'how that was seen internationally', Mr Cairns told ITV. 'The Prince of Wales is one of the most prominent figures that points to Wales, and therefore I couldn't think, in this significant anniversary year, of a better title of someone bridging two communities in his seventieth birthday year,' he said.

In my garden, Alun Cairns is reaching the more satisfying stage of the story. 'When I drive over the Prince of Wales Bridge, I smile every time I do it,' he said, with a broad grin on his face. 'And that so-called controversy? That's just not even a footnote in history. But the bridge is there. And have you noticed the signs?' You would need to be reversing blindfold across the bridge to miss them. Alun Cairns confessed that their oversized presence was deliberate, gesturing their huge width as he recalled: 'After the controversy I said I want the biggest signs possible and that is why they are there. Power!' He laughs, but it is clear that the signs were the only serious tool available to show that the name really had been changed. 'That was basically in defiance of those political campaigners who tried to undermine what should have been a great celebration.'

In the week that the Prince of Wales attended the ceremony to rename the bridge, he went on to attend an exhibition in Cardiff that celebrated the relationship between Wales and Japan, and visited a shire horse farm in Pembrokeshire. A birthday cake was cut at Llandovery railway station to celebrate a significant anniversary, while a garden party was held to mark the seventieth anniversary of the NHS at the hospital named after its founder, Ysbyty Aneurin Bevan, in Ebbw Vale. The next stop was to Tretower Court, and after touring the castle and meeting staff, the Prince found himself with the culture minister, Lord Dafydd Elis-Thomas. 'A lot of work has gone into the garden at Tretŵr, and he was very enthused by it all.' Lord Elis-Thomas was telling me the story. 'It was during that visit that he turned to me and said, "I want to tell you one thing, Lord Elis-Thomas. It's about this bridge." Oh? I said. "I just want to let you know that I knew nothing about it. That I was not consulted".' Lord Elis-Thomas paused, raised both eyebrows at me as if to reinforce the significance of the anecdote, and then continued by recalling his reaction to the Prince. 'Well, they were taking your name in vain, sir, said I, or something like that. And we laughed. But he really wasn't happy at all.' I am confused at first. Given the reports of the Prince's self-deprecating humour and diplomatic experience, I wonder if Lord Elis-Thomas is over-egging the seriousness of the response. So I asked: he was serious, then? 'Oh yeah. And what he told me was, "Of course, I would have called it *Pont y Tywysogion*, wouldn't I?" Hmm. All of them. And that was the point.'

10

To be a King

At 3.10 pm on 8 September 2022 Charles became King. He was at Balmoral, where he had flown from Dumfries House that morning when the Queen's health appeared to be failing. Two days earlier she had appointed her fifteenth and final prime minister, Liz Truss, who would later lament the passing of 'the second Elizabethan age'. In the grief for his mother and the only monarch most of us had ever known, Charles would also be required to fulfil the destiny he was prescribed at birth. He had served as Prince of Wales for sixty-four years and forty-four days from the moment of the Queen's announcement at the Empire Games in 1958 until her death in Scotland. In that instant, Charles became King and the title of Prince of Wales was merged back into the Crown. It could only be created again at his discretion.

Despite the solemn, reflective tone of the television coverage that evening, there was a measured attempt to begin a discussion about whether the new King should use his power to give William the title of Prince of Wales. The debate was started by Lord Dafydd Elis-Thomas, who sat on the sofa for Welsh language rolling news coverage of the Queen's death. Asked what should happen to Charles's former title, he told the presenter: 'I think there needs to be a discussion in Wales regarding what should happen to the title Prince of Wales and what is the use of that title, especially since Wales has become a new democracy,' he said, and posed his own question: 'What sense does it make to have a Prince of Wales who has no constitutional function? But that is a matter for discussion.'

It felt like there would be time for the discussion. The immediate hours and days after the death of the Queen seemed too soon for a debate which would inevitably provoke strong views from those on both sides of the argument. Those who may have been inclined to raise the issue were briefing, privately, that it was best to keep a lid on the strength of feeling that may be stirred about the future use of the title by William, at least until the official period of mourning had passed. Lord Elis-Thomas was an outlier, at least on mainstream media. Beyond a few keyboard republicans on Twitter and Facebook, there was scant other analysis of the future of the Prince of Wales title. If the Welsh people were paying attention to events, they were more concerned with paying their own respects to the Queen while observing the curious ceremonial moments which were playing out on television. As Charles took on the role of monarch, most of us were still trying to comprehend that he was now called King Charles, a phrase previously only uttered in made-for-TV movies.

At 6.00 pm on Friday 9 September Charles made his first address to the nation as King. He was a son in mourning for his mother, and he appeared red-eyed and tired as he performed his first public duty as monarch. Charles was now King of the United Kingdom and fourteen other nations and territories. He spoke with a restrained passion, the emotion showing on his face but not in his delivery, as he paid tribute to his mother's sense of duty to her family and her country.

> I speak to you today with feelings of profound sorrow. Throughout her life, Her Majesty The Queen – my beloved Mother – was an inspiration and example to me and to all my family, and we owe her the most heartfelt debt any family can owe to their mother; for her love, affection, guidance, understanding and example.

In a speech which jutted from deep emotion to the conventions of creating a new monarch, the King added his own commitment to serve the country for the rest of his life.

> Queen Elizabeth was a life well lived; a promise with destiny kept and she is mourned most deeply in her passing. That promise of lifelong service I renew to you all today.

Then Charles turned to his sons, both of whom were caught in the great constitutional change that was occurring in the firm, as well as being captured by grief at the death of their grandmother. William, he said, would assume his Scottish titles and take on the Duchy of Cornwall. These had happened automatically at the moment that Charles had inherited the throne. Then he turned to the one title that was in his gift to confer on his heir.

> Today, I am proud to create him Prince of Wales, Tywysog Cymru, the country whose title I have been so greatly privileged to bear during so much of my life and duty. With Catherine beside him, our new Prince and Princess of Wales will, I know, continue to inspire and lead our national conversations, helping to bring the marginal to the centre ground where vital help can be given.

Swift and surprising, the King's creation of William as Prince of Wales came almost without warning. The Welsh Government's First Minister, Mark Drakeford, said he had been unaware of the planned announcement; a government source let it be known that the palace had called as a courtesy a short time before. In his public statement in response to the announcement, Mr Drakeford said that Charles had 'enjoyed a long and enduring friendship with Wales,' and said the nation 'looked forward to deepening our relationship with the new Prince and Princess.'

Other Welsh party leaders chipped in with their reactions to the news. Plaid Cymru leader Adam Price, speaking for a party brimming with republicans, sought to balance the public mood with his politics. 'There will be time, in due course, for a public debate surrounding the title of the Prince of Wales,' he said. He had surely been hoping that there would have been time for that debate to occur before William was handed the title. 'It is Plaid Cymru's long-held view that it should be the people's democratic right to have a final say on this matter in an independent Wales,' Mr Price added. His predecessor as Plaid Cymru leader, Leanne Wood, put her party's position more simply: 'Wales has no need for a prince.'

For the Welsh Conservatives, the position was also clear-cut. 'A profound, moving address by His Majesty King Charles III,' was the observation of Andrew R.T. Davies, who led the Tories in the Senedd. 'We join him in thanks to Her Late Majesty. And we welcome the new Prince and Princess of Wales. God Save the King.'

Following the King's broadcast, the Press Association reported the comments of a source 'close to the Waleses':

> The couple are focused on deepening the trust and respect of the people of Wales over time. The Prince and Princess of Wales will approach their roles in the modest and humble way they've approached their work previously. The new Princess of Wales appreciates the history associated with this role but will understandably want to look to the future as she creates her own path.

In Wales, the creation of William as the new Prince of Wales was the potential flashpoint, yet the palace PR clearly felt the ghost of Diana could be a more troubling arrival. The speed with which the King created a new Prince of Wales succeeded in stifling most debate about the subject. Concerns about the indignity of a furious political discussion quelled most urges to resist, coupled with a news cycle that was otherwise filled with tributes to the late Queen and the formal events to manage the transition to a new head of state. The moment in history when the monarchy was without a Prince of Wales was the golden opportunity for those who were opposed to its creation. And yet the timing meant that it was an opportunity lost to the formalities of public mourning, and a period of time when the momentum lay with the Crown. This was cultural key-hole surgery, a transplant for which the Welsh public need not be woken from their anaesthesia.

Amid the mourning and the gratitude for the Queen's long reign, there were some practicalities. The Royal Mail had to announce that stamps bearing the image of the Queen remained valid following the accession of Charles to the throne, while the Welsh mezzo-soprano Katherine Jenkins recorded God Save the King in order for it to be played out on BBC Radio 4. She had been with a production team in a small church in Sussex when the BBC rang to ask if she would record the anthem. The crew held a moment's silence, and Katherine said she prayed for the late Queen and the new King. When the anthem was sung, she said it was performed 'in the belief that King Charles III's reign will be happy and glorious'.

Beyond the political, the Welsh public mood at the Queen's passing was perhaps better reflected by Welsh royalty. Sir Tom Jones described her as 'a reassuring force in difficult times, her dedication was faultless and her commitment to duty unrivalled'. Dame Shirley Bassey praised the 'unstoppable force' of the late Queen, while Catherine Zeta-Jones addressed her with a hint of Hollywood melodrama, writing online that 'you have been and always will be close to my humble heart as it breaks today'.

The King's address was also praised by the *Western Mail* leader writer, who said Charles 'struck the right note as he paid a thoroughly deserved tribute to his late mother'. The paper was lukewarm about the creation of a new Prince of Wales, stating that there was 'a need for clarity' about what William would do in the role. 'We wish the King and the Prince well as they begin their new duties,' it ended.

Generous observers suggested that the King's agenda in creating a new Prince of Wales appeared to be less about shock and awe, and more to do with a desire for quiet continuity. In practical terms there was not the time to drag the process out. Lord Dafydd Elis-Thomas was one of the few to predict a swift succession for the Prince of Wales title when I spoke to him a few months beforehand. He told me that he expected Charles 'to choose an opportunity very early on to indicate the succession of the title of Prince of Wales'. His expectation was that there would be 'a big coming-out party at Cardiff Castle. And those who want to, can come, and the others can stay at home'.

Cardiff Castle would play its part, though not immediately for William. A week after his television address, Charles visited Wales as part of the formal tour of the United Kingdom that accompanied his accession. A small group of protesters did achieve publicity at the castle gates, chanting their opposition both to the presence of the King and the creation of a new Prince of Wales. But, on the streets of Cardiff and in the opinion polls, the republicans were in the minority. Thousands of others had stood outside the castle, and queued to get within the grounds, to witness the arrival of the King and his consort in the glorious September sunshine.

With cameras in position, the King's visit was broadcast around the world. I stood on a television gantry, which gave me an elevated view of both the royal arrival and the crowd that greeted them. It was a surprisingly diverse group, with more younger people who skewed the age demographic a little lower than the usual royal walkabout crowds. Charles and Camilla were received warmly, with no hint of dissenting noise from those who had secured a spot within the castle grounds. Their visit included audiences with the First Minister, Mark Drakeford, and the Llywydd of the Senedd, Elin Jones, inside the Victorian gothic state apartments. Around half an hour later the King and Queen Consort met representatives from Welsh organisations that were close to Charles. They included a delegation from Aberfan.

A couple of days before the visit to Cardiff Castle the phone had rung in Gloria Davies's living room. She didn't recognise the number. 'I thought it must be a scam, so I let it go to answerphone,' she told me. When she listened back, it was an official from the Welsh Government's civil service. 'They were inviting fifteen of the Aberfan Wives group to the reception at Cardiff Castle.' She was floored by the message. She began making arrangements, quickly calling the group and working out how many would be able to attend. A minibus was booked. Black mourning clothes were pulled from the wardrobes, and two days later the women stood in a group to meet Charles as their King. Alongside them were representatives of the Royal Welsh College of Music and Drama, as well as the charities and organisations he had backed as Prince of Wales. For a man who had spent decades cultivating his Welsh connections, this was the King showing continuity. Most of those in the room accepted that the relationship would now be different, and that the demands on the monarch would probably mean less focused attention from his office in future. For those that saw a benefit in the role of the Prince of Wales, there was a lingering hope that William would now step into his father's shoes.

11

William of Wales

When William made his first visit to Wales, the Gulf War was wrapping up. It was St David's Day 1991 and the sight of an eight-year-old in a double-breasted blazer was enough to encourage hundreds to line the roads around the centre of Cardiff. William was in the Welsh capital with Charles and his mother, Diana, Princess of Wales, on an outing that would be his first taste of the officialdom and spectacle of a royal visit. After attending a service at Llandaff Cathedral on the edge of town, the focus turned to the launch of a marketing campaign to promote Cardiff as destination for trade and tourism. With a daffodil pinned to his brass-buttoned jacket, William followed his mother's lead in giving cheerful handshakes to the men in suits who lined the lobbies.

In the concrete confines of St David's Hall a small boy handed Diana a bouquet of daffodils. 'Simon's daddy is in the Gulf,' the Lord-Lieutenant, Sir Norman Lloyd-Edwards, said to William. 'He's in the Welsh Guards.' Diana stepped forward to briefly speak to the little boy's mother, their almost-audible chat focused on whether the military wife knew the whereabouts of her Welsh Guard. William stood with the awkwardness of a child dressed as a bank manager. Whatever rehearsals he had undertaken, this was a Prince who could perform. Even as his mother spoke on stage about the business opportunities that Cardiff presented to European investors, William remained undistracted. By the time two men in SuperTed and Spotty costumes appeared on stage to hand William a videotape of the Welsh cartoon show, the Prince had relaxed into a smile that would send press photographs around the world. The walkabout along the street outside was a classic of its type, with the royals allowing the schedule to slip in order to shake just a few more hands before the visit ended.

Sir Norman Lloyd-Edwards recalled how the visit had evolved from a Diana event to the family affair. 'First of all, Diana was coming,' he told me. 'And then Diana decided to bring William on his first ever public engagement, aged eight. So we had to re-print the order of service to include his photograph as well. And then Charles heard that she was coming and bringing William, and he was furious. He said, "For his first visit to Wales, I should be with him," and he said, "Well, I'm coming as well".' The public event was formal and rehearsed; the Windsor melodrama of the early 1990s remained private.

If his brother, Harry, balked at the royal family business model, William was a willing apprentice. From birth he was Prince William of Wales, but the prospect of following his father into the title of Prince of Wales remained a distant concept while the Queen displayed stoic longevity. William's relationship with Wales would be confined to official visits as a child, but his posting to

Anglesey as a search and rescue pilot in his late twenties would equip him with a far deeper understanding of Welsh life than his father achieved during his term at Aberystwyth.

On Anglesey, William and Kate lived in a house on the Newborough estate on the western, rural side of the island. While William flew missions around the Welsh hills and the Irish Sea, Kate was spotted popping into the shops in Llangefni and Menai Bridge.

'I remember seeing Kate shopping in Waitrose in Menai Bridge,' Mark Baker recalled. The conservationist who saved Gwrych Castle is well-connected in North Wales. 'Out of summer season it was pretty dead, so she just blended in with the locals. And William's work with the RAF just embedded him with the local population.' The couple also 'went out and enjoyed themselves,' he said, though he stopped short of providing further details and added his own concern that the couple were facing relentless scrutiny.

The island offered a secluded, private home for the couple. Their rented property immersed the couple in the stunning scenery, with views out to sea and a short walk to the beach. It was their home at the time of their wedding in 2012 and it was where Kate brought Prince George after he was born. The picture of the perfect retreat is easy to conjure, but the reality was a little less romantic. On a visit to a children's centre in Cardiff in 2020 Kate recalled the isolation of parenthood in those months spent with baby George on Anglesey.

I had just had George, and William was still working with search and rescue, so we came up here when George was a tiny, tiny little baby, in the middle of Anglesey. It was so isolated, so cut off, I didn't have my family around me, he was doing night shifts, so if only I'd had a centre like this at a certain time.

Anglesey was an anchor for the young family, a place that defined their early life together and one they could safely return to when their titles demanded more commitment to Wales. The narrative of their time on the island meant it was chosen as the first stop on the itinerary of the new Prince and Princess of Wales when they visited the country a few weeks after the Queen's death. There were no protests on this visit, partly because of the controlled nature of their trip to Holyhead in the morning and, by helicopter, to Swansea in the afternoon. There were no big walkabouts; the couple took the opportunity to engage directly with charities and to be seen to take an interest. There were moments for the cameras with children clutching bouquets, but this was a gentle re-introduction to the Welsh. Smiles seemed genuine, and the affectionate reception came as no surprise to those who had previously seen them in action.

Lord Peter Hain, the former Labour Secretary of State for Wales, said William had been 'very warmly received' at Welsh rugby union games where he had been present. 'People like him. He has got a very modern, engaging manner. More so than his dad.' The generational difference may play to William's advantage, Lord Hain suggested. 'William can talk about anything in anybody's language. I think he will be very popular.' It's a popularity which the former Conservative Secretary of State, Alun Cairns, hoped would override the megaphone of social media. 'I would hope that the palace would take confidence in the scale of events around Prince William's marriage, the wedding of Prince Harry, and the various jubilees that have taken place. The nation gets behind them, even when social media doesn't.'

Opinion polls conducted after William was created Prince of Wales confirmed his popularity. ITV and YouGov asked over a thousand Welsh people:

> Now King Charles has become King, the title Prince of Wales has been given to Prince William. Do you support or oppose Prince William being titled Prince of Wales?
> 66% Support
> 22% Oppose
> 12% Don't know

The opinion poll also showed that the public viewed William more favourably than his father.

> 75% said they had a favourable opinion of the new Prince of Wales, compared with 62% holding a favourable opinion of King Charles — ITV Wales / YouGov

William may yet carve out a distinctive identity as Prince of Wales, even if the comfort blanket of his father's Welsh interests support his first years in the role. The conservationist Mark Baker told me that every Prince of Wales had been different, and that the role ought to continue to be treated like a 'minister without portfolio'. Charles had used the role to focus on conservation and patronage, but the new Prince of Wales may have a more practical, less philosophical approach. 'I think William will be more about the landscape, the outdoors, national parks and things like that,' Baker said.

Rob Osborne said the royal family should have been preparing behind the scenes. Speaking to me before the Queen's death, he posed a question. 'If I were Prince William, I'd be saying: Look, we're at a time now when the union is straining in the four parts of it. What should I be doing? Is he, behind the scenes, really learning Welsh right now? Because if he could come out and make a big Welsh speech, that would be fascinating, interesting. And is Prince George, who is young and will possibly, one day, be the Prince of Wales? Is he learning Welsh? Not that we know of. He might be.' Learning the language would show, Rob argued, that they had learned the lessons that allowed Charles to break through with many of his natural opponents in Wales. It would show the royal family 'to be more ingrained with modern Welsh culture'.

William has a 'huge advantage' compared to his father, according to Justin Albert. 'He is not coming into Wales in the late 1960s and all the strife we had then. The climate crisis is the biggest thing that's coming down on us, and the royal family can help.' Justin Albert sees hope in William's leadership on climate, and how he could promote Welsh achievements in conservation and protecting the environment. 'William is leading on that, with Charles. And we need them both. We need all of them fighting for this.'

Charles earned many plaudits by learning Welsh, and when he spoke he did so quite fluently. He has a love of the language which lifts the soul of those Welsh-speakers who see him as an advocate and an ally for the ongoing campaign to boost the numbers who speak it. The Welsh Government wants one million people to be able to speak Welsh by 2050, and it has backed more opportunities to learn Welsh. There has also been a marked shift in the attitudes of first-language Welsh-speakers towards those who are learning the language. There is now far more encouragement, whereas previously many would have switched to English at the prospect of a conversation with someone who was struggling over their grammatical mutations. In 2021 the language learning app DuoLingo reported that 1.62 million people were learning Welsh through their technology. While William, and Prince George, may yet embrace the Welsh language, they won't have to incubate themselves in the language laboratory at Aberystwyth to get up to the King's standard. Justin Albert hopes that William will 'show that same respect for our culture, our music, that Charles so obviously loves. A genuine love of the culture'.

William's visit to Anglesey as Prince of Wales was followed six weeks later by a first trip to the Senedd. He would meet some of the members who had been critical of the speed at which Charles had created him Prince of Wales, but the trip to Cardiff Bay came with a palace briefing that stated how William wanted to show respect to the institution. Part of that respect came in an off-the-record confirmation to journalists that an investiture ceremony would not be taking place, a move that the palace hoped would settle the matter and allow William's relationship to be built without recurring awkward questions. At the Senedd the new Prince of Wales was seen listening intensely to Senedd members. Devolution brought democracy closer to the people, and in Wales it has led to a left-of-centre government since 1999 either wholly or partly controlled by the Labour party. Those who work closely with the political machinery in Cardiff Bay insist that the crafting of a new Prince of Wales will require a deep understanding of the kind of society that Wales has become.

'There is now a very distinctive Welsh consensus developing,' the Reverend Aled Edwards told me. He had presided over the official renaming ceremony for the Prince of Wales Bridge, but he was also deeply involved in community programmes such as establishing Wales as a nation of sanctuary for refugees. He argued that the 'left-leaning, progressive' politics of the Welsh Government meant the population was backing environmental issues and policies that support the most vulnerable in society. 'We are forging a discourse in Wales that is distinctive. And if I was asked to give a steer, I would think that any future Prince of Wales would have to be very mindful of that shift. It is real and it is palpable.' And he warned against resisting the new Welsh establishment. 'If institutions kick against that dynamic, they will suffer.'

The Reverend, who spoke to me before William became Prince of Wales, said ceremonial occasions such as an investiture ceremony would never get off the ground in this new Wales. 'I am sorry, I sound like a preacher, but that is what I am. I think the antennae must surely say that if you are going into that space in the future, it must be on the basis that some things in Welsh life now have red lines in them, and they must be respected.'

One person who has worked closely with the King on a number of projects in Wales said that the 'clever thing' would be for William to be on the side of the consensus. The rise of political movements, such as the campaign for Welsh independence, may never get a Prince of Wales to support it. But success in building national identity and pride, be it through sport or in pioneering policy areas, should be championed by the Prince if he is to establish credibility as an advocate for Welsh life.

The concept of Wales Week, the annual summer tour, would also need to be adapted and improved. It had become a formulaic exercise for Charles, a template that favoured visits to conservation projects that championed traditional techniques, followed by his Llwynywermod musical evenings. It had also shrunk from a working week to a three-day affair by the time of the last one in 2022. Diversity in royal visits could also be achieved by awarding more royal warrants to Welsh companies. The Royal Warrant Holders Association lists twenty-three companies in Wales as holding warrants, from fire suppression systems to organic farmers. Issuing more warrants, particularly outside south-east Wales, would deepen the royal relationship with new communities and provide new stops on royal tours.

Before he was created Prince of Wales, William's role had not been assessed in any public forum. The dominance of opposition voices in Welsh public life meant any organised discussion about a future Prince of Wales would lead to a polarised debate about the rights and wrongs of the title, rather than a useful exercise in shaping the narrative around how he might undertake his duties. That William visited Wales within a couple of weeks, and ruled out an investiture within a couple of months, spoke to the speed the royal family can employ when it needs to. Social media has made it possible to show a quick public commitment to Welsh events beyond the letter-writing and private visits that Charles preferred. William and Catherine have tweeted their support for high-profile moments like Wales's arrival and departure from the World Cup, while a personal tweet to sympathise with Mark Drakeford on the loss of his wife was followed up, the *Daily Mail* reported, with a letter to the First Minister expressing their condolences.

Small gestures, and the quiet creation of meaningful relationships, will be part of the plan. William has genuine interests which touch areas that his father could not reach, and he has popular support. As parents to young children, both William and Kate can relate to the work of charities that support families in a way that his father could not.

They will also need to grab the unifying moments in Welsh life and be seen to encourage and embrace them.

There is a particular problem with this ambition because of Wales's habit of convalescing around sport. William's patronage of the Welsh Rugby Union fulfils the tradition of giving royal support to the game, and it was a role he took from the Queen as she reduced her patronages in 2016. Yet Welsh rugby ignites such passion in its fans, particularly in games against its big neighbour, that William could never convince the crowds on Westgate Street before a game against the English that he would be rooting for Wales. It was also a patronage that lumbered William with the blazers and committees of the WRU, a male-dominated and old-fashioned structure that was given dinosaur credentials by allegations of misogyny in early 2023. If William fancied throwing greater support at Welsh football instead, he would get a tepid welcome at the Football Association of Wales, not least because he is already president of the English FA. The Welsh national side's success in reaching the World Cup for the first time since 1958 came after a cultural renaissance at the Football Association of Wales which overflowed into the fanbase. Their adoption of Dafydd Iwan's most popular song, '*Yma o Hyd*', about the resilience of the Welsh against the threat from beyond Offa's Dyke, evoked an ambition and identity that was more in tune with the old fringes of Welsh nationalism than with any new 'Carlo'. When William was seen visiting the England team ahead of the World Cup, the Welsh actor Michael Sheen was incandescent. 'He can, of course, support whoever he likes,' Sheen wrote on Twitter, 'but surely he sees holding the title Prince of Wales at the same time is entirely inappropriate? Not a shred of embarrassment? Or sensitivity to the problem here?' It seems unlikely that the new Prince of Wales would want to adopt a formal role at the FAW, despite the vacancy for a royal patron. Following the death of the Queen, the FAW said the issue of royal patronage was 'under review'.

One senior Welsh civil servant said the couple's 'disastrous' Caribbean tour in March 2022 should serve as fair warning for how they need to behave in Wales. William and Kate's trip to Belize, Jamaica and the Bahamas was blighted by a series of PR blunders and tasteless imagery. An open-top Land Rover and photographs of the couple shaking hands with Jamaican children through metal fences created an old-fashioned, colonial impression of a couple who were supposed to signify the monarchy's modern alternative. The civil servant told me that William and Kate needed new Welsh advisors who would steer them away from potentially awkward encounters as they seek to find their feet in Wales. In reality the process is likely to be gripped by the traditional, conservative, softly-softly introduction of William and Kate to Welsh life. Returning to Anglesey for their first visit as Prince and Princess of Wales was a masterclass in playing it safe. Where there may be divergence from Charles, it will be in supporting organisations that help young people with mental health problems or which allow William to expand his own environmental endeavours to Wales.

William and Kate's failsafe visit to Anglesey may set a precedent for a risk-averse, formal approach to Welsh duties. If Wales Week survives under new management, it will likely follow the model established by Charles for highlighting worthy, non-political causes and the charities he championed. Charles may also be loath to relinquish some of the patronages he has nurtured in Wales, including his hands-on role at the Royal Welsh College of Music and Drama. A hybrid approach by the royal family to Wales would allow the links with the King to remain healthy, while William and Kate could gradually expand their interests.

The ceremonial side of the Welsh connection with royalty can take care of itself. At public events and at moments of national significance, William will deputise for Charles without issue. The King's absence will be more noticeable at organisations who have come to depend on his interest and cooperation. Charles may choose to withdraw from public and private statements that seem too controversial for a monarch, no matter how banal the subject may appear. Others hope he will use his new position to continue speaking out. His friend Justin Albert told me he would 'love it' if Charles assumed a leadership role that would allow him, without politics, to lead discussions on the issues the public know that he cares about. 'I would see the role of an intelligent, brilliant, convening King as similar to that of the Dalai Lama or the Secretary General of the United Nations. Somebody who has influence, who can use it benignly for the betterment of all. Without prejudice. Can anyone make those decisions without political bent? Can he talk about buildings and not talk about carbuncles? That is the difficulty.'

Justin had seen Charles do this in Wales, a great convenor of minds to attempt to address issues such as the farm manure that drained poisonous levels of phosphate into the River Wye. They were often issues that stemmed from his passion for conservation, but which also came without the risk of political controversy in either the Senedd or Westminster. There is conventional thought around climate change, the principle of the impact of fossil fuels on the environment is accepted by the overwhelming majority of scientists and most mainstream politicians. There is a clear right and wrong around the pollution of rivers. But there's no consensus on architecture, the skyscrapers of the City of London or the housing estates of the South Wales valleys. Could Charles really advocate passionately just for those causes that have little polarising effect on his audience? 'He needs to be very careful,' Justin Albert said. 'And I think he will be. He is very well advised, with brilliant people around him. These are the areas where he can make a significant difference, and he could be a public voice around them.'

The carbuncle comment, like his admission that he talks to trees, are symbolic of the tabloid approach to Charles's interests that dominated discussion about the future King in the 1990s. He has managed to get on with it, while the world has caught up. He is not an outlier, removed from conventional thought. He is regarded as informed and caring, and no longer a hippy King-to-be.

While the public have come round to many of his big ideas, they have also come round to him. Polling has showed his popularity increasing over the past twenty years, and Justin Albert suggests the impact in Wales has been significant. 'He has come a long way since his investiture to winning over many more people in Wales.' Justin remains an ardent advocate of the 'seeing is believing' mantra about the royal family. 'He hasn't had enough time to meet two or three million of us, but because he is a very personable man, and very charming one to one, even the most ardent republican in Ynys Môn is going to say: Well, I don't like what he stands for, or his values, but I like him. As King he has the opportunity to define the role for a more modern monarchy. And yet the risk of being constrained by convention, and by political exploitation, remains high. He is used as a political tool by all sides, and I would find that unbelievably awful,' Justin Albert said. 'Everybody talking about me and I can't say anything. I know he finds it very difficult. He wants to, but he cannot, defend himself.'

Charles's relationship with Wales will undoubtedly change, not least because of the encouragement he will offer William in assuming a more prominent role as Prince of Wales. If the King steps right back from Welsh life, he will take with him the benefit of a deep engagement with Wales which went far further than that of any previous monarch. It is a relationship that will inform how he bears the Crown. This is a King who previously spent a third of the year in Scotland, and has toured mosques, synagogues and gurdwaras. 'He will be a King for all nations, colours, creeds, sexual orientations – that is what he will stand for,' Justin Albert argued. The country has witnessed how Charles shared his patronage among British society in all its diversity as Prince of Wales.

Charles must step back from some of his close interests if he wishes to assume the dignified silences that were perfected by his mother. He will be tested regularly and publicly. How does a King read a speech by his government, as he must do at the beginning of the parliamentary year, when his people know exactly where he stands on many of its proposals? A bill to reduce carbon dioxide emissions from industrial sites may seem radical to the politicians who drafted it, but we will guess that Charles would have liked them to go further. He will not change his long-held philosophical beliefs, his commitment to the sanctity of human life and the respect he holds for both religious and atheist experiences. But in Charles there is a King who is more engaged with the great variety of attitudes in our society than his mother could have been, and has accumulated decades of credentials to back any claim to be a monarch for all. Whether they want him or not.